SAT* PREP BOOT CAMP
The Real World Strategy Guide to the SAT*

©2013 by Scholastic Test Prep Publishing, LLC®

Published by Scholastic Test Prep Publishing, LLC
Kenosha, WI

Written by Samantha Young
Contributing Writer: Maureen Swade
Book design by Lisa Fisher
Illustrations by Sam Lidester and Brian Sisson

Printed in the United States of America.

ISBN: 978-0-9859447-3-5

Test Prep Seminars® is a registered trademark of
Test Prep Seminars, Incorporated.
visit: www.testprepseminars.org

*SAT is a registered trademark of the College Board.
SAT was not involved in the production of,
and does not endorse, this book.

table of contents

CHAPTER 1
Introduction

Introduction

Why, hello! Welcome to Test Prep Seminars' guide to the SAT. We're glad that either (A) your high school is proactive in your future, or (B) someone who loves you very much decided to force this book upon you, or (C) you're one of those ambitious people who lace up and join the pursuit of happiness like a champ. Whoever is responsible for this treasure map you are now holding, we recommend that you give that person a high-five in the near future because the SAT and ACT[1] will have considerable influence on which route you will be taking in the journey of life. Think about it: you can choose to take the route where you're nearly twice as likely to be unemployed as your

---

1 We have a book for that. Check out *Get Your ACT Together.*

college-educated peers (or, if you are employed, make a mere 40% of their income),[2] or you can *choose* to take the path of higher education and open a world of opportunity for yourself.

With all the educational options out there, many students can't see the importance of an impressive SAT or ACT score. After all, if the local community college will accept them no matter *what* they score, why should they bother to prepare or practice for success?

We will clue you in: because a high test score can mean acceptance into *multiple* colleges and universities—ones with programs specific to your interests or ones that are simply located at the center of the city in which you've always dreamed of living—*and* because high test scores have the potential to turn you into an auctioneer in charge of driving up scholarship bids. That's right ... not only do colleges and universities accept students with impressive test scores ... but they actually *pay* star students to attend their school. With the cost of education rising anywhere from 4 – 24% annually, the competitive offers you receive from colleges vying for your attendance could determine how low your financial contribution will be...piling scholarship on top of scholarship! So take these tests seriously!

If you're already overwrought with anxiety, knock it off and reflect on your advantage: you now have a personal trainer! We are Test Prep Seminars and we're here to get you in shape for the mental marathon that is the SAT so that you can endure the triathlon with ease and leave your 2 million competitors

---

2 http://www.bls.gov/emp/ep_chart_001.htm

in the dust. And since we're strong believers in the humane treatment of all students, we're here to help you reach your goal score the *first* time around so that you don't get involved in an endless cycle of re-testing that allows the College Board to suck the life clean from your marrow. You don't want to show up to prom looking like a 3,000 year-old mummy in formal attire, do you?

Oh, did we not mention that 2 million students are estimated to take the SAT at thousands of testing centers this year alone? As our economy shifts toward educated work, the unemployed are increasingly apt to seek specialized training through a college or university. This means one thing to you: more competition in the scholarship arena. But remember: you, unlike most of them, have Test Prep Seminars on your team and we're here to deliver SAT-specific training designed with a single intention: to maximize your score. *Welcome to the program!*

After studying this handy-dandy book, turn to the TPS workbook and complete practice tests: not in front of the television or the computer, nor while texting your BFF. Rather, treat the practice tests as if they counted toward your SAT score *and* follow up by checking out the answer explanations in the back. We're not trying to prolong the torture, we swear, but the bottom line is that you'll be able to perform better on test day if you've familiarized your body to the SAT's nasty side effects, from bodily cramps to symptoms generally associated with a botched lobatomy!

So give the practice tests your full attention, adhering to both isolation and time limits, and figure out where *and why* you didn't get that perfect score. In your hands, you hold an opportunity to improve your score the *first* time around: don't dismiss it.

NOTES:

college
Board

Student, Meet SAT.
SAT, Play Nice.

The SAT, which originally stood for Scholastic Assessment (or, alternatively, Aptitude) Test and now stands for **Superlative[3] Abasement[4] Torture**, was designed by the cabal of evil scientists and educators of the College Board in 1927. This standardized evaluation of students' ability to perform at a college level contained verbal and math tests in order to gauge the efficiency of *how* students problem solve under pressure.

While your high school education may have focused on specific facts as part of a general knowledge base, the SAT is more like an IQ test in that it examines your brain's power to do brainy things, like *rationalize* and *conceptualize* and all of those other -ize verbs that you learn to do over 13 years of education. Oh, and communicate. But that doesn't end in -*ize*.

3 Definition on page 187
4 Definition on page 126

For students who didn't do much *izing* in high school other than that of the social persuasion, the SAT is a trade-off. They can temporarily abandon life as they know it, with its sleeping and socializing and sanity (all over-rated), in order to prepare themselves to be successful testers and, consequently, do some damage control to cover up their embarrassing GPAs.

As for serious scholars who have consistently sacrificed many or all of those S's for four years, the SAT is a regret-propagating device: their untainted collection of A's will only be a secondary signifier of their intelligence. Whatever you do, Mr. 4.0, don't become despondent. The SAT isn't exactly a slap in your scholarly face because *technically*, you have been training for this test for the entire duration of your education. Just think of it this way: you're taking the skills you've learned in school and applying them to something new.

Speaking of new, when The College Board could no longer find satisfaction in the frustration caused by their original labyrinth of torture, they released an expanded test in March of 2005 that they call the *new* SAT[5]. Yay!

The new SAT is an elaboration on the original: the Verbal section was changed to the Critical Reading section, the Writing section was added, and advanced Algebra was sprinkled into the Math section (but hey, Quantitative Comparison questions have been removed, for whatever that's worth). This crime

---

5 If you feel the need to blame *someone*, look at California. In 2001, U. of California suggested that the University cease using the SAT as its admission test. Not wanting to miss out on the sweet, sweet anguish of sun-kissed students, The College Board revised the test to appease California and, well, here we are today.

against humanity lasts three and three-quarters of an hour: that's two 225 minutes (or 13,500 seconds, if you're curious). But hey, that's a bit better than the dreaded vocabulary section that used to be there! So this current taste of eternity will be split as such:

SAT Test Durations

Test	Length (min)	Length (sec)	Number of Questions	Sections
Critical Reading	70	4,200	67	2, 25-minute 1, 20-minute
Math	70	4,200	54	2, 25-minute 1, 20-minute
Writing	35	2,100	49	1, 25-minute 1, 10-minute
Essay	25	1,500	1	1, 25-minute

If you're paying attention, you probably noticed that there's 1,500 seconds missing (we know you're looking at seconds). Totally not a mistake.

We told you that The College Board is comprised partly of evil scientists, right? Well, what is an evil scientist's favorite activity? That's right: experimenting on humans. Against your will, you will be partaking in an additional 1,500 seconds (25 minutes) of experimental testing in one of the three areas. The worst part is that they hide it in your test so that you won't be able to differentiate between the real test (which counts toward your score) and the part in which you play the role of guinea pig (and, since rodents don't generally attend college, will have no effect on your score). Even though the test has its critics, colleges have remained faithful to College Board's system of ranking students according to their aptitude in critical reading, math, and often writing. So please, don't rely on your favorite blogger's exposé on the SAT conspiracy as an excuse for a low score. Instead, be the anomaly and knock some standardized test tail!

"And at which score should I start looking for a favorite blogger?"

Look, we already told you that such an excuse won't work. Pay attention!

If what you meant to inquire was which score you should shoot for, it's relative to what you're looking to accomplish, and which school you'd like to attend. Each test subject is scored on a scale of 200 to 800, making a perfect score the coveted 2,400 and a comatose patient's score the perplexing 600. But unless you're trying to receive a full-ride scholarship to the University of Prestige with a full-access pass to the teachers' lounge (we hear rumors of a daily omelet bar and donut buffet), you're not going to need anything near 2,400, so relax. As a matter of fact, the mean composite SAT score for seniors during the 2012 school year was 1,498 (496 in Critical Reading, 514 for Math, and 488 for Writing[6]). If you're not sure what your goal

6 http://nces.ed.gov/programs/digest/d09/tables/dt09_144.asp

score should be, check out your potential schools' websites or call their admissions officers. Each university has different admission standards and will often provide prospective students with minimum score requirements for admission as well as scores to shoot for if you'd like to be one of their fortunate scholarship recipients.

"Just how do all those answers roll up to a good score?"

OK, so the way your SAT score will be calculated is similar to the process by which magical unicorns are born: someone, *somewhere* has to be privy—but we'll probably never know how the magic moment goes down. Even though The College Board's hoard of wizards seems to follow a pretty consistent recipe that transforms raw scores into SAT scores, no one outside of the company has ever mastered the exact recipe. However, you can request a **Student Answer Verification Service** at the time you register for the test date or up to five months after you take the SAT test. This will cost you some change but it may help you sleep better at night. Visit www.collegeboard.com and click on Registration.

Raw Scores

This we can determine. The raw score is the sum of all questions answered correctly, less a fraction for each incorrect multiple-choice answer. (Except for student-produced responses in the Math section, which receive no penalty.) Essays are scored from 2–12, or receive a 0 in the case of illegible, off-topic, pen-scribed, or non-existent responses.

Percentiles

Used to compare one student's raw score to another's, the percentile reports the percentage of students that you out-performed. If you score in the 72nd percentile, for example, you tested better than 72% of your fellow testers across the nation.

Like we said, we can't put your raw score into a top hat and pull out your SAT score. However, according to the following approximation chart provided by the College Board, we can approximate what the SAT score for an average tester would be if the magic trick were performed on his results by one of the official SAT wizards.

SAT Scores and Percentile Rankings

Score	Critical Reading	Math	Writing
800	99	99	99+
750	98	97	99
700	95	94	96
650	89	85	90
600	79	74	81
550	66	61	69
500	49	45	52
450	32	28	35
400	17	15	19
350	8	6	8
300	3	2	3
250	1	1	1

NOTES:

Now before you get all sassy about how *obvious* the correlation is between the SAT score and the national percentile rankings, recall that this is a book and it cannot respond. Also, even though the average Critical Reading score corresponds with the

49th percentile, *it's a coincidence*. Every year, the SAT score-percentile relationship fluctuates, and as you can see, an SAT score of 500 in Math is only in the 45th percentile. So where in the world do they come up with these numbers?

First of all, part of the strange system has to do with separating students' perception of grades from SAT scores. Since the SAT was designed by college and high school professors to provide an objective evaluation of a student's ability to perform at levels found in a university setting, its reporting system had to be designed in a way that manages to cram *every* student from *every* city across the nation onto the *same* level playing field (here's hoping the guy next to you took a shower). Or, more bluntly, it was designed to eliminate grade inflation (you know, where A's are handed out like free balloons at the county fair). Well, if students who generally perform at an average level receive an SAT score of 70 instead of the 90 that they've grown to expect, The College Board would probably never hear the end of it. Therefore, it's perfectly logical—and actually quite wise of them—to avoid a 100-point scale and adopt a scale dissimilar to the norm. And so we have a possible score of 800 in which 560 sounds significantly better than the comparable 70%.

SAT Scores vs. ACT Scores

We're asked this all the time, so we've produced a chart that compares 2010-11's SAT[7] and ACT[8] composite scores based on their percentile rankings. (Since the ACT's scale is 0-36, its percentile rankings often overlap.)

Percentile	SAT	ACT
99+	2,300+	33+
95	2,040	29
90	1,930	28
85	1,850	26
80	1,780	25
75	1,730	24
70	1,680	23
65	1,630	22-23
60	1,580	22
55	1,540	21
50	1,500	20-21
45	1,460	19-20
40	1,420	19
35	1,380	18
30	1,340	17-18
25	1,290	16-17
20	1,240	16

7 http://professionals.collegeboard.com/profdownload/sat-percentile-ranks-composite-cr-m-w-2010.pdf

8 http://www.actstudent.org/scores/norms1.html

NOTES:

"I'm a terrible test-taker. Is there any hope for me?"

That depends. Are you involved with a baffling number of extra-curricular activities? Have you successfully juggled a demanding job and your education simultaneously? Are you a star athlete at your high school? Do you have family members that are alumni of the university or who've donated a large sum of money to the university? Do you have a letter of recommendation from Chuck Norris? (They won't say no. *No one* says "no" to Chuck Norris.) Have you been perfecting your application essay ever since you first realized at age 12 that "dolphin trainer" is a real profession and there's no way that you're *not* going to have a business card that says, "Jo Quincy, certified dolphin trainer"?

What we're trying to say here is, "Of course there's hope!"

Even though your SAT score isn't the only factor that determines whether or not you'll be admitted to your college or university of choice, many admissions officers will form an opinion of an applicant based on this score because it is a quick, efficient indicator. So even though your essay may be stellar and your list of extra-curricular activities impressive, a score well below that of the university's mean acceptance score will be detrimental to your chances because it will influence the way the admissions officer perceives everything else on your application. Luckily you have Test Prep Seminars in your corner to beef up your preparedness and get you ready to knock out your score!

After all, without having to know *you* personally, our experience in test preparation has taught us that there are five main factors *probably* holding you back from your best possible score:

- ✓ Lack of test-taking strategies
- ✓ Anxiety
- ✓ Poor time management
- ✓ Exhaustion
- ✓ Lack of some "tips of the trade"

And voila! Without even having to arrange for a private assessment, we already know your needs and how to fulfill them!   Yay!

The PSAT – Opt In.

If you are dedicated to doing well on the SAT, there's no excuse for bypassing the PSAT (well, "My pants are *literally* on fire" might be an acceptable excuse, but since you're probably lying, "pants on fire" is hereby nullified). The PSAT ("P" standing for preliminary) is similar in structure and content to the SAT, minus the essay, and is usually given during 9th/10th grade. Like the grown-up version of the SAT, the PSAT measures aptitude in critical reading, math problem solving, and writing.

Although the PSAT's questions may be a little different than the SAT's (especially in the math section, since the PSAT only tests up to Algebra I and the SAT tests up to Algebra II), the resulting score will not only give you a preview of the real deal, but it also provides feedback on your college preparedness for each area. This will allow you to fine tune your study habits to accommodate your personal needs. Additionally, a good score may qualify you to enter into the National Merit Scholarship Corporation (read: smart people's lottery in which all players win because just holding a ticket makes you look all kinds of classy in the eyes of a university). With nothing to lose and plenty to gain, you should definitely opt to take the PSAT.

NOTES:

Costs

To add insult to injury, you have to actually PAY for this torture. And it's not cheap! Take a look:

Various, Ridiculous SAT Fees[9]

Fee Type	Cost	Why!?
Registration	$51	Applicable to all students registering to take the SAT. Waivers are available for eligible students.[11]
Rescheduling by Phone	$15	Once a student is registered for the SAT, this fee is charged for rescheduling additional test dates over the phone.
Change	$27.50	To change test type[12], center, or date.
Late	$27.50	For registering between the regular and late registration deadlines.
Standby	$45	Once the late registration date has passed, a student may register as a standby.
India and Pakistan Testing	$40	In addition to any other fees incurred, charged for testing in India or Pakistan.

9 as of 2013

10 Waiver eligibility guidelines can be found online at http://sat.collegeboard. com/register/sat-fee-waivers

11 Type refers to SAT and SAT II, the latter of which contains subject tests. For more information on SAT II, hop online and go to http://sat.collegeboard.com/ about-tests/sat-subject-tests

A note on registering as a standby: In the event that there is additional space, material, and staff present after properly registered students have arrived, standbys are admitted in order of their arrival to the testing center. Standbys should arrive at the testing center as early as possible and will not be informed of their admittance until 8:15, when admittance is cut off. There is no guarantee that any standbys will be allowed to test. This is a last ditch resort and costs big bucks, so avoid this option like the plague if you can!

As you can see, the fees add up. And they don't include transportation ($5-10), preparation material ($20+), or the box of #2 pencils you'll break in the study process ($2.50) and during the exam ($0.50, bringing us to a minimum grand total of $75). Are we discouraging you from taking it multiple times? No way! Taking it multiple times gets you closer and closer to your fantastic, dolphin-training dreams! But we are trying to say…make each go count! Do your absolute best each time as if it's your only time; treat each test as if Squeakers' happiness, your BFF bottle-nosed dolphin, depends on it.

Sunday Test Dates

Most students take the SAT on a Saturday between October and June. If, however, for religious reasons this day is not fitting, you may opt to take your test on a Sunday. While this alternative will not cost you an additional fee (I know, we couldn't believe it, either!), proof is required in the form of a signed letter from your clergyperson on official letterhead and you must fill in the 01000 test center code on your application. Once this process has been completed, any further testing must also be completed on Sundays. Please note, however, that testing on Sunday rather than Saturday provides zero benefit to your score and locks you into Sunday-only testing. Don't go through the hassle just because there's going to be a huge house party on Friday and you want to be "responsible" and take the test when you're feeling more bright-eyed and bushy-tailed. Only use this option if you actually abide by religious convictions that prohibit you from partaking in Saturday testing.

Early Decision/Early Action

If you wish to meet the deadlines for Early Decision or Early Action, you will need to schedule your SAT test date in either October or November. Early Decision is a program in which you commit yourself exclusively to attend a college if they choose to accept your application. *Early Action* is a similar program, though non-exclusive, in which a student may apply to multiple schools with the understanding that an attendance promise is not being made. Even though the *Early Decision* is

NOTES:

not contractual, putting in multiple applications of this sort has the potential to get you "blacklisted" from those universities involved. (Not as cool as it sounds, actually.) If you're feeling like Bigfoot at a shoe store and simply *can't* find a school that fits just right, don't put in any Early Decision applications. Go for Early Action.

Obtaining Your Score

SAT scores can be obtained in three ways: by harassing the mailman every day when he walks past your house because you're "anticipating a very important letter," by paying $15 to listen to a recording of your results over the phone, or by pre-registering at Collegeboard.com *prior to your test* and logging in (for free!) after your test has been scored. The latter option, which doesn't waste 15 bucks and only requires a few clicks to see your entire testing history, is obviously preferable. However, if you're only now (for some baffling reason) looking at this book and your mailman has obtained a restraining order against you, you can always just call 1-800-SAT-SCORE (1-800-728-7267). You will need to provide your birth date, testing date, and registration or Social Security number. Oh, and don't forget a credit card.

Registering to Retest

Once the College Board has collected enough of your personal information during your initial registration that they could basically steal your identity (OK, maybe a slight exaggeration, but you get the point), scheduling for additional tests is as easy as making a phone call or using that website on which you've already created an account (right?). To reschedule by phone, call 1-866-756-7346 and follow the instructions. Otherwise, if you'd prefer to reschedule your test online like the suave computer stud that you are, visit... www.collegeboard.com/student/testing/sat/reg.html.

Sending Your Score

During registration you are given an opportunity to send your scores to a maximum of four colleges and universities by providing their school codes. This option will save you a few bucks, but *don't even think about it*! We recommend you hold off and dish out a couple extra bucks to do it later.

Why? In March 2009, the College Board weighed the pros and cons of allowing students to choose which scores to send and which to stuff in their closets with all of their other dark, dark secrets. And so it became an option to avoid filling in school codes and only send scores that you want your potential educators to see. (Actually, while this may shock you, The College Board is actually doing you a solid here: they decided to let you hide your skeletons because they figured you'd be at least a *little* less stressed out so your score would better reflect your capabilities. Say, "Thank you.")

The College Board offers a service called Score Choice ™ that allows you to choose the scores you want to send to your college(s). Before you decide to take this option, you need to do your homework and understand the score–reporting rules adopted by each school. There is an easy to use tool on www.collegeboard.com that enables you to do those searches quickly.

Once you've decided that you're happy with the score you've received, you can send it to the college(s) of your choice by phone (a costly choice, but if you must...) at 1-866-756-7346 or online at www.collegeboard.com/student (again, only available to students who've preregistered).

NOTES:

Yes, the SAT looks scary. Yes, it will impact your future. Yes, you've heard horror stories and you've probably had nightmares. Like that one in which *you* were the unfortunate soul who booked the last possible test date for the season, and *you* stayed awake the night prior in order to study, and then *you* ended up falling asleep during the first section of the test. Ahhhh! And, yes! *You* are probably thinking, "Oh, come on. Don't be so dramatic." But that exact scenario has, indeed, been experienced more than once (honestly, we've met a few of those unfortunate souls). Don't let it happen to *you*! … Ooooo!

Ahem.

We know, we know...you aren't going to make such a silly mistake because, no matter how awful our jokes are, you're going to keep reading and learn how to stay nonchalant[12] in the face of the stolid[13] College Board's attempt to torture yet another generation of students. That's because you're just so dang impressive.

---

12 Definition on page 168
13 Definition on page 186

Preparing for T-Day

On the big day, you're going to want to know the format and the directions. The test is timed, and the time is ticking, so we can't have you musing over how peculiarly the directions are written, or over the validity of each question's premise. We're going to teach you to read, comprehend, and react directly to the instructions. No tangents[14].

A note on the vocabulary used in this book: To help you get started with your vocabulary, you'll notice superscripts in the beginning of this book (did you notice?). Sometimes they'll be a page reference to the indicated word's definition. We've compiled and defined a plethora[15] of the vocabulary frequently seen on the SAT, which spans from page 126 to 197. Oh yeah... it's long. So, you may wish to begin creating notecards for this list as soon as possible. If you prefer to study digitally, perform an Internet or phone application search for "flashcard." As long as you're willing to create the flashcards (or if you don't think a stack of pre-made notecards is actually worth the ridiculous price they're sold for in stores), blank notecards are cheap and there are plenty of free programs out there. Beyond being fiscally responsible, making your own flashcards will help you assimilate the vocabulary. You will have to study them eventually, right? Why not use the creation process as your study time and spend the cash you'll save on something more enjoyable, like anything other than SAT-related goods?

---

14 Definition on page 189
15 Definition on page 175

Conditioning yourself to dive in and annihilate the test is going to take some training, though, including learning how to read efficiently, expanding your vocabulary, bulking-up your problem-solving skills, and fine-tuning your writing. So let's figure out how to get you into test-toppling shape.

Block Out Time

SAT preparation is time-consuming! It cannot be effectively done during commercial breaks to the jingle for the new, improved, technologically advanced quad-ply toilet paper; nor while you blindly bounce through the hallways en route to class, ricocheting off your peers as if you live in a pinball machine; nor on every other weekend when you just can't seem to find anything better to do. If you're going to be properly prepared, it is absolutely necessary that you block out time slots in your schedule that will be dedicated solely to studying for the SAT.

The best way to create a workable schedule is to lay out all of your current obligations. Include school, homework, extracurricular activities, work, and that one T.V. show that you couldn't possibly fathom *not* watching.

Here's an example:

Sun	Mon	Tue	Wed	Thu	Fri	Sat
Work 9-4	School 8–2:45	School 8–2:45	School 8–2:45	School 8–2:45	School 8–2:45	Work 9-3
	Softball practice 3-4:30		Softball practice 3-4:30			Softball practice 3-4:30
				Home work 4-7		
	Home work 6-7	Home work 4-8				
			Home work 6-8		Work 4-10	
Home work 7-10	Dancing with the American Stars 7-8					Friends and/or Family

Now remember that you need to bathe at least once a week and eat at least one real meal per day (given that staying conscious is of interest to you), and that teleportation devices have yet to be invented (so, unfortunately, you'll need to budget transportation time).

Keeping these mandates in mind, block out time slots that you will dedicate to studying for the SAT, like so:

Sun	Mon	Tue	Wed	Thu	Fri	Sat
Work 9-4	School 8–2:45	School 8–2:45	School 8–2:45	School 8–2:45	School 8–2:45	Work 9-3
	Softball practice 3-4:30		Softball practice 3-4:30			Softball practice 3-4:30
SAT 5-6:30	Home work 6-7	Home work 4-7		Home work 4-7	Work 4-10	**SAT 6-7**
Home work 7-10	Home, MD. 7-8	**SAT 7-9**	Home work 6-8			Practice test 7-7:15

Notice how hectic this schedule looks? And how you probably wouldn't do such a terrible thing to yourself if you hadn't created a plan that you're going to promise you'll keep? That's why we created this template for you to complete with your own schedule.

Don't forget to sign at the bottom. Now you can tear it out and post it in a special place to remind you of your promise.

LEGAL CONTRACT

I,_____, on this day, _____ ,
Name *Date*

do solemnly swear to abide by the schedule that I have created. Though it may be modified at a later date, I hereby recognize my contractual obligation to follow through with the plan and, in the event that I become frustrated, reassess my priorities, as needed, in order to remind myself that doing well on the SAT is, indeed, important to me.

	Sun	Mon	Tue	Wed	Thu	Fri	Sat
7 A							
8 A							
9 A							
10 A							
11 A							
12 P							
1 P							
2 P							
3 P							
4 P							
5 P							
6 P							
7 P							
8 P							
9 P							
10 P							

Student: _____   Date: _____
Signature

Witness:_____   Date: _____
Signature

Designate a Brainiac Zone

Getting "in the zone" sometimes requires actually designating a zone. Insomniacs, for example, are often told first and foremost to designate their beds as sleep-only zones. The reason for this simple alteration's effectiveness is pretty straightforward: As creatures of habit, we become readily conditioned to act in accordance to our expectations for any given environment. This explains why the children responsible for the loud screeches typically heard on a playground can, upon entering a library, become partially mute and funnel their excited screams through wide-eyed expressions. Likewise, doing homework in bed conditions students to be mentally active in this zone; so, when they crawl between the sheets, instead of drifting off into a cozy slumber, they lie awake with calculations running through their heads. Or, on the other hand, they've become so conditioned to pass out on their pillow that even an exposé on the heated debate over true white versus off-white paper production can't stave off slumber.

Now, not only do you know that you should *never* do homework in bed, but you also know that setting up a personal Study Zone will help you slip into study mode.

This goes for separating where you work and where you play, as well. Unfortunately, a lot of students play PC games on the same computer that they use to research and write papers. If you can get away with designating a spot that *doesn't* share space with your computer, you'll do a better job of ignoring your favorite game or FaceSpace as it beckons your attention.

Assemble a Kit

To trim SAT preparation prep time gather all of the tools you anticipate needing to study, including this book, notecards, a few pens and pencils, highlighters, notebooks, a calculator, a dictionary, et cetera. Keeping these things together in a kit will ensure that your preparation time will be spent productively instead of searching, searching, *searching* for that notebook that you've been filling with all of those important tips and tricks (where did it go?).

Furthermore, during your online registration (seriously, if you haven't done that yet, we're shunning you), you probably cruised the SAT website. Did you notice the Official SAT Question of the Day™ or the free Official SAT Practice Test? They're completely (gasp!) free and at your disposal. Incorporate them into your kit by bookmarking these sites.

Create a Plan That Works for You

We can't coach you all that specifically on this process. We can only give you a few pointers and trust *you* to be honest with yourself in determining your specific needs.

The best way to customize your plan is to take the PSAT and use its results. It's the most up-to-date real-deal test that you could possibly use: it's written by the same authors as the SAT, it's proctored in the same fashion, and it comes with an objective review of your results. If, however, you're reading this too late and the PSAT is no longer an option for you, try completing a few sample tests from the TPS workbook and use the answer key/explanations to determine where you stand.

In either case, once you have an idea of your current performance, compare it with how well you're aiming to do. If you're scoring significantly lower than you'd like, you're going to need to dedicate significantly more time to SAT preparation than if, for example, you're on par with your goal score.

Before you blurt out, "Oh, good! I'm already at my goal score!" and slam this book closed, consider the cost of college. (Nope, we're not going to let you forget.) It's huge! If you're already on par for your goal score and you still have the time, why not try to pump it up even more and make yourself a tasty temptation for those scholarship committees? Sure, you could take out $30,000 or more in loans to pay for your education; sure, you could live off dehydrated noodles for ten years in order to pay off the balance; sure, you could sell your organs on the black market and pay off the tab in one swoop—but why not just study for a couple weeks, do well on the SAT, fill out a couple applications, and just maybe have Team Moneybag$ throw some scholarships your way? Or, if you do *really* well on the SAT, have Team Moneybag$ straight-up pay for your entire education? It could happen, smarty pants.

Now that we've gotten *that* out of the way ....

The schedule you've signed on page 29 should only be a general outline of *when* you plan to study. In addition to determining when, we recommend that you work up a sort of subject-specific schedule that rotates between test areas once the bulk of the test has been covered.

Weekly Study Plan

Week I: Read through book title and think about possibly reading the actual book

Week II: Monday: read introduction
Tuesday-Friday: read critical reading section
Saturday: 15 minute practice test #1, work on vocabulary cards
Sunday: take a break!

Week III: Monday-Wednesday: begin reading math section
Thursday-Friday: continue with math section, work on vocabulary cards
Saturday: 15-minute practice test #2, work on vocabulary cards
Sunday: get some sunshine

Week IV: Monday-Wednesday: read writing section
Thursday: begin journaling/writing practice essays
Friday: thoroughly edit any practice writing and finish vocabulary cards
Saturday: Read conclusion
Sunday: definitely time for a bike ride with friends to de-stress

Week V: Monday: 15-minute practice test #3 and #4. Determine where you need training.
Tuesday: begin developing a schedule to focus on where YOU specifically need assistance. And remember to use your teachers: they want you to succeed!

Working on a rotation will allow your unconscious mind to assimilate some of the information that you were unable to effectively incorporate into your knowledge during the time you were studying.

What? You think that contradicts the whole idea of studying?

Well, have you ever spent an evening studying, only to resign to the cold, harsh reality that there's approximately zero chance that you'll understand AP chemistry by the following morning— but then you wake up, and when you're breezing over your notecards in a last-ditch effort to save your hide, you realize that it all makes *perfect* sense? (Well, maybe not *perfect*, but at least you can now understand your teacher's lame joke about hydrophobic molecules being terrified of utility bills.) That, my friend, is the power of your unconscious mind. Let it work for you!

For the curious-minded: Scientists have trained mice to complete a maze while wearing silly hats. The hats, which look similar to a colander, actively scanned the mice's neural activity. Worn 24 hours a day, the resulting map of data showed the mice repeating the maze over and over in their sleep. After the night's rest, it was found that the mice were able to complete the maze in a shorter time than they had done before sleeping, suggesting that the mice were learning from the unconscious repetitions.

As you rotate between subjects, keep a journal of your experience. Was a particular session more frustrating than usual? Do you feel like you've learned zip, zero, zilch? These assertions aren't as terrible as they might feel because, since you've recognized your problem areas, you're now able to directly address them. This may include adjusting your schedule by moving more difficult subjects to days when you're less swamped with homework, reassigning the amount of time you spend on each subject, or splitting your daily SAT study time into two sessions because two straight hours is simply longer than your brain is willing to cooperate; this may *also* include seeking help.

Ask for Help

Students generally develop a pretty negative view of their teachers, which is devastatingly unfortunate. Almost *all* of your teachers sought a career in education because they *wanted* to help students; they had a *desire* to assist students in achieving their full intellectual potential. The perception students have of their teachers is more often a projection of their negative feelings toward education than anything else. And the teachers—surrounded by students who despise them for caring—become frustrated, and perhaps even jaded. The poor teachers are cursed by their students to play the role of a crabapple. But you can save them! You can free your teachers from disillusionment and *ask for help*.

Sure, there will be teachers who've been lost forever to the crabapple curse, but you have everything to gain and nothing to lose by asking for help. Give it a shot.

Learn to Love Testing
(Just kidding. Move along.)

Reward Yourself

This only applies to those who've earned it. If you've barely skimmed this book, or it's week six of your SAT preparation and you've only accumulated a "massive" four hours of study time, please turn to page 18 and compare its content with the content of your piggy bank. Please reassess your priorities.

But you—you, with the impressive preparation plan and the positive attitude—you need to pencil in some time to reward yourself! Positive reinforcement is just as powerful as negative punishment, so couple your goals with a reward. Anticipating a reward in the near future will do a lot more than thinking, "*Some*day, maybe 10 or 15 years from now, I'll look back on this day from the comfort of my champagne-filled hot tub and think, 'I'm glad I studied for the SAT instead of going out on a date with that, albeit extremely attractive, underachieving loser.'" Yeah, you will probably have forgotten about all that hot stuff by then, plus, do you really think it'll be satisfying to *forecast* a reward? Not nearly as satisfying as a couple carnival rides, or the giant wad of cotton candy that, despite the killer stomach ache, you have no regrets having eaten.

Test Prep Seminars, for example, is fond of this one: "For every 100 students who gain admittance to a quality university after partaking in a TPS seminar, employees shall be granted an extra day of paid vacation."

It's probably best that you shoot for realistic rewards, like going to a movie. Perhaps in 3D?

NOTES:

Keep the Prize in Mind

Even though your end goal—being able to afford a champagne-filled hot tub or, you know, being able to live a comfortable life—may not be a very good reward for your present-day tribulations, it shouldn't be altogether forgotten. Life, as many teenagers know it today, comes with only a fraction of the happiness and freedom that they could experience tomorrow: today, they're drenched in confusing hormones and trying to appease many different people with vastly different expectations. As an adult, however, when their individual dreams are to revitalize downtrodden antique cars, design their own clothing, give their children a safe and happy home, or be a philanthropist, a good first step for each and every one of them is to soak up some knowledge. Whether that knowledge is used to afford their personal comforts or the comfort of others, the rule of thumb for success is obtaining an education.

Stop. Don't you *dare* start citing Bill Gates, Steve Jobs, and Mark Zuckerberg as proof that a college education isn't necessary for success. No. Please, just stop.

These heavyweights are *exceptions* to the rule. The only reason you know their names is because, unlike the majority of us, they either (A) were geniuses from the beginning and dropped out of college because they had already surpassed the intellectual prowess taught in undergraduate programs, (B) stumbled across a technological breakthrough that was hastily gobbled up by the public, or (C) gambled big time on an idea that (thank goodness) paid off.

Let's do a little exercise. In the left-hand column, jot down the names of a few of your acquaintances who either dropped out of college or opted not to go altogether. In the right-hand column, list some of the people cited in the argument against higher education. (We'll give you the first three on this side.)

Your Acquaintances	Celebrity Billionaires
	Bill Gates
	Steve Jobs
	Mark Zuckerberg

Now, draw a line to connect the names listed in both columns. Oh, there aren't any matches? Oh, *weird*!

So, are we done here?

Whatever you wish to do in the future, your best shot is to get educated, and if you just so happen to be the exception to the rule, what does the cost of college matter? Nada. That's right. Poor ole extremely rich you with the four wasted years of learning neat facts and meeting interesting people....

Get Focused

Growing up in the age of the internet normalizes multitasking to the extent that we often have difficulty focusing on one thing at a time. While multitasking is a super-awesome ability to have in a non-academic setting, the SAT requires you to focus all your attention on a *single* task. And since this is no longer second-nature to most students, TPS says, "Exercise your concentration!" The most effective way, really, is to beast through some of those practice tests in a single shot.

One of the best ways to get focused is to block out audible distractions—be it some irritating proctors chitchatting, or some nervous kid's incessant tapping of his foot. You can block them out by shoving something in your ears. Wait! Not a crayon! Go to your local convenience store *and* buy a pair of earplugs.

Know Your Potential

After all of your intense studying, you'll have a better understanding of what *you* do best. As you enter into each subsection, tackle the question types in the order of your adequacy. Right off the bat, you'll be able to bank in on the points from questions that you're most likely to answer correctly *and* you'll have a nice little confidence boost.

Be Positive

Never underestimate the power of positive thinking. Many of
the head honchos of the business world will tell you that they
got to where they are by visualizing themselves wiping their
bums with $20 bills. Well, not in those words. But you know
that saying, "Dress for the job you want, not the job you have"?
These guys took it a step further. To become the successful
CEOs that they ultimately became, they visualized themselves
living the life they wanted, not the one they had. By assuming
their success, they were able to better achieve it. So, how
does your future look?

(Feel free to use this space to draw yourself flying a pterodactyl,
swimming through a hot tub of fudge, or singing a duet with
Elvis—the real thing, no impersonator.)

Take Your own notes here.

SAT-Conquering Day

Once you're prepared, there's nothing left to fret over. Still, you're probably going to feel a little stressed out on the big day. This is a completely normal, healthy response that you should anticipate, so when you wake up on the big day and immediately begin to sweat, don't beat yourself up. Worrying about your worrying is only going to perpetuate the anxiety. Instead, repeat the following phrase:

"The SAT is about to experience the whooping of a lifetime."

Go ahead: talk yourself up. If you've gone through the training, you've earned the right to assume dominance over the test. Just don't get *too* cocky.

To minimize silly mistakes (i.e., showing up without a pencil or forgetting your calculator—now that would stink), create a checklist for yourself *today* and customize it as you go.

On the day of the SAT, you will need to:

- ✓ Get a good night's rest before your exam
- ✓ Bring an acceptable photo I.D.[16]
- ✓ Have your admission ticket in hand[17]
- ✓ Arrive at your testing station *no later than* 7:45 A.M.[18]
- ✓ Believe in yourself and have the confidence to succeed (we'll coach you on this bit)

---

16 Acceptable photo identification includes current (i.e., unexpired) driver's license, state-issued I.D., school I.D. card, a valid passport, a completed Student I.D. Form (can be obtained from your school), or a Talent Identification Program I.D./Authorization (applicable only to students in the 7th and 8th grade). *Important reminder:* During registration, you must now provide a picture of yourself, full frontal, no disguises! If you registered on-line, the digital upload can be in a .jpg, .gif or .png format. If registering by snail mail, your picture must be between the sizes of 2 x 2 in. to 2.5 x 3 in.

17 If you somehow manage to lose this very important piece of paper—you know, the one that you absolutely must have with you in order to take the test—visit Collegeboard.com, create a student account, and follow the directions for lost tickets.

18 Doors open at this time and close definitively at 8:15 A.M.

But wait! There's more! You should also come equipped with:

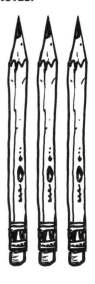

✓ Several #2 pencils with soft rubber erasers, most sharp and a couple dull

✓ A bar eraser or two

✓ An acceptable calculator with a replacement battery[19]

✓ A watch with absolutely no beeping, blooping, or ringing

✓ A snack for break time

✓ A bottle of water

If you need any other items, such as an inhaler or lozenges, pack those along as well. Better safe than sorry!

Clothing

Even though this seems like a silly thing to discuss, your clothing is rather important. Any form of distraction, from being itchy to being cold, will negatively influence your score. The clothing you choose will determine whether you spend nearly four hours concentrating, squirming away from an itchy seam, shivering, sweating, or pulling up the back of your pants every five minutes when a breeze passes over the Grand Canyon. Be wise: worry less about how you look and focus on comfort. The SAT awards zero points for fashion, so embrace sweatpants that can be hiked up and layers of shirts that can be easily added or removed as per the climate fluctuations in your testing zone.

---

19 Acceptable calculators are limited to graphing, scientific, and four-function calculators. This means no computers, no calculators with a keyboard, and no using your cell phone. For more detailed information, visit SAT.Collegeboard. com/register/sat-test-day-checklist#calcPolicy

NOTES:

Things to Leave Behind

Now that you're all ready to go, let's talk about some of the things that you should *not* bring.

Blank "Scrap" Paper
The test booklet will provide plenty of blank space for you to complete the necessary calculations and make notes for yourself. Disguising cheat sheets as scrap paper is way too easy so don't even bother arguing with your proctor.

Study Guides
As far as study guides go, they're great—but not on test day. At the last moment, you should be concentrating on staying calm and thinking through your strategy to spank the SAT. Come test day, the knowledge you'll need to do well is either part of your repertoire, or it's not. A few nervous moments in your car before the test aren't going to do you any good. Nor will trying to drive and study in tandem. (Note: car accidents are considerably time-consuming. Don't cram on the way!) Take the time to study *before* the big day and *relax* come the fateful Saturday.

Cell Phones
Your cell phone shouldn't make it into the test center. If you need to bring it with you, leave it in the car. Can you imagine the horror if you forgot to silence it and *La Cucaracha* were to blare in all of its obnoxious glory? If you're thinking, "But what if I have a really important phone call that I just *can't* miss?"

Well, Mr. Important, reschedule your test. If you're anticipating a phone call, you won't be 100% focused.

Music Players

Feel free to get psyched in the car, but leave your MP3 player at home. You won't be able to listen to music while testing, nor during the break. Additionally, in the unfortunate event of your pocket turning on the device, your butt blaring get-pumped tunes would only pump your proctor to punt you out the door. Yes, your proctor can remove you if you become a nuisance, and no, your money will not be refunded.

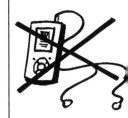

Coffee and Energy Drinks

Though coffee and energy drinks are helpful for shaking off the sleeps and for maintaining consciousness while reading extremely boring material, don't be fooled: come SAT testing day, they are some of your greatest foes. Beyond stimulating your mind, caffeine stimulates the production of urine. With strictly regulated breaks during the SAT, diuretics are dangerous business, so stay away from coffee and all other caffeinated beverages an hour prior to, and during, your test.

Yoga Mat

We're going to teach you how to stay Zen during this high-stress time of your life, but there won't be room to do the downward-facing dog between your and your neighbors' desks. Leave the yoga mat behind and use the following de-stressing and uncramping techniques. While you may think that we're pushing the limit on the "cheese factor," we promise these tips can be quite useful!

NOTES:

Keeping Your Cool

Butt-in-seat safe, all of these techniques will help you relax both prior to and during the test.

Pull Your Hair
… but, you know, gently (unless you have a thing for bald spots, whatever). Though it seems odd at first, consider the places you recognize tension. We're going to guess that a few of those places are your shoulders, neck, head, and (perhaps) eyes. Well, in that same vicinity, you also carry a good deal of tension in your scalp. One way to relieve the build-up of tension in the scalp is to place your fingertips on your hairline and, with your fingers slightly spread, slide them through your hair to get a handle on your roots. Squeezing the sides of your fingers together, gently tug outward to lift the scalp away from your skull, thereby stimulating blood flow. Only pull as firmly as is comfortable or your peers may think you're having a mental breakdown during the test.

Rest Your Eyes
Drop your lids and slowly roll your eyes both clockwise and counterclockwise, stretching their rotation in every direction. Keeping your eyes closed so that the proctor doesn't think you're teasing him, cross and uncross your eyes repeatedly. Lastly, use cupped hands to cover your eyes and block out the majority of the light. Giving your eyes a good rest will consume 15 or so seconds, but defeating tired eyes will be well worth the sacrifice. If you feel a tension headache coming on, blocking out light is particularly helpful.

ROLL 'EM

Roll Your Neck

Begin by letting the weight of your giant brain pull your head forward. Rest your chin on your chest for a second to stretch the muscles that run down your back, and then gently roll your head clockwise, stretching your neck only as far as feels refreshing[20]. Make a complete rotation, pause, and resume rotation in the opposite direction. Closing your eyes tightly, turn your head to the far right (exaggerating the closing of your eyes will save you from suspicion of being a checking-out-your-neighbor's-sheet cheater). Pause, keeping the stretch, and return to facing forward. Repeat facing left.

Stretch Your Shoulders

Sit up straight and push your shoulders back to feel the stretch through your chest. From this position, slowly roll your shoulders up to your ears, pause, and then roll them forward until you feel a slight stretch through your shoulder blades and neck. End the stretch by pushing your mid-back forward and shoulders backward.

Shake it Out

Extend your hands at your sides and perform some extreme jazz hands: stretch your fingers out until you can feel the stretch in your palm and *shake, shake, shake* the writer's cramp right out. You'll also be able to expend a good deal of the excess energy that your bouncing legs just can't seem to jog.

---

20 Overstretching muscles, especially those in your neck, can lead to more soreness than relief. Do not force any more stretching than feels natural.

Take a Breath

Sometimes you just need to give your lungs an opportunity to shine. Stop reading for a moment and slowly take in a deep, deep breath through your mouth: allow your diaphragm to drop, your stomach to extend, and your lungs to fill with all of the oxygen they could desire. Focusing on the physical sensation, slowly breathe out this mega breath through your nose until your lungs feel empty. Before inhaling again, experience this emptiness. Repeat. This technique, called "sigh breathing," will calm you in both mind and body. Does it sound too good to be true? Try it!

Feeling a little too self-conscious to do some of these de-stressing exercises? Don't want to look like you're freaking out in the middle of the exam and pulling out your hair? Iffy on breaking out your sweet jazz-hand moves? Worried that the kid one desk over will think that you're crying when you cover your eyes to give them a rest? Consider the amount of money you're wasting on this test if you don't allow yourself to look a little nutty. Plus, who's going to see you anyway? Everyone else in the room is going to be zoned in on his or her own test or lost in his orher own anxieties. No one is looking at you. Stop being such an egomaniac and do whatever weird little stretch you need.

NOTES:

In the Event of Things Going Awry

... it's not the end of the world. Yes, it'll be inconvenient to have to retest, but if you'll recall… you don't have to *admit* that you ever scored a 750! And since most students do better the second time around, you're bound to increase that score to *at least* 800!

Plus, even though your SAT score is important, it won't be the only factor that will be taken into consideration on your college application. As long as you get a decent score, your awesome GPA, *long* list of extracurricular activity, and *stellar* application essay should show off just how bright of a star you are. Just remember that you are not that one embarrassing score you got: you are years of spectacular performance and a knowledge machine that can always try again!

Now that we have all the legwork done for our preparation, let's get to chasing your future by going over some TPS tips and tricks!

NOTES:

TPS Presents:
SAT Tips and Tricks

First of all, did you know…

✓ There aren't intentional trick questions

✓ There is only one (1) correct answer for each question

✓ There isn't a pattern in the answers

✓ The whole "C is the best option" thing isn't true (at least on the SAT) because the College Board strives to randomly distribute the answers

✓ Questions increase in difficulty with each subsection

Are you surprised by any of these points? We tend to meet a lot of students who *are* taken aback when we point out these facts! Because of the SAT's importance and the veil of secrecy that The College Board suspends over its heinous[21] activities, it's no surprise that students create and pass on urban legends like, "The best SAT answer sheet looks like a crop circle!" Or, "Never guess on the SAT because incorrect answers are worth negative points!"

"But incorrect responses are worth negative points!" We hear you screaming at the top of your lungs. Calm down. Yes, you're right. But the conclusion you've probably drawn is incorrect relative to strategy, so let's address guessing right off the bat:

21 Definition on page 155

NOTES:

The Guilefully Gory Guise of Guessing

Guessing can be dangerous business on the SAT, but this assumes that you'll be *blindly* guessing on four or fewer questions throughout the entire test, when the average student is likely to face the temptation of guessing on a heck of a lot more than that.

And *why* is randomly guessing on *more* than four questions better than randomly guessing on, say, two? Statistics, my dear, statistics!

If you have 5 options, and you randomly choose one, you have a (⅕ × 100%) 20% chance of guessing the correct answer. This means that, statistically, if you *randomly* guess on 1, you have a 20% chance of getting it correct; if you randomly guess on 2, you have a 40% chance of getting one of them correct; and so on. If, however, you randomly guess on exactly 5 questions, you are statistically likely to correctly answer 1 and incorrectly answer 4. The College Board recognized this game of chance, and to negate the hours of four-leaf clover hunting and rabbit-foot rubbing, they erased the effects of luck by taking off ¼ point for each incorrect response. They can't, however, erase the effects of an *educated* guess!

Consider: You are given 5 options (A—E), so each has a 20% chance to be correct. However, if you can cross out one obviously wrong answer in each question, you can increase your odds to have a 25% chance of getting the correct answer by guessing. If you can cross out two bad answers in each, you can increase your successful guessing probability to 33%, and if you can cross out *three* bad answers, there's a 50% chance of filling in the correct bubble.

"Ah, yes, but even with the odds far in my favor, I still have a 50% chance of being wrong and hurting my score."

Young grasshopper, you are on your way to being wise—but you're not quite there. Remember how an incorrect answer is worth - ¼ and a correct answer is worth +1? Incorrect answers only have 25% of the weight of a correct answer, so even sheer statistics will tell you that gambling *wisely* on the SAT is a *good* thing. If you don't believe us, we've put together an analysis of the possible guessing outcomes for 25 questions. The first row is for blind guessing (i.e., the question itself was a mystery) and the last row is for educated guessing (i.e., all but two possible answers have been eliminated).

Number of Options	Points for Correct Guesses	Penalty for Incorrect Guesses	Overall Points for Guessing
5	25 × 20% × (+1)	25 × 80% × (- ¼)	5 – 5 = 0
4	25 × 25% × (+1)	25 × 75% × (- ¼)	6.25 – 4.69 = +1.56
3	25 × 33% × (+1)	25 × 66% × (- ¼)	8.25 – 4.13 = +4.12
2	25 × 50% × (+1)	25 × 50% × (- ¼)	12.5 – 3.13 = +9.37

Did you notice how blind guessing has zero detrimental effect on your score, and educated guessing has a positive impact? And a wave of peace and understanding rolled across the young grasshopper's spirit as he unmasked the simple statistics of *guessing*.

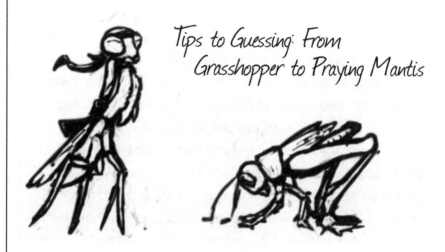

Tips to Guessing: From Grasshopper to Praying Mantis

(A praying mantis would take a grasshopper any day, if you're wondering.)

Becoming a guessing master is doable by anyone. But before you spend all day studying the ways of the confused, remember that guessing is no substitute for knowing the answer. These tips are to be used only in the event of a brain hiccup!

Search for Commonalities

This tip is best understood by example. Consider a question in which the options are:

(A) $\dfrac{x \pm 2}{y + 3}$ (B) $\dfrac{x - 2}{y + 3}$ (C) $\dfrac{x + 2}{y - 3}$ (D) $\dfrac{x \pm 2}{y - 3}$ (E) $\dfrac{x + 2}{y + 3}$

The most common numerators are x±2 and x+2, so we can eliminate (B). The most common denominator is y+3, so we can eliminate (C) and (D) for being y-3. We're then left with (A) and (E). Just by identifying commonalities, we can increase our chance of correctly answering this question from 20% to 50% *without ever reading it.*

Identify Trends

Within many sentence completion problems are trends among the vocabulary that will assist you in eliminating bad answers. Consider the following:

There will be many -------, seasoned competitors; you, however, will be the most -------, prepared competition the College Board has ever challenged.

> (A) mediocre, adroit
> (B) haphazard, keen
> (C) intelligent, confounded
> (D) wise, perspicacious
> (E) indifferent, adept

Searching for a trend, we recognize that two people with similar traits, "seasoned" and "prepared," are being compared. Keeping with the positive tone that accompanies preparedness, we can analyze the first portion of our possible answers: (A) is out due to *mediocre*, (B) due to *haphazard*, and (E) due to *indifferent*. If you stop at this point, you're choosing between two options for a 50% chance of correctly guessing.

If you were able to eliminate *haphazard* without knowing its precise definition, you'll probably be able to do the same in the second column and eliminate *confounded*. Consider how these words relate to those that you already know: the same way *haphazard* reminds you of the word *hazard*, confounded could remind you of the word *confused*. Is being *confused* any good when you're taking the SAT? Not at all! So drop *confounded* and choose the correct answer, (D), without ever having to know what *perspicacious* means (we bet you know that it's a good thing, though!).

Seek Frequency

Consider a question in which the options are:
- I.   Broken camera
- II. Letter from your grandmother
- III. The Tooth Fairy

(A) I only
(B) II only
(C) I and II only
(D) I and III only
(E) III only

Try not to think too hard about the question that caused such a smattering of options, because this is about guessing and we couldn't think of a question in which all three options would make any sense anyway.

If you're as baffled as you ought to be, your only chance of correctly answering this question is by choosing the answer that reflects the greatest frequency. And what does that mean? Let's start by completely ignoring these *super* random nouns and just boil it down to Item 1, Item 2, and Item 3.

Now let's look at your options. **Three** of your options contain Item 1 (A, C, D), **two** options contain *Item 2* (B, C), and **two** options contain *Item 3* (D, E). Based on frequency, one of the three answers containing *Item 1* is the correct answer. Based on this tip, you have narrowed five answers down to three (A, C, D), increasing your probability of randomly guessing the correct answer from 20% to 33%.

Keep it Random

True randomness in the answer arrangement would result in clusters of answers, such as two, three, or even *four* A's in a row. But these tests are *supposedly* assembled by humans who intentionally *avoid* patterns, so when they recognize random clusters, they respond by mixing-up the answers. This means you should be a wee bit suspicious if you see three identical answers in a row. If you see *four* identical answers in a row, consider yourself a resident of Dangertown.

Knock-Off Answers

"But you said there *aren't* any trick questions!" We hear your fretting—and we don't blame you. This could be confusing. What there *won't* be are questions that have multiple correct answers or *zero* correct answers. What there *will* be are knock-off answers: answers that are so close to the correct answer that rushed students will haphazardly choose them and lose a quarter of a point on a question that could easily have been a slam dunk—*if* they had been more careful! In the same way that you should be skeptical when you're tempted to buy a $250 watch from a street vendor for the low, *low* price of $25, you should take a moment to read the fine print before you end up presenting a shabby *Timax* to your sweetheart on his/her birthday and end up *blinding* the poor kid's eye. Oh, we're being melodramatic? That's not what your boyfriend is going to think when a spring from his knock-off *Timax* shoots out and stabs him in the eye. Yeah, you should have considered that!

Which is why you need to …

Slow Down and Read Carefully

Just because the test is timed doesn't mean that you'll gain bonus points for flying through questions all haphazardly. While you should be able to answer the first few questions of each subsection in a brief moment, for the latter questions— you know, the harder ones?—quick doesn't equate to efficient. You're better off reading questions at a pace slow enough for your mind to comprehend; a good number of the available answers will be *so close* to correct and *so similar* to each other that if you don't pay close attention to the specifics of the question, you're likely to choose one of the *wrong* answers in lieu of the correct one.

Time Management

Every student is allotted less time on each section than he or she would prefer. *That's just how it's designed.* Instead of succumbing to Time Panic, remember that *everyone* in the room is in the same crunch as you, and that half of the people in the room are probably making one or more of the following mistakes:

Flub: Freaking out because they aren't sure how much longer they have to finish the section. They've just spent three minutes trying to remember the definition of *gubernatorial*[22] and developed amnesia. "*Gubernatorial...* goober... nation... editorial... *gubernatorial, gubernatorial—* wait, where am I!?"

Remedy: Write the end-time for each section on the front of your booklet. Simple, accurate, a deterrent for amnesia: *priceless.*

Flub: Dismissing themselves from the exam because they need to make an appointment with a chiropractor ASAP. You see, they're health-conscious people with serious concerns about the whiplash they've developed over the past hour by recklessly craning their necks at a million miles an hour to check the clock hanging on the wall behind them.

---

22 Definition on page 154

NOTES:

Remedy: Bring your watch, take it off your wrist, and place it on your desk directly in your line of sight. We recommend a digital clock because it is possible to become so involved in the Pythagorean Theorem that all knowledge of telling time has disappeared. Also, no sun dials.

Flub: Grooming themselves by nibbling off that small piece of snagged nail, which inevitably turns the mild imperfection into a large, jagged hangnail that beckons to be gnawed at for 93 seconds.

Remedy: Keep your nails trimmed and filed, both coming up to and during the test. Nail-biting is a compelling expression of anxiety with potential to turn a measly chipped nail into a giant project. Plus, do you have any idea how dirty it is beneath your fingernails? Yuck!

Flub: Becoming mildly hypnotized by the swirly motion of filling in their bubble sheets and finding themselves lost in a sea of graphite. Consequently, every four answers are followed by 20 seconds of searching for a reference point and mumblings of, "What the heck question was I answering?"

Remedy: Finish an entire page of questions *in the test booklet* prior to filling in the answer sheet. By minimizing the number of times that you need to reorient yourself as you shift back and forth between bubble sheet and test booklet, you'll drastically reduce the amount of time you spend de-confusing yourself.

Flub: After (sloppily) finishing a subsection, returning—as a big, fat cheater—to a previous section to "tie up some loose ends."

Remedy: Big. Mistake. First of all: *it's cheating*. Notice how, before Sir Cheater McCheaterson went about his deceitful ways, the booklet told him:

STOP

IF YOU FINISH BEFORE TIME IS CALLED,
YOU MAY CHECK YOUR WORK IN THIS
SECTION ONLY. DO NOT TURN TO ANY
OTHER SECTION IN THE TEST.

Apparently he didn't. If you return to another section to work, you're as bad as this jerk. Second of all: if you get caught, *you'll be given the boot*. No test score, no refund, no benefit to you.

Flub: (Since we're on the subject of cheating…) Analyzing the proctor's eye movements to determine the most opportune time to look over at their genius neighbor's bubble sheet.

Remedy: Do your own studying. After all, even though Mr. 2400 might be getting a perfect score, those foolish enough to copy his bubble sheet are *probably* filling in the correct answers, *but in the wrong section.* Yep, the test sections are all the same from one test booklet to another—they're just presented in a different order.

Flub: Setting down their pencils *where the pencil cannot do anything.*

Remedy: Seriously, why would you put down your pencil? Unless you're going to stretch your fingers or shake out a cramp, *never* put down your pencil. Trust us, there's *nothing* that you can't do while holding a pencil, and there are *very* few things that a finger can do better than your pencil. Take this time to check your work. Look:

uhmm...?   hrmm...   yes, yes...

Flub: Reading the directions like a total dunce.

Remedy: Know the directions before you ever see a legit SAT test booklet. You may not know what the exact questions will be, and you may not know the answers right off the bat, but you *can* have control over the SAT by knowing the directions long before you ever introduce yourself to your testing seat. Doesn't that sound reassuring?

NOTES:

Now that you've trimmed all those wasteful seconds, you have a significantly roomier window of time with which you can work. Here are some tips on how to use that additional time wisely:

Don't Forget: Questions Get Harder

Yikes. If you didn't know this, we're so, so sorry, because it's not some cruel joke that TPS is playing on you. You see, each subsection begins with rather easy questions, but they will increase in difficulty as you proceed. *This gem of knowledge comes with some powerful advantages, though.*

In the beginning of each subsection, you can assume that the "obvious" answers—the ones that just jump out at you—are, indeed, correct matter how thoroughly you inspect them. These are most likely the easy guys with the obvious answers, *so don't waste time over-analyzing them!*

Later on, you can assume that the "obvious" answer is the trick answer (i.e., the answer meant to *distract* you from the correct answer). When an answer screams out for your attention, show it you're not some sucker: be a detective and search for its flaw before you welcome the answer into your bubble sheet.

Hiding in the gray area between the two extremes are questions with numerous *almost* correct answers. These types of questions are a bit tricky because you can't rely on either of the two aforementioned tricks.

A note on non-answers: Knowing that the questions increase in difficulty will also help you determine whether or not to give that "non-answer" option a thought. At the beginning of a subsection, the "None of the above"-type of answer is more likely to be correct than later. Why? Well, the College Board likes to create a false sense of security in this reply early on so that when a student can't figure out the answer to a more difficult question, he or she panics and erroneously plugs in the non-answer.

Develop Your Own Annotation

While working through the test, you'll come across questions that you can solve quickly, ones that baffle you, and ones that you're *pretty* sure about (Well, maybe. You think you've got it.). Instead of mulling over the same question for *way* longer than you should, or allowing it to haunt you as you "move on" to the next question, designate some quick symbols to questions that you want to double-check and ones that you left blank. Don't try to draw a dragon every time you want to indicate, "This question is ridiculous!", or sketch a confused koala every time you want to remind yourself to double-check an answer. Make your notations short, sweet, and discernible, like a giant ✗ when you've skipped a question or a ? when you're iffy on your answer.

And what we consider to be one of our most important tips:

Don't take a practice exam, no matter how much you want to, with fewer than 48 hours between you and the SAT. Taking a practice exam is nearly as draining as the real thing (of course, this only stands true if you take the practice exams in the proper fashion), and burning yourself out right before your test is counterproductive. Plus, what if you get a disappointing score on the practice exam? The College Board will do plenty spirit-breaking for you, so spend your final 48 hours doing something pleasurable, like getting some fresh air and relaxing in the sun. You can always contemplate your method of attack from a hammock, right?

If you're concerned about being sharp in the early A.M., try using a crossword or Sudoku puzzle; these can get the blood flowing to your giant brain without prematurely tapping into the wealth of knowledge you've stowed away for the SAT.

Speaking of stowing away knowledge, let's get to it!

CHAPTER 2
Critical Reading

Critical Reading

In this section, you'll have 67 questions to complete in 70 minutes: 19 sentence completion questions to test both your vocabulary and your comprehension of advanced sentence structures, and 48 passage-based reading questions to test your ability to process literature. Sentence completion questions consist of *single* sentences (phew), but the passages can be anywhere from 100 to 850 words long.

You may be thinking, "Big whoop. Do a little reading and take over an hour for 67 multiple choice questions." But before you blurt it out and embarrass yourself, consider this: fixing a stand-alone sentence may only take a few seconds, but some passages will need to be read *very* carefully (and sometimes a once-through, as meticulous as you may read, might not suffice). And, unfortunately, you will probably get all flustered at least once—especially when the questions get increasingly harder (which they do)—but TPS is here to help you overcome this jarring agitation.

To avoid the embarrassment of having filled in a total of only four ovals in this section, you're going to want to know your reading speed. Remember how we mentioned that you shouldn't be fooled by 67 questions in 70 minutes sounding easy? Even though this breaks down to 62 seconds per question—a whole 62 seconds to choose just *one* letter from only *five* possible letters—there's also the whole reading thing.

What we're trying to say here is, don't be deceived by the whole time-to-question ratio; it's not nearly as manageable and casual as you may think. Get to know how long it takes you to read, how long it takes you to understand the question, how long it takes you to seek out the supporting evidence, and how long it takes you to match the evidence to the options. Sounds a bit more difficult when we put it that way, doesn't it?

Between reading the question, your options, and then *thinking*, you're looking at a time allocation closer to 40 seconds per question. And if you work wisely, you should be looking at even less time on the sentence completion questions so that you can reallocate the extra time to the reading passages' questions. Regardless, the 40-second estimate may be drastically different, depending on how quickly you read. To determine how *you* should allocate your time personally, we recommend that you go through and calculate the amount of time it took you to complete each question on a practice test. This way, if you would like to increase the number of questions that you complete in the limited time alloted, you may attempt to move more quickly through your practice tests and see if it pays off. Pay attention to which *types* of questions you can afford to speed through and which you need to handle in a more meticulous fashion.

NOTES:

Efficiency in Critical Reading

Generally speaking, the most efficient way to navigate through the critical reading section is by tackling questions in the order of: sentence completion, short passage, long passages. This order is determined by two factors:

☆ Sentence completion takes the least time; meaning you'll be able to address more questions than if you began with the reading passages, which are more time consuming.

☆ Furthermore, shorter reading passages take less time to read than longer reading passages. This provides the opportunity to answer more questions in the alloted time.

Being that no *one* question is worth more than another, correctly answering more questions—even if they are the easier ones—is the key to scoring big on the SAT. So choose the order of your subsections carefully!

Speaking of subsections, remember how we told you that questions become more difficult as you progress? Well, that gives us two more keys to efficiency:

☆ As you work through a subsection, anticipating an elevation in difficulty can save you from obsessing over a tough question and wasting precious time. If you have determined your prime speed to be 38 seconds per question, but you're already approaching a full minute, make an educated guess and *move on.* If you'd like to circle it and return to it later, feel free, but don't let one point devour the time of two.

☆ Since vocabulary will become more advanced as you work through the subsection, there is no reason for one of the very first answers to be one of the more obscure vocabulary words. So if you come across a word in the very first page of vocabulary that not one of your study buddies has ever heard of, you may want to consider it an *incorrect* option.

Remember: increasing difficulty has to do with *subsections*, not sections as a whole. This means that you'll be doing something a little like this:

SAT Coaster

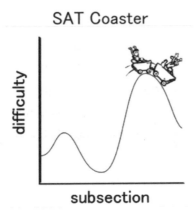

Pretend it's a roller coaster: even though it's getting really hard toward the end, you'll have a joyride to the bottom shortly.

Sentence Completion

The title says it all. Your job will be to choose the *best* possible word(s) to complete a sentence, like so:

Canadian Lynn Johnston was named cartoonist of the year in 1985, the first woman to be so -------.

(A) inspired
(B) entrusted
(C) honored
(D) employed
(E) eminent

Your task is simple: determine which one makes sense *in context*. While many of the options presented to you will be grammatically correct (because the College Board is tricky and will do whatever it can to foil you), the *best* answer will be the one that doesn't make your English teacher have a panic attack in the janitorial closet.

Whether you're choosing one word or two (like in the next example), all SAT sentence completion questions follow this same format, so you'll know exactly what to do when you see this:

If the laptop doesn't -------, first check the -------.

(A) happen . . switch
(B) turn off . . USB connection
(C) power up . . battery
(D) drive . . ignition
(E) greet . . street

OnCe again, only one option Can really Complete this sentenCe logiCally. (hint, hint)

Unfortunately, the sentence completion question that you'll see on the SAT will be a bit more difficult and is used as a means to test your vocabulary. Each question thrown at you can be lumped into one of two predictable categories: *contextual* or *logical*.

Contextual questions require you to recognize *how* a specific word is being used in a unique sentence. Contextual questions come in the formats of

Blah blah blah -------, definition of the blank.

&

Blah blah ------- and ------, definition of the first blank and definition of the second blank.

Examples of these guys would be:

She was an -----, for she spent most of her time with her own thoughts and rarely expressed her feelings.
(A) tenet
(B) *introvert*
(C) vigilante
(D) puissant
(E) catalyst

&

This book is filled with ------- and -------, clever jokes and wise sayings that will help you with the SAT.
(A) kiosks, barristers
(B) improprieties, invective
(C) *quips, aphorisms*
(D) apexes, jaunts
(E) labyrinths, scribes

Logical questions require you to know the definition of a word
and to be able to identify how it is being used within a complex
sentence. Logical questions come in the formats of

After observing this thing, prior notions of *x* were changed to
-------.

&

Although this thing *x*, we see the opposite characteristics of
x including -------.

And examples of these are:

After witnessing his impressive dunk, the coaches dismissed
Joe's "novice" status and declared him to be a ------- part of
the team.
(A) obstreperous
(B) *salient*
(C) ubiquitous
(D) uncouth
(E) bereft

&

Though it is assumed that certain breeds of dogs make poor
pets, the family was surprised to find ------- in their new pit
bull.
(A) *fidelity*
(B) suffrage
(C) victuals
(D) gainsay
(E) nexus

But, as we've told you once and we'll tell you again, don't ever underestimate the College Board. They like to trick you, and when it comes to sentence completion, it's usually done by mixing up a good deal of contrast and continuation signal words.

college
Board

Logic Reversal Words

Contrast signal words indicate that you're looking for two competing thoughts or ideas, such as can be found in the statement:

> I woke up in a *great mood* this morning because I was convinced that the government had banned the SAT, **but** now I'm *depressed* because I realize it was all just a sweet, sweet dream.

How sad!

As you can see in the sentence below, we *italicized* the contrasting thoughts and **bolded** the signal word. As long as you can do the same with more complex examples, you'll be just fine. The logic reversal words that you should be on the lookout for include:

Actually	Instead of
Although	Nevertheless
But	On the contrary
Despite	On the other hand
Even though	Rather than
Except	Still
Far from	Unless
However	Unlike
In contrast	While
In spite of	Yet

So if you were to be given "**Rather than** being -------, Emily preferred to share the cookies with her classmates.", you're going to look for something that is *opposite* of what you'd call a person who shares. Think: *If Emily* weren't to *share, she'd be* … greedy." And you're on the right track!

Continuation Signal Words

Continuation signal words indicate that you're looking for two *agreeing* thoughts, as are seen in the statement:

> Your jokes are *lame, cheesy* **and** *couldn't amuse a baby*, even if the punch lines came equipped with a basket of candy and fluffy bunnies.

Now you're just being mean.

Once again, even though you're way too sassy to ever need our help (we know you agreed with the example), we've *italicized* the agreeing thoughts and **bolded** the continuation signal word on the sentence below. Continuation signal words that you should watch for include:

Also	In addition to
And	Likewise
As well as	Moreover
Furthermore	Such as

For example, if you were to be asked to complete the sentence

"Here at Giant Corporation, Inc., we admire persistence; **likewise**, we applaud persons with ------- personalities", you would ponder as to what characteristic is similar to "persistent." Think: *If the Giant business likes persistence, then they probably also like assiduous people.* (You'd say that because you've begun making your vocabulary cards and, since it starts with an A, it was part of the first batch you made. Yay, you!)

The TPS Sentence Completion Method

The biggest pitfall with these questions is *created* by students overcomplicating the test. To save you from your own self-induced agony, TPS has devised the following blueprint for spanking sentence completion questions:

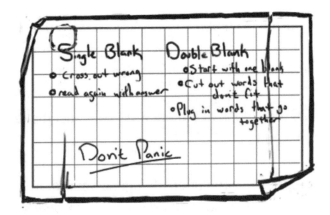

Begin by reading the sentence, keeping an eye out for contrast signal words, and skip over the blank(s).

For sentences with a single blank:

1. *Without sneaking a peek at your options*, read it again, this time intuitively plugging in sensible words. This "stab in the dark" will prepare you for sifting through the options.

2. Get to sifting. Read *all* possible answers, mark those that are similar to your own, and cross out those that make zero sense.

3. Plug in the answer that you think fits best and reread the entire sentence, inserting your choice. Does it make sense? If not, cross it out and try another.

Let's try it!

Ever since Columbus, the Americas have been host to a highly ------- culture, mixing European, Asian, Native American, and African influences.

Remember... don't look at the answers yet! Just make a guess as to what it could be.

OK, so we're talking about many things, so our "stab in the dark" would be something like *variable*, or *heterogeneous*.

Now, let's take a look at the options

    (A)   mundane
    (B)   sporadic
    (C)   complex
    (D)   diverse
    (E)   uniform

And hey, look at that, we have *diverse*, which is pretty much the same as *variable*! Our answer must be (D). But let's assume we don't know what *diverse* means, so let's try eliminating some options.

(A) ~~mundane~~ variable is *far* from boring

(B) ~~sporadic~~ *occasional* doesn't make sense!

(C) complex

(D) diverse

(E) ~~uniform~~ this is the exact opposite of variable

Now we're down to two possibilities: complex and diverse. Which is the *best* answer? Why, diverse, of course. For it means *showing great variety*.

For a sentence with two blanks:

1. Begin by determining if the sentence contains a reversal word.

   ☆ If yes, then one blank must be positive (+) and one must be negative (-).

   ☆ If no, then both blanks are either positive (+) or negative (-).

2. Assign a + or - value to each word in your list.

3. Eliminate options based on whether they fit the sentence structure, i.e., if it contains a reversal word or not.

Let's try it!

> While the public often ------- the negative television ads during election campaigns, research shows that such tactics can sway voters and win votes for the more ------- candidate.

>
> (A)   reviles, exuberant
> (B)   enjoys, wishy-washy
> (C)   applauds, patriotic
> (D)   berates, aggressive
> (E)   respects, inexperienced

Do we have a sentence reversal word? Hopefully you saw it right away! If not, try again: "While the public often…". See it now? *While* tells us that we're going to have a positive (+) and a negative (-) word to complete the sentence, so let's go through and see how many words can be given a +/- value.

> (A)   reviles -, exuberant +
> (B)   enjoys +, wishy-washy -
> (C)   applauds +, patriotic +
> (D)   berates -, aggressive +
> (E)   respects +, inexperienced -

Now, looking back at the original sentence, we see that the last blank must be something positive—because only good things get a candidate more votes—and the first blank must be negative because *while* dictates one negative and one positive. So, we need our choice to be -, +

    (A)   reviles -, exuberant +

    (B)   ~~enjoys +, wishy-washy -~~

    (C)   ~~applauds +, patriotic +~~

    (D)   berates -, aggressive

    (E)   ~~respects +, inexperienced -~~

(Wondering why aggressive isn't a negative here? Don't be tricked into giving a word the wrong sign. The word "aggressive" for example is often labeled as negative. But think about it, do you really want the attorney you hired to keep you out of jail to be anything other than aggressive? So some words can be either.)

At this point, a guess would give you a 50% chance, but understanding the connection between *negative* ads and *aggression* will be the key to successfully answering D.

Whatever you do, don't dwell. If you *think* you know the answer, make a guess; if you're baffled, skip it. Either way, mark the question in your booklet in case you have time for a second sweep and move along.

There's also a few other tips that TPS would like to share:

On *After*: When found in the *beginning* of a sentence, you know that the second half of that sentence is affected by the first.

After being told that she'd stepped in a "cow pie," Anne's appetite quickly diminished.

> (Her appetite diminished *because* she'd *suddenly* understood that "cow pie" meant cow manure and was not a nickname for cheesecake.)

On *Although*: When used in one clause, a conflicting thought will be found in another.

> *Although* she was generally a sweet girl, she awoke in a foul mood on the day that she was to meet with her hairstylist.

> (She's usually very nice, *but* she was rude on that fateful day. Consequently, her notoriously luscious locks were hacked into a horrible mangle. The moral of the story: reschedule your hair appointment if you wake up on the wrong side of the bed.)

On *For*: When used as a transition, the second half of the sentence will explain the first half.

I'm extremely disappointed in the stagnancy of commercial technology, *for* I'm inclined to think that something must have been invented since the release of the mePhone.

(The speaker thinks that the technology market should be filled with new, innovative products. Why? Because she finds it strange that there haven't been any breakthroughs since Pear released the mePhone. ...and the mePhone 2... and probably 3 and 4 and 5. Repeats aside, isn't there anything else out there?)

NOTES:

More on *For*: When used at the beginning of the sentence, a contrast is *often* being indicated.

> *For* handing in such an amazing essay, her paper on the art of chewing bubble gum was given a zero.

> (She handed in a pretty impressive thesis paper, but a quick Internet search exposed her as an academic fraud. She probably ended up getting kicked out of college. Learn from her mistake.)

So when is it an exception? Generally speaking, this is when we can take the information in front of the comma and just move it right before the period and still get the same idea across.

> *For* his amazing act of bravery in rescuing the child from a burning building, he was given the Medal of Courage.

becomes…

> He was given the Medal of Courage *for* his amazing act of bravery in rescuing the child from a burning building.

But if we try it with the first sentence, we end up with:

> Her paper on the art of chewing bubble gum was given a zero *for* handing in such an amazing essay.

…which, logically, doesn't make much sense!

On *Double Negatives*: If the College Board is going to trick you
on a sentence completion question, it'll probably be done by
throwing in two contrast signal words, such as in:

> The miser wouldn't pay an extra $0.25 to
> turn his hamburger into a cheeseburger, so
> the waitress wasn't shocked when he ------
> a $0.10 charge for sprinkles on his
> ice-cream cone.

> (A)   consented to
> (B)   permitted
> (C)   endured
> (D)   disputed
> (E)   authorized

The fix? Read the *entire* sentence and identify *all* contrast and
continuation signal words *before* speculating on the possible
answers.

Since we told you that this would be a double negative, you
know that you're looking for something that agrees with a
man being a miser and refusing to pay a $0.25 charge, even
though everyone knows that cheese makes *everything* more
delicious. So even though the trick was for you to be *shocked*
and assume that the miser was going to do something out
of character, you were on the lookout and saw the second
negative: the poor waitress *wasn't* shocked (neither when
he refused $0.35 in delicious toppings, nor when he left a
$0.04 tip). So you know to find something that *agrees* with the
personality of a miserly old man. Perhaps one that *disputes* ten
meager cents?

On *You Versus Political Correctness*: If you're trying to decide between your opinion and a statement that is politically correct, *go with the latter*. The SAT tries very hard to be P.C., so you're better off choosing the option that sounds most publicly acceptable. Just imagine you're running for senator and ask yourself, "Which of the options is least offensive. Or better yet, which is the most positive?"

On *Really Difficult Vocabulary:* Sometimes you just actually need to know the word. If possible, work *around* really difficult vocabulary by paying attention to the context. Take this question:

Even though he was ------- of heights, Brad did a spectacular job of overcoming his consternation and confidently performed a high-wire balancing act that filled the auditorium with elated cheers.

(A)   fond
(B)   terrified
(C)   appreciative
(D)   inattentive
(E)   supportive

Do you need to know the meaning of *consternation*, or do you only need to consider that he did some daring high-wire balancing acts, something atypical of a person who is ------- of heights? Without wasting a moment on the definition of *consternation*, we can determine that the answer is (B), terrified. Thus, really difficult vocabulary sometimes exists only to waste your time. Before you're 40 seconds into the analysis of con-ster-na-tion's pieces, see if you can't take a detour around it altogether.

Deconstructing Tricky Sentence Structure

If you're having a hard time dealing with the construction of a particular sentence because of its use of contrast or continuation vocabulary, we recommend that you simply go through your options and assign each option a positive (+) or negative (-) value, as discussed earlier. Once you have your vocabulary list simplified to plus and minus signs, you can significantly decrease the size of your list by removing pairs that don't fit the sentence structure.

Take a look at this tricky guy:

> As a scientist, Leonardo DaVinci was capable of _____ but his mistakes were remarkably few in light of his _____ .

   (A) error ... accomplishments
   (B) artistry ... failures
   (C) genius ... works
   (D) trivia ... lapses
   (E) innovation ... achievements

Do you see the reversal word "but?" This tells us that one part of the sentence is going to be negative and one part will be positive. It is pretty clear that the first blank should be a positive word, as it speaks of being capable. It is also relatively clear that the second half of the sentence will be negative, as it is providing a "but" to being capable. So the first thing you do is look for answers where the first word is a positive word and the second word is negative:

(A) error- ... accomplishments+

(B) artistry+ ... failures-

(C) genius+ ... works+

(D) trivia isn't really either. (Some words may not necessarily demonstrate a positive or negative, and are simply considered neutral) ... lapses is negative - So we have a neutral here and a negative

(E) innovation+ ... achievements+

So you can see here that just by quickly assigning +/- to each word, we have already narrowed our possible answers to either (B), or possibly (D). If you have to guess on this one, at least you were able to increase your chances from 20% to 50%! And when you plug in the 2 options left, B becomes a very obvious answer. Voila!

Here's another, though less obvious, example:

> For its tiny size, ocean plankton has ------- impact on the
> planet's ecosystem.
>
> (A) a negligible
> (B) no
> (C) an enormous
> (D) a minor
> (E) a small

Even though we don't have any of the classic logic reversal
words, it's clear from the sentence's structure that it is designed
to indicate a contrast between the smallness of plankton and
its effect on the environment. Without having to know what
plankton is, we can eliminate (A), (B) and (D) for this reason
alone. While (E) could work, it doesn't really make a statement.
Consequently, answer (C) works best: "For its tiny size, ocean
plankton has *an enormous* impact on the planet's ecosystem."

Sentence completion seems easy enough, right? That's why
you're probably going to want to do them before you move on
to the portion covered in our next section.

Reading Passages

The majority of the critical reading section is composed of long and extremely dull passages from which you must answer a bunch of questions. Are we exaggerating just how boring this section will be? Not at all. As a matter of fact, in the eyes of the SAT writers, boring is beautiful: the more disinterested you are in the passages, the less closely you'll read them, which makes it easier for the writers to craft "difficult" questions for you.

"Oh no!" we hear you crying. "How do I prepare my mind to confront these insipid passages and somehow protect it from turning into mush?"

You sound so smart with your advanced vocabulary.

And that's a good question. *However*, there is some good news *and* some bad news. The bad news: There isn't a quick, direct way to nail down the analytical skills that you'll need to do well on this section. But before you freak out, here's the good news: You've been, in an indirect sense, preparing for this section since you first learned how to read. Can you say that about any other part of the test?

One thing that we can suggest is pushing your reading speed. The faster you can read—while, of course, still comprehending what you're reading—the more time you'll be able to allocate to analyzing the questions. Your best bet is to practice reading faster and faster, and then test how much of the material you retained.

NOTES:

Since you'll probably go insane if you force your brain to endure a thousand practice tests, we recommend that you pump your speed by reading a variety of literature and, directly after, recollecting on its content. This can be done by either writing a detailed summary or by creating a list of important points and supporting evidence. Completing this last step will ensure that you're truly reading and not haphazardly skimming, which is only as good as not having read at all when you're asked to recall details. After practicing different reading speeds, verify your progress with the scores from an SAT practice test.

We hope you're not taking this suggestion as, "Read only what you like, then only what you loathe," (i.e., the boring, schmoring SAT material). If you're going to be successful in your endeavor to become a quick analytical reader, you need to give yourself some variation. Try rotating between your favorite comic book, *The New York Times*, an article from some magazine that you generally enjoy, *The Atlantic Monthly, National Geographic*, and whatever other publications you can find in your public library. Becoming familiar with many different styles of literature will keep the journey interesting *and* prepare you for whatever mundane article gets thrown your way.

Plus, if you don't keep it interesting, you'll probably give up. Right? Right. And that's not the goal here. So, instead of taking Negative Nancy with you on this journey, shove her out of the passenger seat and welcome Positive Patty aboard: the better your attitude, the better you'll fare.

As you do your reading—whatever sort it may be—do so actively. If your eyes are the only part of your body doing any work, there won't be much of anything to which your memory can connect. If, however, you could just get the speech centers of your brain active, you could do a significantly better job of recalling the information.

Reading Actively

Here are a few ways to avoid mindlessly eyeballing a block of text. Try some of them out and use whichever one works best for you. (Notice the one part? Don't consistently use them all; you'll never get past the first passage on the test.)

Teach Your Speech to Do the Macarena

What we mean is … as you finish each paragraph, try to repeat its movements: **What is the point? How did it support the point? How does the point relate to the passage?** (You know, Macarena mentally. But don't just bask in your newly attained knowledge; use your words.) This way, if you're not sure what to say, you know that you need to reread *this* particular paragraph. The difference between needing to reread a paragraph and needing to reread an entire passage is like the difference between retracing your steps since you last had your car keys and frantically searching an entire city for a neon green rabbit's foot keychain that wasn't so lucky after all.

Know What You're Looking For

Before you get started, skim the questions so you know what to seek and *then* get to reading the passage. Know what you're looking for *before* you start looking! As you find material relevant to the questions, circle or underline it and *move on*! Don't ever stop in the middle of your reading to answer a question, because you'll almost always be asked questions about the main idea which, without having read the passage in its entirety, you may not be able to answer. Once you've finished reading the passage, the marked areas will tell you where to look for the answers.

Circle Strong Vocabulary and Phrases

The most inspired writing occurs when authors are in harmony with their thoughts. Since you're looking to dissect their thoughts, circle strong phrases, imagery, and vocabulary (especially adjectives and verbs) as you read. **Getting in tune with the author's tone and attitude helps with comprehension, which will help you read more quickly and answer questions more confidently.**

Underline Important Bits

An extremely effective way for some students to read actively is to become wise underliners. What we mean by *wise* is that you can't just underline everything you see; rather, you need to underline the <u>important bits</u>, and the <u>important bits</u> only! Most students become so pleased by the neon colors of their highlighters that they forget the whole point of underlining and

highlighting: to indicate the *extremely important information*.
And what does that entail?

Well, most prose generally contains the following:

- ○ An introductory paragraph with the **main idea**
- ○ Supporting paragraphs with **evidence** and **examples**
- ○ A paragraph with **counter-claims** and **rebuttals**
- ○ A conclusion indicating the **implications** or future **plan**

It is these four things that you should be <u>underlining</u> as
you read. As you come across the supporting paragraphs,
<u>underline</u> the main idea of each and write "EX" in the margin
to indicate examples. If you can find these four main pieces,
you'll be able to swiftly navigate the passage to find the
information you need.

Wondering why we suggest <u>underlining</u> and never highlighting?

- A. Highlighters aren't allowed on the exam
- B. Even highly trained highlighter users become enamored
  with the pretty colors and forget the device's purpose
- C. It's super tempting to sniff something so bright and
  beautiful, but we need you to have as many brain cells
  as possible

So wean yourself away from the highlighter and get used to
good ole #2.

Play Possum When the Longest Passage Comes Around

This tip is really the exact opposite of reading actively, because we're suggesting that you not read a particular part at all. But we have good reason! See, with such a long passage, a surprising number of students don't do the best job of *actively* reading on this one. If you have time to do it, fantastic. But make it the last one you do, as longer questions don't get more points.

The reason we suggest this is that the long passage tends to be so long (*twice* as long as the other long passages, as a matter of fact), and the questions tend to be so difficult, that few points are typically awarded to the average student for all of his hard work in this area. Consequently, TPS advises students to do the longest passage last, or if need be, *skip* it altogether and use that time to *actively* read *other* passages and revisit questions that were marked as skipped or were unsure guesses (you marked those guys with a ?, right?). The reasoning goes right back to the fact that all questions have the same worth: why spend several minutes reading the longest passage and spending time on the most difficult questions, when you could return to easier passages and pick up a few extra points? And, hey, if there's time left over, do some educated guessing on those long passages and maybe pick up a few extra points!

An Important Note

Before we comment on the different types of reading passages, we want to make one thing clear: all necessary information to answer the question will be located *within* the reading passage. Why did we find this so darn important? Because you should not, in any circumstance, allow your outside knowledge to complicate the question. If your outside knowledge counters what the passage says, *don't let it impede on your choosing the answer that reflects the reading passage.* You're looking to answer the questions based solely on the passage—not on what you already know, smart guy.

Hopefully this won't ever happen to you though, because even though the College Board will go out of its way to make your life difficult, it *won't* go so far as to make itself look bad. As a matter of fact, they're very interested in keeping a sparkly clean public image. (How else would they get parents to keep handing over their children?) Consequently, they avoid including passages that contradict common knowledge and opinions; this means no essays on the health benefits of long-term radiation exposure and no excerpts from *How Women Ruined the Workforce.* The College Board isn't about to bring up a controversial issue that would turn your conscience into a warzone.

Passage Types

The passages vary from test day to test day, and from season to season. There are, however, a few things that you can anticipate:

 There will be a few short passages, each about 100 words and accompanied by two or three questions

 There will be five long passages, each between 450 and 850 words that span 50 to 80 lines

 There is *always* one scientific passage

 There is *always* one excerpt from a narrative

 Each passage will be preceded by an italicized introduction *which should be read carefully* as it could contain information crucial to understanding the passage.

The Scientific Passage

We chose to start here because, for reasons unjustified, students tend to be terrified of the science passage. "But I want to attend a music academy," they cry. "Why do I need to know anything about science?"

Wipe your eyes and take a breath, because *you don't*. The scientific passage might ramble on about bimolecular nucleophilic substitution reactions in organic chemistry and how a sp^3 hybridized carbon atom is attacked from the opposite side of the leaving group (gasp!), but there will *always* be an explanation of this jargon in layman's terms. Even though your instincts are going to push you toward panicking, your fears will be dismissed when you read, "That is, two molecules come together when one part of a molecule is replaced by an 'attacking' molecule from the opposite end." The College Board is banking on your inability to fight off hyperventilation before making it to the "that is" part.

Let's practice! Do your best to make it through this excerpt and question without breaking a sweat.

An alcohol is a molecule that contains an OH group; that is, it has a branch composed of oxygen and hydrogen. While most people think of alcohol as an intoxicating beverage, alcohols are also used in detergents and to lubricate jet engines.   It also surprises many people to learn that the same fermentation process that produces alcoholic beverages is being researched as a means to produce alcohols that can supplement global energy needs.

Based on the information in the passage, we can conclude that:

(A) alcohol has a very limited range of uses
(B) alcohol alone is an effective detergent
(C) alcohol is a great fuel for jet engines
(D) alcohols contain at least one oxygen atom
(E) alcohol is the energy of the future

How'd you do? Just a little perspiration, but then you arrived at the "that is" part and regained your cool?   We're so proud of you, because that's the hardest part of the scientific passage! And while some of those answers mix together aspects of the paragraph, only one, (D), is explicitly stated in the passage.

The Minority Passage

Next up, we have the minority passage: the passage that you should be *oh* so glad exists. You see, the minority passage came into existence in the 1970s in response to accusations that the College Board had designed an inherently biased exam, and that this bias was evident when the scores of minority groups were compared to those of the majority group. To ensure that they wouldn't lose a single victim, a minority passage was added to the critical reading section in an attempt to say, "See, we love torturing all *equally!*"

And here's why you should be glad that it exists: *the questions that couple minority passages are some of the easiest you will encounter.* Since you know *why* the minority passage is included, you don't even have to consider what the tone will be, which is of *course* an appraisal of some minority group. And best of all, the questions that ask you what the author is trying to express can be simplified to the following question: Which of the following five options are something that you would like to be said about you?

Without even needing a passage, then, you should be able to correctly answer the following:

The author expresses ------- toward the Cuban community for enduring their trials and tribulations.

(A) contempt
(B) ambivalence
(C) disinterest
(D) reverence
(E) envy

Oh, how the author *revered* the Cuban people for the struggles they endured! Easy peasy.

NOTES:

The Art Passage

The art passage covers all sorts of subjects from modern literature, to sculpture, to music. The passage could be on a medium, a particular style, or even on a single artist, and it's generally written as a compliment of the subject. So while the author may have some sort of criticism, it's usually delivered as a compliment sandwich with a side of chips: some good things, a bad thing or two, and some more good stuff. (The chips are usually good, too, making the passage have an overall positive tone.) As you read, underline the beginnings of each pro and of each con; the questions are bound to ask something about the author's criticism and how it relates to his overall perspective.

The Historical Passage

Historical passages are commentaries on a time period or a cultural movement, be it politics, fashion, or spirituality. The authors will provide their interpretation of a period or movement, providing examples to support their claim, and will often cite other experts who agree with their viewpoints. The authors may also present and refute colleagues with whom they disagree. As you read this passage, circle all names and dates, and when you arrive at the list of examples, surround the whole chunk in nice, thick brackets so that you can skip over them later if you need to re-skim the passage in order to comprehend the overall meaning of the text.

The Fiction Passage

The fiction passage tends to be the trickiest because it relies on a set of fine-tuned skills that are picked up over years and years of paying attention in your English class. You will need to read this particular passage very closely to pick up on style and tone, and to sort through literary techniques such as analogies and extended metaphors. When it comes to the latter aspect, your challenge will be to work with what's *actually* there and not to get carried away: to pick up on the authors' *intended* meaning, not to cook up some profound message that's barely related to the text.

The Paired Passages

There will be a coupling of two independent passages that are related by subject, tone, or conclusion. For example, you may have two passages written by philosophers from different times and places, one written on war and one on the concept of love. Although they may begin with two different subjects, they will both end with a commentary on the importance of respecting the autonomy of strangers. Therefore, while these passages initially seem unrelated, they complement each other nicely. See how that works?

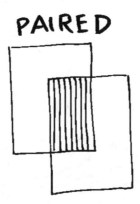

PAIRED

The double passage is set up like this:

(1) Introduction
(2) First passage
(3) Second passage
(4) Questions on the first passage
(5) Questions on the second passage
(6) Questions concerning both passages

But you'd be wise to go about dealing with the double passage like this:

(1) Introduction
(2) First passage
(3) Questions on the first passage
(4) Second passage
(5) Questions on the second passage
(6) Questions concerning both passages

Think about it: passage one will be freshest right after you've read it, and passage two will be freshest, you know, right after you've read it. And since you can't answer questions that concern both passages until you've actually *read* both passages, you should save them for last.

As for the content, the paired passages could be of any of the aforementioned types, so deal with them individually as you would if they were isolated.

To help with the connectivity of the two passages (how they agree, disagree, or complement one another), you may wish to jot a note on how they're related just prior to answering the second passage's questions. The issue of connectivity will be largely ignored as you work through the second passage's questions, as the relationship issue will be reserved for the third round of questions; therefore, it may be helpful later on if you make note of the relationship while it's still fresh.

If you're concerned that you may not understand why the particular passages are paired, fear not: the relationship between the passages is often commented on in the italicized introduction. It may say that they have commonalities, or that they have two different views; but even if it doesn't explicitly come out and say their relationship, TPS has a trick for you:

★ If both passages are on the same subject, or written by two contemporary authors, the passages probably oppose one another or use very different reasoning to arrive at the same conclusion.

★ If the passages are on different subjects, or were written by authors separated by time or space, the passages probably agree or complement one another.

Why? Well, if two very similar passages were chosen (both in subject and authors, as any given time period and place tends to have its own unique style), and both authors agreed in pretty much every sense, the differences would be far too easy to identify. And if they were written on different subjects, but had nothing to do with one another, then the College Board would have a doozy of a time coming up with questions for the third section.

The You-May-Want-to-Skip-This Passage

This ruthless 100+ liner was put into the SAT to make even the nerdiest of bookworms break down during the critical reading section. Whereas the paired passages have a nice little break in the middle where you can answer questions and take a breather from the authors' dull jabbering on advanced ice cube freezing techniques, the big one ruthlessly chugs along for 1,300+ words and only stops when it arrives at the junction of "These questions are ridiculously hard" and "When the heck did this boring waste of ink ever say that!?" And this, dear, is why we recommend that many students never hop on this train and instead journey to happier places, i.e., other passages where the points can be nabbed more easily. In a nutshell, save this big ole baby for last!

Buuuuuuuut, for our smarties out there, and the admirable, brave souls who refuse to back down from the College Board's rudest use of print, TPS has a tip for you:

While the questions for all passage types are *usually* posed in the same order as their answers appear in the original text, this predictable sequence is nearly *guaranteed* for the super long passage. This means that you should jot the question number in the margin beside the line in which you found its answer, because you can be confident that the next answer will be found *after* that line. This gem is *especially* valuable when you have question 4 indicating a vocabulary word in line 62 and question 6 citing a phrase from line 76, because you'll be able to narrow your search for question 5's answer to lines 62 through 76.

Before you try to get away without reading the passage, we're going to warn you that *context can change everything*. This means that you'll need to consider lines 62 through 76's context, because its relationship to the passage as a whole could drastically change its meaning. It will often be the case that one of your options will be an answer that only makes sense if the word or phrase in question were taken out of context. Don't fall into the trap!

Question Types and Strategies

Good news! SAT writers are boring and predictable, so even though they design questions with the sole purpose of causing the maximum amount of suffering, they're generally pretty bad at it! Even though the first couple waves of students faced the agony of the College Board's reading passage questions, later testers were saved by the translucence of the meticulously followed plan: when observant students realized that all questions could be easily categorized into six question types, they took action to prepare themselves. Lucky you, they were humanitarians and shared their discovery.

1. General (Main Idea)
   a. The author is primarily concerned with …
   b. The argument in the second paragraph is best summarized by …
   c. The primary purpose of the exploding bottle of soda is to show …

Consider the topic and concluding paragraphs, and briefly revisit the topic sentence of supporting paragraphs. Like anticipating answers for sentence completion questions, trying to answer the question in your own words prior to scanning your options can be helpful. These questions are testing your ability to identify different ways to restate the same thing. While the passage may say, "We ought not blindly allow the use of dangerous chemicals, called by the less threatening name of *pesticides*, to be sprayed across the American fields," but the correct answer may be phrased as, "The primary purpose of the passage is to argue that unnatural forms of pest control in agriculture should be monitored."

2. Explicit (Facts)

Ex

> According to the documentation of rogue thumbtacks attacking the posteriors of principals across the nation, ...

These questions are based on snippets of information, usually paired with a line reference, that force you to determine their function or significance: what did this bit of information mean, or what purpose does it serve? Well, if that excerpt came from an essay on bullying in school, it would suggest that it is not just students, but also authority figures, who deal with bullying in the classroom.

3. Extended Reasoning (Inferences)
   a. Based on her belief in this particular unstated assumption, it can be inferred that …
   b. Which of the following statements would the author most likely (dis)agree with?

Inferences, or conclusions made based on the author's words, are often indicated by words and phrases such as *apparently, it can be inferred, probably, seems, suggests,* and *the author implies.* These questions can be paired with any type of passage and frequently include faux answers: ones that *look* right at first glance, and ones that merely restate a fact without answering the question. Avoiding the trap is as easy as following this process: formulate your own answer and try to find one similar to it that is *supported* by the passage and not merely by your attitude toward the text. And again, *always read all of the options before choosing one.*

4. Author's Logic
   a. What tone does the author take when recounting the plight of the AWOL left sock?
   b. Which of the following best describes the development of the passage?
   c. The author cites the court case of "Kid on Crutches vs. Banana Peel" in order to …

If you circled vocabulary and imagery as you read, glance over it again. Just a few key words and phrases, and knowledge of how they were used within the passage, will give you everything you need to know. Your task is to determine *how* the author develops and delivers his ideas in the passage.

5. Vocabulary-in-Context
   a. The word "accost" in line 12 means …
   b. The phrase "quailed away like a startled chicken" (line 13) refers to …
   c. Which of the following best captures the meaning of the word "gainsay" in line 14?

These questions often deal with particularly advanced vocabulary or with words that have multiple meanings and rely on your ability to determine the word's meaning based on its usage in a particular sentence. These questions can be dealt with the same way as sentence completions. Likewise, your option can be swapped for the word in question to check for sensibility.

6. Double Passage Comparison
   a. Which statement from passage 1 does not have a parallel idea in passage 2?
   b. How would the author of passage 1 respond to the idea of banning mushrooms as a food source as suggested in passage 2?
   c. Which statement regarding ostriches as an alternative to motorcycles is best supported by the two passages?

Remember that tip we told you to jot down before answering the second passage's questions? You can use these notes as a guide to answering the comparison questions. It is also helpful to focus on the validity of your options for *one* passage at a time. Eliminate all false options, and review the remaining possibilities to check their validity for the other passage: this method will limit how much the two passages blur together as you cruise your options.

Question Key Words and Phrases

....because sometimes it can be difficult to understand what the SAT is even asking of you (we know your pain).

Word or Phrase	Your Goal
According to the author/passage	Answer the question based on the passage. Do not consider outside factors, such as what you know, think, or believe.
Best	Sift through the options, many of which will be correct, and find the *one* that most effectively answers the question. You may also find yourself trying to decide which one of numerous *almost* correct answers is least incorrect.
Chiefly, Mainly, *or* Primarily	Determine the most central aspect or most important reason from among numerous true options. You will have to consider the weight or impact of different parts of the passage and decide which is most influential.
Except	Identify which word, phrase, or statement is the odd man out. This may be something true among incorrect statements or something false among correct statements.
The author implies/suggests *or* It can be inferred	Using evidence from the passage, choose an option that is representative of the author's implied conclusion. The answer will not be directly stated, so you will need to understand the big picture.

NOTES:

Tips and Tricks for Passage-Based Reading Questions

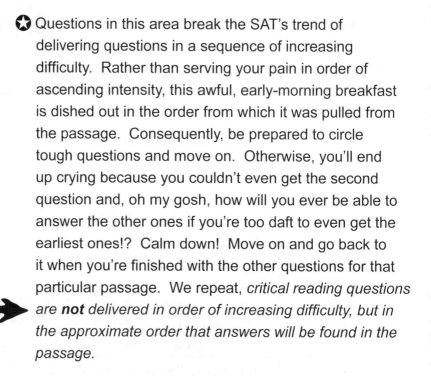

⭐ Questions in this area break the SAT's trend of delivering questions in a sequence of increasing difficulty. Rather than serving your pain in order of ascending intensity, this awful, early-morning breakfast is dished out in the order from which it was pulled from the passage. Consequently, be prepared to circle tough questions and move on. Otherwise, you'll end up crying because you couldn't even get the second question and, oh my gosh, how will you ever be able to answer the other ones if you're too daft to even get the earliest ones!? Calm down! Move on and go back to it when you're finished with the other questions for that particular passage. We repeat, *critical reading questions are **not** delivered in order of increasing difficulty, but in the approximate order that answers will be found in the passage.*

⭐ Don't ignore adjectives: they can be the key to understanding the author's intent, tone, and attitude.

⭐ Be able to support all answers with information found directly in the passage.

⭐ Vocabulary questions that use a word with multiple meanings *rarely* intend the common definition. For example, *grave* in the following sentence refers to something other than a burial plot. "The *grave* expression on her face told us that something was seriously wrong with the sow." And what about the word *sow*? Does it refer to the action of scattering seeds, or to the animal (i.e., a female pig)?

✪ Don't be made a fool. Recognize that an option may be *both true* and *wrong*. As always, the correct one is that which **best** answers a question, *not* one that simply states something true.

✪ Don't play hopscotch with your passages. Handle the question set for one *entirely* before moving on to another passage.

✪ If trying to choose between two answers, the least *absolute* is most likely the correct one. i.e., "it is *always* true that" versus "it is *often* true that" and "we *never* go there" versus "we *usually* don't go there." Bad answers often contain such absolute vocabulary and should stick out like a sore, very wrong thumb!

✪ Questions with a line number reference: read four lines before and after that line to put the info into context.

✪ If you circle a question with the anticipation of returning to it, make sure to do it *before* moving onto the next section. This includes both sentence completion and passage reading questions, but we've put it here because it's a particularly important tip for dealing with questions on rather long or bland passages (i.e., all of them) because, if you move on for even five minutes, you'll probably forget all of the rationalizing you've already gone through, or even the actual reading that you were unfortunate enough to have done.

NOTES:

⭐ Inference questions: If an option seems far-fetched, it probably is. The College Board uses prose from good writers, so understanding an SAT passage won't be like deciphering the "IDC" from a text message. (Does "I don't care" really mean "I don't care," or does it mean "Wow, that sounds like the worst idea ever but I'm bored so I guess I'll go."? How are you supposed to know?)

⭐ If you're running short on time, locate questions with line references—specifically vocabulary questions—because they can usually be answered after only reading three or four lines, whereas main idea questions require a complete reading and comprehension of a passage.

And last, but not least,

⭐ Beef up your vocabulary.

How? By reading on into the next section, of course!

CHAPTER 3

Vocabulary

Vocabulary

Having a well-developed vocabulary is extremely helpful as you move through the critical reading section of the SAT. While there are some questions that can only be answered with certainty by a person who knows the precise definition of a particular word, most questions will merely be made *easier* and less time-consuming by a person with an impressive vocabulary. For these brainy students, this means more time to deal with other, non-vocabulary based questions.

If you don't consider yourself to be a "brainy student," you're still in luck: if you can master word prefixes, suffixes, and roots, you can disassemble and comprehend words that you've neither seen nor heard. We recommend that all students freshen up on these components before moving forward to the vocabulary. And why do we think that adding *more* is going to help you? Because they'll be shortcuts in your learning process for that giant stack of notecards you're assembling!

Latin Prefixes

Prefixes come just before the root word and add to the definition of the word. An easy one that you're probably privy to is the combination *co* and *operate*, a word that means to *operate together*. One you might not be familiar with, however, is *antedate* from the chart below: if you know *ante* means before, you get "before date," which is *exactly* antedate's definition: precede in time.

Prefix	Meaning	Example and Definition
a	without	amorphous – without shape
ambi	both	ambiguous – multiple meanings
ante	before	antedate – precede in time
circum	around	circumnavigate – navigate around
co	together	convoke – call together
de	away, off	deter – discourage, send away
dis	none, away	discord – lack of harmony
inter	between, among	interject – to interrupt by saying something
post	after	posthumous – pertaining to after death
pre	before	presage – indicate before something occurs
re	again, back, backward	redundant – done over and over and over and over and over and over
retro	back	retrograde – moving backward
sub	under	subvert – to put underneath
trans	across, beyond, through	transcontinental – across continents

NOTES:

Now these guys aren't Latin, but they're super helpful just the same!

Other Helpful Prefixes

Prefix	Meaning	Example and Definition
bene	good	benefit – something advantageous
contra	against	contravene – to conflict with
dict	speak	dictate – to say or read
homo	same	homogeneous – of the same kind
hyper	above	hyperactive – more active than normal
hypo	below	hypoallergenic – causes less allergic reactions than normal
mal	bad	malodorous – unpleasant smelling
necro	dead	necrology – the study of death
mis	wrong	misnomer – incorrect name
multi	many	multitude – a large number
neo	new	neologism – newly introduced word, term, or phrase
poly	many	polymorphic – changes shape numerous times
sanct	holy	sanctify – to make holy

hypoallergenic hippopotamus

Latin Roots

Now we're to roots, the *core* of a word! These guys are frequently manipulated to mean a plethora of things, so if you can remember the roots, you'll be half-way to understanding the more complex vocabulary word.

Root	*Meaning*	*Example and Definition*
duc	to lead, bring, take	conduct – to guide, to *bring* together
ject	to throw	projection – presentation of image on a surface, to *throw* the image up
pel	to drive	impel – to urge to move forward, to *drive*
pend	to hang	pendulum – object suspended, *hanging* from a fixed point
port	to carry	import – to bring into the country, to *carry* from another place
scrib or script	to write	subscribe – to sign, to *write* one's name inscription – something written
tract	to pull, drag, draw	extract – to remove, to *draw* out of something
ver	truth	veracious – *truth*ful
vert	to turn	invert – to *turn* in

NOTES:

Latin Suffixes

And we have suffixes, the tail end of a word that functions just like a prefix. Why not just prefixes then, you ask? Because with the ability to use *both*, you're looking at complex words made out of small, easy to remember bits of information! In *Latin Prefixes*, we showed you how *circumnavigate* means to navigate *around*, but if you have *circumnavigable*, all of a sudden it's *able* to be circumnavigated. See the worth in suffixes and prefixes? Read on!

Suffix	*Function*	*Example and Definition*
able *or* ible	forms adjectives that mean "capable or worthy of"	transferrable – capable of being transferred visible – capable of being viewed
ation *or* ment	creates a noun out of a verb	cerebration – thought (from cerebrate, which means to *think*) blandishment – flattery
ify	forms verbs that mean "to make or cause to become"	vivify – to make vivid
ity	creates a noun out of an adjective	austerity – severity

Now that you're privy to some of the important components of our language, you can use it to deconstruct vocabulary that is unfamiliar to you. Here are two examples to try:

The wart-covered, malevolent hags placed a *malediction* upon their enemy.

mal: bad | dict: to say = to say something bad

Could they be placing a curse on their enemies?

Sasha's *interjection* forced Joe and Carl to put aside their tiff and search for her missing Fluffykins.

inter: between | ject: to throw = to throw between

Did she throw her words between Carl's and Joe's?

Since English can be annoyingly peculiar, deconstructing vocabulary can be a bit of a tricky process—but once you adopt the habit, it's amazingly useful! This is why we *highly* recommend memorizing the above prefixes, roots, and suffixes before moving on. With that knowledge locked away in your noggin, without ever knowing what *impending* means, you'll feel something *hanging* above your head, and next thing you know, it will hit you: *impending* is *about to happen*. Just like this list of most commonly used SAT vocabulary.

NOTES:

abase – to degrade or dishonor

> Think of it this way: stealing a base is acceptable in baseball, but in other scenarios, stealing is dishonorable.

> He was greatly abased when the only girl on the baseball league managed to sneak a base right in plain sight.

abash – to embarrass

> It sure would abash you if you'd accidentally bashed yourself over the head.

abate – to lessen

> If Abe ate half of your ice cream sundae, then he would abate the amount you'd get.

abhor – to loathe or hate

> I abhor Abe for eating my ice cream!

abominate – to loathe or hate

> Abominate rhymes with hate. Think of a cheer: "Don't hate. Don't abominate. Just mediate!"

> Ever since he ruined an otherwise perfectly good snowboarding trip, Jeff abominated the Abominable Snowman.

abstruse – difficult to comprehend; profound

> Abstruse and obtuse have similar meanings, and obtuse is often used in mathematics. Perhaps you may find the study of mathematics to be abstruse if you struggle at mathematics.

acclivity – upward slope

> It might help if you look at the "acc" and think of accelerating. If you approached an acclivity while driving up a hill, then you would rely on the accelerator to help get you to the top of the hill.

> Let's climb the acclivity so we can get maximum acceleration on the way down!

accolade – award, honor

> A college student who takes studying seriously will be more apt to receive top academic accolades for being studious.

accost – approach and speak to

> The shrewd tourist accosted the shopkeeper to negotiate a cost for the necklace he wanted to buy for his niece.

acquiesce – to agree without enthusiasm

> You may acquiesce to spruce up your spiffy new vocabulary skills with your cantankerous acquaintance instead of studying with your clever best friend.

acronym – a word formed from the initials of a group of words, a phrase, or a name

> Acro implies "beginning" and nym implies "word," thus acronym roughly translates to "beginning of a word." Think SCUBA (self-contained underwater breathing apparatus).

acute – keen, sharp, quick witted

> Owning a leopard seal with a cute set of big eyes might seem like a cute idea, but they are very acute and can drown a person if they feel threatened.

adamant – unyielding, resolute

> When your pal Adam comes knocking on your door, you must remain adamant and send him packing. It's time to study!

admonish – warn against error, mild rebuke

> Since Nicole was admonished for sneaking out past curfew, the likelihood for her to repeat such daft behavior was severely diminished.

adroit – skillful

> Utilizing a droid to execute neurosurgery would take advantage of its particularly adroit abilities.

adulate – flatter excessively

Oh, you adulate me!

adulterate – to make impure

Babies are born pure; adults become impure.

adumbrate – to foreshadow by disclosing partially

Great writers always adumbrate a bit about the next book in their series as a teaser.

aesthetic – the artistic side; visual beauty

Cosmetics are used to increase aesthetics.

affinity – natural attraction

Females have a biological affinity for masculinity.

affray – public brawl

I would be afraid to be in the middle of a raucous affray.

affluent – rich, wealthy

A flu does not discriminate if someone is affluent or poor; a person will still be stricken with illnesses.

agape – a wide-open mouth

If you want to eat a large grape, your mouth must be agape.

aghast – horrified

I was aghast when my boyfriend passed gas at my parents' dinner table.

al fresco – outdoors

Al relishes the feel of freshly cut grass and a refreshing breeze when he studies this vocabulary list al fresco.

alacrity – enthusiastic willingness or readiness

You should study this vocabulary with awesome alacrity.

alias – false name

Alice's alias was "Mrs. Plumb."

alimentary – supplying nourishment

If a pharmacist specialized in vitamins, might she go to alimentary school?

allay – to soothe

> Aloe will allay sunburn.

altercation – a physical dispute

> Long-lasting frustrations tend to lead to altercations.

amass – to collect

> A mass of dust amassed in the corner and created an army of dust bunnies.

amalgam – a mixture or combination

> An anagram is an amalgam of the letters in a word, such as anagram becoming "nag a ram."

ambiance, **ambience** – the feel or character of a place

> The overall ambiance of the lounge was extremely homey.

ambulate – move or walk

> If you see an ambulance headed your way, you may want to ambulate out of its way.

ambivalent – uncertain

> A decade later, we're still ambivalent about who let the dogs out.

ameliorate – to make better

> Amelia was know for ameliorating her surroundings until her world was the best of all possible - until it was perfect.

amity – peaceful relations

> Opposite of enmity (enemy) = ally.

> After years of being enemies, the two nations finally agreed and experienced amity.

amok – uncontrolled frenzy

> The calmness of a monk is the exact opposite of amok.

amorphous – lacking shape; ghostly

> Focus on "morph." If you've had your fair share of Saturday morning cartoons, you know that this means to change shape.

> The amorphous entity shifted between human and bat before taking on the form of a truck.

anarchy – absence of government or control

> People go crazy on Black Friday: WalStore enters a state of complete anarchy!

anecdote – a short amusing story

> A short note; an anecdote.

> Since studious Sally didn't have much time to talk on the phone, her grandmother would give her quick anecdotes as words of encouragement.

antagonist – a challenger

> An antagonist is *against* a main character.

> The antagonist unsheathed a broadsword and challenged the hero to a duel.

anthropoid – human-like

> Just picture C-3PO or R2-D2 teaching anthropology, and you will remember anthropoid.

> So many of our jobs are being done by robots nowadays that it's only a matter of time before an anthropoid cyborg is serving us our morning coffee!

apathy – indifference

> Apathy makes one a pathetic person; he or she lacks a passionate opinion.

> Apathy causes us to walk past the homeless without considering offering a helping hand.

aphorism – a wise saying, adage

> The aphorisms of your ancestors should be respected.

apostate – unbeliever, turncoat

A prophet is the foil of an apostate.

apex – peak

Peter Parker painted six peaceful apes on the apex of Pike's Peak.

arbitrary – chosen randomly

Don't arbitrarily fill in your bubble sheet or you'll end up in the bottom percentile.

arcane – secret or mysterious

You could go buy a brand new, titanium cane from the store, but the best canes are old, wooden, and contain arcane knowledge of the past.

archetype – a standard model

Unique individuals are notorious for straying from archetypes and doing their own thing.

ardor – passion

If you adore someone, you must have a burning ardor for that person.

askew – crooked

If a screw enters wood askew, it won't lay flat.

assuage – to ease or pacify

A massage would assuage tired shoulders.

astute – exhibiting a keen mind; shrewd

Might you call a cunning school of technology an astute institute?

atrophy – wasting away

You'll never win a trophy if you sit around letting your muscles atrophy.

atypical – not normal

Atypical things are not typical.

NOTES:

audacity – boldness

Audacity is the capacity to do something bold.

I can't believe she had the audacity to spit out my cookies!

august – majestic

Picture Augustus Caesar wearing an august robe in August.

The king wore an august robe covered in rubies and diamonds.

austerity – severity; strictness

It would be a rarity for someone of austerity to loosely give to charity.

avant garde – reflecting the most recent trends

It's hard for the elderly to keep up with the avant gard.

aversion – dislike or distaste

Those who oppose change will have an aversion to new versions of their favorite songs.

awry – twisted; askew

If you hang a picture on the wall and it ends up hanging awry, you may want to retry with a level.

baleful – of evil influence

If a lump of straw had evil intentions, might it be called a baleful hay?

baneful – poisonous, harmful

> If you eat something baneful to the human body, you'll have a whole other understanding of "painful."

barrister – lawyer

> A barrister can either put you in or keep you from being put behind bars.

bawdy – obscene; humorous

> His bawdy jokes made the sensitive girl bawl.

beatific – joyful

> When we're joyful, we tend to enjoy music with a beatific beat.

begrudge – to envy or resent

> Has "grudge" right in it!

> After years of being voted captain of the soccer team, Jose was loved by most, but also begrudged by some of his jealous teammates.

beguile – trick

> It was extremely easy to beguile the gullible guy!

belated – late

> Again, has "late" right in it!

> Since I missed your actual birthday, let me wish you a belated one!

beleaguer – to harass or annoy

> The league of brats beleaguered the pedestrians in the park until they packed up and left.

benevolent – kind

> The world would be a better place if benevolent deeds were more prevalent.

berate – to scold

> If you make your parents irate, they may berate you.

bereft – lacking a necessary thing

> If you suddenly find yourself bereft of your pants, you are probably the victim of a hilarious theft.

betroth – to become engaged

> If you're betrothed to Mr. Roth, you'll soon be Mrs. Roth.

biennial – every two years

> bi = two; ennial = years.

> The biennial kitten mitten drive has, once again, raised enough kitten mittens to last the kitten club a whole two years!

blighted – ruined; withered

> A bloated, old bird would be blighted for flight.

boisterous – noisy and energetic

> The boys' sleepover was far too boisterous for the parents to get a wink of sleep.

bourgeois – middle class or conventional

> The bourgeois of America is disappearing as the gap between the rich and the poor widens.

brandish – to wave menacingly

> Her instinct was to brandish a sword as the troll came near.

brandish

brevity – briefness

> Think "briefity."

> The mark of a good writer is brevity. The mark of a not-so-good writer is a bit of rambling because (s)he can't quite get out those thoughts in a few words but needs a lot of them.

brine – salty water

> The Rhine River is fresh water, *not* brine.

broach – bring up for discussion

> The coach broached the need for more defensive strategy.

brusque – brief; curt

> Brusque conversations are perfect for brisk weather.

bumptious – self-assertive

> The bumptious jerk bumped into me and stole my place in line.

burgeoning – flourishing

> After a little bit of fertilizer, the community garden was burgeoning.

burnish – to polish

> Always burnish your furnisher before you have guests. (Yeah, we know it's spelled *furniture*, but you'll remember it now!)

cache – hiding place

> Store your extra cash in a strategic cache; then you will have a pleasant surprise when you stumble across it five years later.

cajole – to coax

> Cathy cajoled Joe into trying Cajun food even though he was hesitant to eat new cuisines.

callous – unsympathetic

> Coach Cal callously dismissed Calpurnia's calluses caused by tennis and made her practice her serve for two more hours.

calumniate – to slander

> Calvin was humiliated when Anne calumniated his good name.

canard – misleading story; a hoax

> The canary put on a canard by pretending to be a duck.

candor – frankness

> Frank was named for his candor: he was, after all, incredibly frank and to the point.

cantankerous – quarrelsome

> With her frequent fits of spoiled rage, Cassie was known as a cantankerous little girl.

capacious – spacious; massive

> A capacious place is very spacious.

capitulate – to surrender

> The poor people were forced to capitulate their capital to the invaders.

captious – apt to seek out faults

> CAPTCHAs are captious in a computer's ability to read a picture.

caricature – an exaggerated likeness, a cartoon

> A caricature turns a normal person into a real character.

carpetbagger – a swindler or corrupt politician who takes advantage of others

> Mr. Moneybags was exposed as a carpetbagger after a scandal involving the thefy of charity funds.

carrion – rotting flesh

> Carrion-scented perfume would be a *terrible* idea (unless you're trying to lure a vulture).

carte blanche – full authority to do as one wishes

> Mom gave her son carte blanche to buy anything he wanted on their shopping spree.

castigate – criticize severely

> To this day people castigate Nixon for Watergate.

catalyst – a person or thing that brings about change

> Her catalyst to become a vegetarian was the cute cattle frolicking around in a grassy field.

catharsis – a cleansing or mental breakthrough

> Carol felt much better after a couple cathartic minutes of crying.

caustic – burning; critical or sarcastic

> The caustic chemical caused one heck of a burn.

cauterize – to burn tissue

> The surgeon had to sanitize and cauterize the wound.

cavil – to raise unimportant objections

> Tired of the petty bickering, the judge banged his gavel when the attorneys began to cavil.

censor – to remove inappropriate ▮▮▮▮

> Movies aired on television go through a lot of censoring to be family-friendly.

censure – to criticize or blame

> She censured him for his proclivity to not censor himself.

cerebral – of the brain or intellect

> Use your cerebral powers to win this argument!

chagrin – embarrassment

> He tried to grin away his red-cheeked chagrin.

charlatan – a fake; a person who pretends to be something or someone other than he is

> Charlotte the Charlatan couldn't be true to a single person in her life.

chaste – pure; unspoiled

> The chaste young woman was chased by her admirers.

chasten – to correct by punishing

> We had to chasten the dog for constantly chasing down the mailman.

chic – smartly dressed, stylish

> A pretty chick is dressed really chic.

chicanery – deception by trickery

> Think "trickanery." Again, spelled wrong, but you get the idea.

> Melissa used some sly chicanery to get out of paying the library fee that she very well knew she owed.

chimerical – bizarre; very strange

> The chimerical monster was a mix between a fish and a kitten.

choleric

choleric – hot-tempered; easy to anger

> Cholera, an illness marked with a high fever, is the origin of the word "choleric."

> Chelsea was choleric and often blew up on her classmates for the slightest offenses.

churlish – rude

> The childish little boy was very churlish when he refused to share his toys.

circumspect – cautious; prudent

> Think about *circumnavigating* a situation to *inspect* it before you enter.

> Eager Edger was a very circumspect scientist and was cautious about never experimenting with combustibles.

clemency – cool-tempered, especially toward enemies and in sentencing criminals

> The judge granted Kobayashi Takeru clemency by sentencing him to eat 100 Klements hot dogs in 30 minutes instead of facing jail time.

coerce – to bring about by force

> The police officer coerced a false confession from the poor kid.

cogent – clear-minded; well thought out; logical

> The agent remained cogent despite the gunfire around him.

cogitate – to consider with great care

> To cogitate is to meditate.

> Prior to choosing a school, cogitate each of your options to make sure you are making the right choice.

cognizant – fully aware and well-informed

> I was totally cognizant of the dangers associated with being awesome, but I chose to be this way anyway.

cohesive – sticking together

> Adhesives make items cohesive.

> They were a very cohesive group, so they worked very well together.

collusion – conspiracy or plot

> Thirteen men were busted for a collusion to mint their own U.S. currency.

colloquial – informal wording in conversation

> Think of *local* slang.

> Since gonna is not in the dictionary, but is often used in spoken language, it is considered a colloquialism.

comely – attractive; agreeable

> If you'd like to be more comely, try combing your hair!

commensurate – equal; proportionate

> Your award will be commensurate to your performance.

commiserate – to sympathize; to share in the misery

> The comely couple commiserated over the misery caused by the injury of their pet lizard.

NOTES:

comport – behavior

> Teachers often report on how students comport themselves.

compunction – uneasiness caused by guilt

> He was filled with compunction after puncturing his friend's tire.

concur – to agree

> Would you concur that concur and agree have a similar, if not the same, meaning?

concurrent – at the same time

> Speak any Spanish? Con is *with*.

> Two people speaking at the same time are speaking concurrently.

congenital – existing at birth

> Think of genetics and how you're born with your genes.

> You were born with a congenital condition of being awesome.

conjecture – statement made without supporting evidence

> The judge lectured that there'd be no more ridiculous conjectures in her courtroom.

conspicuous – obvious or visible

> If you're trying to not be suspicious, you should avoid being conspicuous.

contiguous – touching or joining

> Think about the 48 contiguous states.

> Alaska and Hawaii are not considered part of the 48 contiguous United States because they do not touch other states.

contort – twist; bend

> The contortionists seemed to be able to bend their bodies in even the most unnatural of ways.

contrite – feeling guilty

If the con tricked a person and did not feel right, then he would start to feel contrite.

copious – lots

Your stomach couldn't cope with such copious amounts of cheese.

corporeal – of physical nature

Mr. Spooky here is *in*corporeal but Mr. Sooki is corporeal.

correlate – to put in connection

The judge couldn't convict Kim because he didn't have evidence to correlate her with the big heist.

co-related – remember your prefixes!

"Together" related, or having a mutual relationship Plants and animals are co-related because one needs oxygen and produces carbon dioxide while one consumes carbon dioxide and produces oxygen.

countermand – to cancel an order

Countermand is to counter a command.

Wishing for peaceful relations, the lieutenant countermanded his superior's orders to attack enemy troops.

crass – not cool

If you throw trash in the grass, then you are a very crass individual (and should be ashamed).

credulity – gullibility making one easy to trick

If you don't check someone's credentials before forking over your cash, you suffer from incredible credulity.

crepuscular – occurring during or relating to twilight

Considered to be nocturnal, bats are crepuscular little guys: they do most of their hunting during the quiet twilight.   (By the way, it's pronounced kri-pes-que-ler.)

crestfallen – dejected; overcome with sadness

> Even though he brushed daily with Crescent toothpaste, he had four teeth fall out, and he became quite crestfallen.

cull – to select from a group

> To have a productive garden, it is best to cull the best seedlings from the store and care for them daily.

cupidity – extreme greed, usually for money

> Mark's cupidity caused him to lose most of his friends: while he was always happy to join his friends for dinner, he was known to short-change his portion of the bill at group dinners.

cursory – quick and superficial

> Cursory means superficial, like moving your mouse cursor: it's a quick movement across a superficial screen.

> Being too lazy to actually read over her essay, Beth did a cursory scan of her paper and turned in a first draft.

daunt – intimidate; frighten

> Reading the entire dictionary in one day seemed like a daunting task.

dearth – scarcity

> There is a dearth of wealth on this earth.

delude – to deceive

> She deluded him into thinking that delude meant to compliment.

NOTES:

deluge – to overwhelm, or flood

Have you drowned yet in this deluge of vocabulary?

demure – reserved; modest

The demure girl blushed with every compliment.

denizen – inhabitant

A bear is a denizen of its den. Also, it rhymes with and is synonymous with citizen.

deplete – to lessen a supply

Our supply of pleated skirts is seriously depleted!

depraved – morally empty

If you're feeling depraved, try praying.

derided – ridiculed

His peers derided him for not riding the horse bareback.

derogate – to detract; to remove; to cause to seem inferior

The fact that it was printed on wrinkled paper seriously derogated her otherwise spectacular thesis on the harm caused by derogatory language in school yards.

descry – to catch a glimpse of

I hope no one descries you sitting at your desk, crying over how long this vocabulary list is becoming.

desultory – aimless; haphazard; disconnected

The kitten had a very desultory way of exploring the blankets.

deter – to prevent or discourage

The snow storm deterred the tourists from sunbathing.

devoid – void; empty; without

If the first two letters are removed from the word, then it would be "void" and therefore devoid of its prefix.

The freezer was devoid of pizzas after Jake spent a weekend at home without his parents.

dexterous – very skilled in bodily movement, especially with hands

> Dexter is eerily dexterous with a butcher knife.

diabolical – devilish; scheming with evil intentions

> Diablo is a diabolical character in the game franchise because he is well known to be evil.

diaphanous – translucent

> She was mortified to learn that the flashes of cameras shone right through the diaphanous material of her dress.

discern – to distinguish via senses

> It can be difficult to discern the smell of sulfur from the smell of eggs.

discord – out of sync; lack of harmony

> Black Friday is the embodiment of discord: people pushing each other, goods falling to the floor, and a breakdown of normal manners.

discreet – secret or hidden

> If we want to keep this agreement a secret, you'll have to be very discreet.

discrete – apart from others

> Public restrooms usually have a discrete boys' room and a discrete girls' room.

disparage – to belittle someone or something

> After making a million dollar mistake, the CEO was disparaged by the media.

disseminate – to dispense; to distribute

> If a politician wants support from a community, he must disseminate his ideas to every household.

distraught – anxious; worried; distressed

> The monster truck driver seemed distraught over the idea of crushing his dream car.

NOTES:

divers – several; various

> Unable to make up her mind, Pauline randomly selected divers of people to accompany her to the bowling alley.

doleful – sad; mournful

> Look at that sad banana!

> The doleful child cried after dropping his chocolate covered banana in the mud.

dubious – doubtful

> I was fairly certain that our dubious plan would fail.

ebb – a decline

> The waves ebb and flow onto the beach.

ebullient – bubbly; happy

> If a charismatic Internet tormentor scared a victim into giggling and smiling, might the tormentor be called an ebullient e-bully?

efface – to erase; rub out

> Efface that mascara dribbling down your face.

effete – weak; ineffectual

> Some might argue that Canada is an effete nation because it really doesn't go out of its way to make enemies like other aggressive countries.

efficacy – power to produce

> Solar power has surprising efficacy in lowering our dependence on fossil fuels.

NOTES:

effigy

effigy – a three-dimensional representation of a person, usually used for ritual

> It is common for participants in a revolution to burn effigies of ruthless dictators as a way of expressing their anger.

egregious – extreme

> Greg's essay was scored poorly due to egregious grammar errors.

elation – extreme joy

> When Zoe won the lottery, she felt complete, utter elation.

elicit – extract a reaction

> The prosecutor elicited a response from the defendant that was sure to win him the case.

elude – escape or evade

> The nude dude couldn't elude the police; they caught him, cuffed him, and put some pants on him.

elucidate – to make clear

> Further explanation of the Pythagorean theorem elucidated the solution to my math homework.

emaciated – thinned; weakened

> After doing nothing but playing video games the entire weekend, Joe's muscles were emaciated and made Monday morning dodge ball quite difficult.

emulate – imitate

> Emulate nearly rhymes with and copies the definition of imitate.

> Baby Joe emulated his father's dance moves to a T.

enmity – hatred

> My *former* best friend forever and I have developed great enmity for one another ever since we became enemies.

epitaph – memorial inscription on a tombstone

> It was my epitaph to say, "Here lies the coolest corpse you know. She died saving a school full of penguins from a raging fire. Coolest. Person. Ever."

epitome – a simplified representation of something; can also mean a perfect example of something

> The typical diagram of an atom is an epitome of the real thing because it doesn't truly represent electron clouds.

equestrian – pertaining to horseback riding or the horseback rider

> Many literary characters from classic literature went on a quest equestrian-style since horses were popular modes of transportation and cars did not exist.

equipoise – state of equilibrium or balance

> After careful shifting, the seesaw had finally reached equipoise and lay parallel to the ground.

equivocal – unclear; ambiguous; capable of two or more interpretations

> Literary geniuses make some details of their stories equivocal so that the reader is forced to explore many possible meanings.

equivocate – waffle or waver

> Using equivocal language is also used to deceive people because it allows the speaker to equivocate between multiple interpretations so that it fits his specific audience.

erode – to gradually diminish or destroy

> Over time, rain water will erode the details of even the most meticulously carved statue if it is left outdoors.

erudite – very learned

> Since she never left the library, Erin was erudite in pretty much every subject.

eschew – keep clear of; habitually avoid for moral reasons; shun

Eschew chewing your nails.

esoteric – understood only by a select few

Theoretical physics is an esoteric subject because you have to be extremely well-versed in physics to understand it.

ethereal – of a spiritual or delicate nature

It looked like we could put our hand right through the ethereal body of the ghost.

euphemism – a mild substitution for something unpleasant or offensive

"A little thin on the top" is a pleasant euphamism for balding.

evoke – to summon forth

The smell of pumpkin pie evokes memories of Thanksgiving dinner with my family.

exact – to demand or compel

When the hospital's generators ran out of power, authorities were forced to exact generators from nearby homes.

exhume – to extract from a grave

Grave robbers exhume ex-humans from their graves.

exhaustive – to test all possibilities

Exhaustive means what it sounds like: over-complete.

Really, really, *really* wanting to find her favorite stuffed animal, Annie ordered her entire family on an exhaustive search of the house for Buttons.

exigent – required urgently

With her hair ablaze, water was exigent to extinguish the flame.

exorbitant – over the top, going beyond usual limits

This amazing paper towel has exorbitant absorbency!

explicate – to clear from involvement; to explain or make clear

> She was explicated from the crime when the true thief explicated the means by which he broke into the bank *and* was his own get-away driver.

extraneous – existing outside

> There are extraneous circumstances that make this case difficult to judge.

fabricate – to mentally devise something, often with an intent to deceive

> Do you know what a fable is? Use the "fab" of fable to help you remember fabricate, because a fable is a made up (or *fabricated*) story.

> Not wanting to tell his Sue that he'd forgotten their anniversary, Paul fabricated a story in which he was robbed of a beautiful, expensive necklace he'd purchased just for her.

facet – a plane or surface, such as on a gem

> The diamond had many facets, making it even more sparkly.

facetious – provoking laughter, often over an inappropriate subject

> Picture a laughing face.

> Mark often made inappropriate and offensive jokes, unaware that his facetious humor was a bit too much for his particularly sensitive roommates.

fastidious – meticulous; demanding; impossible to please

> Gordon Ramsey is a fastidious restaurateur and head chef as he screams and curses at his employees until they perfectly recreate his signature dishes.

fatuous – lacking intelligence or rational thoughts

> If you don't exercise your muscles, your body becomes fat. If you don't exercise your mind, your brain will become fatuous.

fawning – showing overwhelming affection

> The children fawned over all the newborn kittens.

feasible – possible; reasonable; doable

> Scoring above average on the vocabulary section of your exam is feasible if you keep studiously studying.

fervor – intense feelings or heat; passion

> I have a fervor for dancing. Some call it "dance fever."

fetid – foul smelling

> Get your fetid feet off my sofa!

fictitious – false; imaginary

> Glittery vampires are fictitious characters.

fidelity – loyalty

> After taking their wedding vows, each partner expected complete fidelity from each other.

filch – to steal

> Filthy Phil foolishly attempts to filch francs from German five-star generals.

flagrant – deliberately and openly bad

> She finds his new floral fragrance quite flagrant, and she sneezes every time she walks past his office.

fluctuate – to waver or be irregular; move up and down

> Your heartbeat would fluctuate, too, if you flew an airplane while you had the flu.

florid – ornate or gaudy

> Florid floral arrangements are often found at funeral parlors.

foible – a flaw in character or behavior

> Despite being a great show dog, digging holes and chewing shoes were Shaggy's foibles.

forbearance – a calm patience

> Her ability to calmly bear through four bad movies was a testament to her forbearance.

formication – tactile hallucination of something crawling on or under the skin

> The girl squirmed as she was experiencing formication after watching a movie on arachnophobia.

forte – strong point

> With such an imaginative mind, creating unique and beautiful homes from abandoned, condemned buildings was John's forte.

frenetic – anxious, fast, disordered activity; frantic

> Fran's frenetic movements knocked every glass off the table.

forward – disobedient; unruly; brash

> I found his harsh comments on the quality of the dinner to be shockingly forward.

frugal – cheap or economical; thrifty

> If you want to retire early in life, you should learn to be frugal as soon as possible!

furtive – stealthy or sneaky

> The undercover spy had a furtive twinkle in his eye.

gainsay – to declare false; speak against

> I gainsay that, contrary to what everyone thinks, the earth is actually a cone.

garbled – distorted

> The space ship's garbled transmission sounded more like "Houston, we half lid off."

gambit – strategy to gain advantage

> The chess player's gambit was to trick his opponent into thinking he was sloppily exposing his knight.

garish – like florid or gaudy

> A middle-aged woman dressing like her teenage daughter is a garish sight, especially if she garnishes her hair with hot pink hair extensions.

garrulous – wordy; talkative

> Garry was so garrulous that we opted to cover his mouth with duct tape.

germane – relevant and appropriate; pertinent

> Water is germane to both the germination and sustentation of life.

gestate – to incubate; maintain conditions favorable to development

> A fetus in the womb is gestating.

gesticulation – to make signals; gesture

> If you speak with your hands, you're a pro In gesticulation.

gibe – to insult or mock

The bully gibed his victim until she broke down and cried.

gloaming – twilight or dusk

With gloaming come the chirps of the early bird.

gossamer – delicate; light; tenuous

The gossamer threads of a cobweb shivered in the gentle breeze.

gradation – gradual progression

Evolution is the gradation of a few species into many diverse species.

grandiose – impressive due to excessive largeness, scope, or effect

The beautiful noise of the live mariachi band was grandiose.

gratuitous – complementary; unnecessary or unwarranted

Coffee or tea served after dinner in South Korea is gratuitous and has made many a foreigner paying the dinner bill quite grateful.

gregarious – social; outgoing; extroverted

Being more of a home-body and loner, Ashley wasn't known to be very gregarious.

grimace – facial expression of disgust or disapproval

Grimy faces cause Mr. Monk to grimace.

grisly – gory; gruesome

Unless you have a strong stomach, avoid looking at the gory aftermath of the "grisly" bear attack.

gruesome – grisly; gory; horrifying

Jack the Ripper will be remembered by generations of scared British children for his gruesome acts on the streets of London's East End.

gruff – rough speech or action; hoarse

> A collie barking on Halloween might sound gruff after yelping "ruff ruff" to the trick or treaters.

gubernatorial – relating to the governor

> The gubernatorial dinner party served only the most important people in politics.

guile – craftiness, cleverness

> Some bawdy party crashers had just enough guile to sneak into the mansion without an invitation.

gullible – easily tricked; naïve

> *Gulliver's Travels* might be a dreadful book for gullible people as the stories may trick them.

hackneyed – commonplace; over-used; stale

> The image of hippies playing hacky sack is a hackneyed one.

haggard – emaciated; wasted

> The skunk was so haggard that we weren't so much afraid of it as we felt pity for it.

hallowed – holy; honorable; sacred

> Halloween originated as a hallowed holiday.

harangue – a ranting, may be spoken or written

> The melody of his harangue provoked chills that ran down the audience's spine.

haughty – arrogant; overly proud

> Even though the content of his presentation was worthy of praise, his haughty attitude dissuaded the judges from giving him an award.

hedonism – a philosophy that focuses on pleasure as the chief good in life

> Ignoring all she had learned at church and religion class, Suzie indulged in all sorts of gluttonous hedonism such as over eating, never working, partying too much at night and sleeping all day.

heinous – evil; depraved

> In my opinion, Hitler was a heinous man for all his crimes against humanity.

heresy – a subversive opinion (against the norm or dogma)

> Galileo Galilei committed heresy against the Catholic church when he declared the earth to be round.

hierarchy – social order with grades of importance or power

> A hierarchy claims that some people are in a higher social position than others.

hiatus – a break or interruption

> Take a hiatus from vocabulary study!

Ok, now back to studying!

hirsute – covered in hair

> A hairy suit will be hirsute.

hoary – elderly; gray or white from age

> Hoary is close to hairy. If it helps, imagine an old man with white hair coming out of his ears as he is now hoary and hairy.

homily – a lecture with a lesson; sermon

His homily contained a message from the Holy Father.

homonyms – words that are spelled or pronounced similarly, but have different meanings

"Homo" means same or similar and "nym" means name or word. Remember your prefixes and Latin!

Fare means how much you owe, and fair means to be equal: very different meanings, but pronounced the same.

iconoclast – one who attacks or destroys religious or cultural traditions or symbols

The iconoclast demolished our icon.

ignoble – commonplace; not noble

He behaved ignobly when he ignored the customer.

ignominious – shameful; dishonorable

The ignorant foreigner had no idea that his actions were considered ignominious in our culture.

imbibe – to drink; to comprehend

We had to bribe the child to sit still long enough to imbibe the day's lesson.

imbroglio – a mess; entanglement

Why is it that headphones always end up in an imbroglio?

imbue – to influence; to inspire

This book has imbued you to study hard and kick the SAT's butt, right?

immolate – sacrifice; burn up

The effigy was immolated over an open fire.

immutable – unchangeable

The talkative nature of the girl was immutable.

impale – to skewer with a sharp object

I'm going to impale your pale, study-tired eyes out with a pencil if you don't keep studying!

impasse – an unsolvable predicament; a dead end

An impasse is impassable!

impassive – lacking or not showing emotion

He was surprisingly impassive after he lost the championship game: he didn't shed a tear or yell a syllable.

impartial – fair; objective

The SAT is judged impartially by a machine.

impeccable – flawless and blameless; incapable of wrongdoing

The amateur chef's dishes were far from impeccable.

impending – imminent; about to occur

After failing to complete the vocabulary list, Crystal felt an impending doom on test day.

imperious – dictatorial; tyrannical

An imperious ruler is overbearing, bossy, and domineering.

implacable – unbending; stubborn

The spoiled girl was implacable about *every* detail of her outfit.

implicit – implied or understood

If you have a driver's license, it is implicit that you know the rules of the road (so don't bother saying, "But officer, I didn't know!").

NOTES:

impropriety – an improper or inappropriate act

> He displayed impropriety when he stole his neighbor's personal property.

impugn – verbally oppose or attack

> The robber was impugned by the perfume shop owner.

impunity – immunity from punishment

> The officer granted the criminal to be too young to know any better, so the 4-year-old thief was granted impunity.

inadvertent – thoughtless or careless; unintentional

> Dale's mother inadvertently told her son's friends that he was afraid of the dark until he turned 14.

incessant – uninterrupted; unceasing

> The dullness of this vocabulary list is incessant!

inchoate – incomplete

> At 5am, most people's minds are inchoate.

incite – to bring to action; provoke

> The clown's creepy face paint incited terror in the unsuspecting children.

incontrovertible – not open to question

> Freedom of speech is an incontrovertible right in America.

incubus – a nightmare, especially of an evil spirit; mental burden

> My dreams are haunted by a gooey incubus with glowing red eyes.

indolence – laziness

> In his indolence, Jack refused to clean up his room.

indomitable – invincible; unconquerable

> The indomitable Spartans could not be dominated.

inept – unqualified; foolish

> If you wear your pants below your butt, you might as well shave "inept" into your hair.

NOTES:

infer – to conclude based on a set of premises

> After watching the debate, the country inferred that the monkey was, unfortunately, unfit to run the country.

ingenious – creative; imaginative; resourceful

> A genius can develop an ingenious plan.

ingenuous – straightforward; frank; childlike simplicity

> You, on the other hand, are probably only capable of developing ingenuous plans. (Just kidding! But really, belittle yourself a little and remember the difference between these two very similar words.)

inscrutable – mysterious; enigmatic

> The unreachable center of the earth is inscrutable.

insidious – sly; seductive; subtle, yet having a cumulative effect

> Inside each spoonful of oatmeal was an insidious dose of arsenic.

insipid – tasteless; boring; flat

> Remember how disappointed you were with your first tray of insipid school lunch? Yeah, you'll remember that forever.

intangible – unable to be touched; difficult to be seen or understood

> Love is an intangible emotion.

invective – abusive speech

> The inebriated, frustrated customer slurred invective insults at his waiter.

inveterate – habitual

> A morning cup of coffee was an inveterate part of her life.

invidious – obnoxious; offensive

> Avoid, at all costs, invidious topics for your SAT essay.

irascible – irritable; snappy; hot-tempered

> Not getting enough sleep makes me super irascible.

jaded – fatigued; made dull or cynical by life

Having been dumped by four different girls in one year, Carl had become extremely jaded and swore off women forever.

jaunt – day trip; pleasure hike

When we realized school had been canceled, we went for a jaunt in the park.

jingoism – over the top patriotism

The jingoistic terrorists hated all citizens.

jocose – jolly

The jocose man laughed when he was poked.

jocular – playful

The jocular puppies jumped to play with the stuffed toys.

jocund – jolly

The holiday song would not be the same if it were sung, "Have a Holly, Jocund Christmas."

judicious – prudent or thoughtful

We have judiciously created memory aids for you; ergo, you can be judicious in your thanks to us.

ken – range of understanding

> Ken's ken can span quite far.

kinetic – relating to movement

> A kinetic jolt went through the car when it hit a pothole.

kiosk – small booth with information or with items for sale

> If a small booth sold door-related items, might it be called a key key-osk?

kismet – fate

> It is your kismet to kiss me right now!

kleptomaniac – compulsive thief

> A kleptomaniac stole some ke s f om m ke boa d…Can you guess which ones she took?

> Hint: Y and R. Hee, hee…just trying to see if you are still awake with all this crazy vocab!!

knave – tricky evil-doer

> The knave crept out with a stolen diamond in tow.

labyrinth – a maze in a three-dimensional space; winding series of passageways

> The mouse got lost in the laboratory labyrinth.

lacerate – to tear roughly; maul

> A badger lacerates its prey to shreds.

lackadaisical – lacking life or spirit; listless

> His lackadaisical attitude toward cleaning made the room smell like stinky socks.

laconic – brief; concise; lacking extra words

> His laconic response was, "Yes."

lambaste – to assault; attack, may be physical or verbal

> She doubted a baby lamb could lambaste a human, until it ripped off her hand as she tried to take its picture.

languid – mellow; lacking energy; sluggish

> The languid sloth couldn't even get off the couch to open another bag of potato chips.

larceny – stealing

> I declared it pencil larceny when my classmate failed to return the borrowed writing utensil.

lascivious – lewd; openly sexually charged

> The lascivious preview ensured that the upcoming movie would be a sellout.

lassitude – fatigue, mental or physical

> I almost collapsed from lassitude when my mother assigned me yet *another* chore.

latent – dormant

The previously latent virus finally suddenly became active, causing a headache, a runny nose and a sore throat.

laud – to praise

The local newspaper will laud the local man for having saved three children from a housefire. He will be the new town hero!

lecherous – lewd; excessive or offensive sexual desire

The lecherous letters between the two lovers were discovered and consequently ruined their reputations as quiet, proper members of society.

lethargy – laziness; indifference

My lethargy was expressed by lounging in bed *all* day.

lewd – vulgar; obscene

The lewd comments about her clothing made her hide under a large sweater.

libation – beverage

Soda is my guilty libation of pleasure.

licentious – lewd; lacking moral restraints

Many people should go to jail for their licentious acts against others.

litany – repeated responses

I gave him a litany of reasons to hire me as part-time help at the pizza shop.

lithe – flexible; graceful; nimble

The lithe ballerina swept across the stage without a single misstep.

litigious – involved in legal action

The litigious landlord sued his tenants for rent after they moved out.

loathe – to hate

> She loathes it when people wear loafers with athletic shorts.

loquacious – talkative

> My loquacious friend told the entire world about my crush on the new kid.

lucid – clear; understood

> After a splash of cold water, I was lucid and ready to drive to school.

lucubration – meditation; laborious study

> Serious lucubration results in deep understanding.

lugubrious – sorrowful; mournful

> A lugubrious day, be it due to rain or snow, is notorious for causing a bad mood.

lurid – gruesome

> The monster's lurid appearance struck fear in the hearts of anyone who saw him.

macabre – gruesome; focused on death

> The macabre science project on decomposition disgusted the judges.

magnanimous – heroic; noble; generous

> The magnanimous donation allowed the homeless shelter to remain open.

malaise – a condition of unease; depression; sickliness

> Malodorous mayonnaise puts me in a state of malaise.

malcontent – unsatisfied; not content

> You should now know that "mal" means "bad," and if you do not, then you have put me in a state of malcontent.

malediction – bad speech; a curse

> After thoroughly upsetting his mother, a spiteful slur of maledictions rained down upon him.

malevolent – malicious; ill-willed; spiteful

> The malevolent dictator ordered all citizens to throw out their orange juice because *he* didn't like it.

malice – desire to cause injury to another

> Mad Alice looked at the white rabbit with malice since he was the reason she ended up in Wonderland.

malign – to defame; slander

> The maligned president watched as his approval rating plummeted.

malodorous – foul smelling

> The cats left a malodorous scent behind that no amount of vinegar could cure.

maneuver – to move cleverly or with skill

> I maneuvered closer to the only student who brought a calculator, hoping he'd show some pity.

maudlin – foolishly affectionate

> My maudlin gifts of flowers and cash were fruitless.

marital – relating to marriage (also, the exact opposite of *martial*, which is war)

> Their marital vows promised to abstain from martial tendencies and, instead, to practice peace.

maritime – relating to the sea or a ship

> The maritime explorations made quite a few sailors seasick.

martial – relating to war or combat

Mars was the Roman god of martial combat.

meander – to wander aimlessly

We casually meandered our way around town, exploring whatever came our way.

melancholy – sadness; depression; despondency

Mel and Chloe were in a state of melancholy when their collie ate their melon.

mellifluous – melodious; flowing with sweetness

There is a mellifluous sound coming from the babbling brook.

mendacious – dishonest; lying

Mendacious men lose the trust of their loved ones.

mendicant – a beggar, or the act of begging

My mendicants for a new PlayCenter system was ignored by my mother.

miasma – a poisonous vapor or atmosphere, often in a swamp

Miasma upsets my asthma; a mimosa helps me relax.

minuscule – itty bitty; tiny

A minute is miniscule in comparison to a year.

misnomer – a wrong or inappropriate name

Don't call me Shirley! That's a misnomer. I'm Samantha.

misconstrue – to wrongly analyze or explain

She misconstrued the facts and came to the wrong conclusion.

mitigate – to make less hostile or severe

Picture feuding neighbors building a gate between the two houses to create distance and peace.

Unable to come to a consensus, the hostile neighbors were forced to bring in a third party to mitigate their dispute.

NOTES:

mnemonics – any learning or memorizing technique

> We've exhaustively created mnemonic examples to help you remember this extensive vocabulary list.

modicum – a little bit

> Saying "Give me a modicum more" might be a modicum awkward. (as is this sentence)

monotonous – tedious; single-toned; drab

> Monotonous, monochromatic, monosyllabic material makes my mind melt.

mollify – to soothe

> Molly Weasley would mollify her children, especially when evil struck.

mordant – sarcastic; sharply spoken

> The mordant teacher sarcastically said, "Oh, but of *course* I'll accept week-late homework!"

morose – gloomy; sullen

> A moldy rose would be a morose sight if roses could mold.

myriad – a large or perhaps indefinite number

> My walk-in closet presents a myriad of outfit options fit for a princess!

nadir – the lowest point

> The nadir of his nose had a huge wart.

nascent – coming into existence; emerging; beginning to develop

> The nascent butterfly looked extremely fragile as it emerged from its cocoon.

nebbish – a person who is timid or submissive

> A newbie is often nebbish on the first day of work.

nefarious – wicked; evil

> Some nefarious sorcerer turned all the townspeople into ducks.

nemesis – a retributive or vengeful enemy

> My nemesis replaced all my shampoo with mayonnaise!

neophyte – a beginner or novice

> As a neophyte plumber, I was unable to clear the clog and had to call in a more experienced professional.

nettlesome – causing annoyance or difficulty

> The nettlesome squirrel chased away the beautiful birds.

nexus – a connection, link, or tie between things

> Broadway is the nexus of live musical performances.

noisome – physically harmful; offensive to the senses; objectionable

> Exceedingly loud noise emitting from your headphones is noisome to your Eustachian tubes.

nonchalant – appearing unconcerned or indifferent; casual

> He did a backflip nonchalantly, saying "Yeah, I'm flexible."

nonplussed – puzzled; perplexed

> The cat was nonplussed as his own image came into view in the mirror.

novel – new; strange; unusual

> This new novel about monkey butlers is a novel one.

nonpartisan – free from party affiliation or bias

> The nonpartisan panel unanimously voted to give themselves raises.

novice – beginner; inexperienced; untrained

> The novice gambler foolishly bid his entire pot on a pair of twos, which lost him all his money.

noxious – harmful, either to health or morals

> I had to leave the kitchen because the noxious cleaner started to sting my lungs.

nuance – a subtle difference or variation

> If the weather fluctuates by one degree, then there is a nuance in temperature change.

nullify – to invalidate or neutralize

> The fact that the kids had already planned to stay inside and watch movies all day anyway, nullified the effect of the fact that it turned out to be a dreary, rainy day.

obdurate – resistant to persuasion; stubbornly persistent in wrongdoing

> The security officer called for backup when the suspect was obdurate about emptying his pockets.

obfuscate – to make obscure

> The scientific equations were obfuscated by obscure symbols.

oblivion – the state of being forgotten or unknown

> She was in a complete state of oblivion after the car wreck: she didn't even know her name or where she was from.

obsequious – excessively attentive or compliant

> Our class brown noser was known for being obsequious.

obsolete – no longer used or useful; outdated

> Floppy discs are now obsolete.

obstreperous – resistant to control; unruly

> Obstreperous children are easy to spot at a grocery store: they'll be the ones screaming in the candy aisle.

obtuse – blunt; lacking sensibility or intellect; difficult to comprehend

> I tried to explain how to operate the toaster, but he was simply too obtuse to figure out the machine.

obviate – to anticipate and prevent; to make unnecessary

> The automatic timer on the lights obviated the need for a switch.

occult – pertaining to the action of influence of the supernatural

> The cult dabbled in the occult; they liked to raise oranges from the dead in California.

odious – repugnant; hateful

> The odious librarian added restocking fees on top of late fees.

officious – meddlesome; opinionated

> While decorating, Mrs. James' husband was officious about moving everything *slightly* to the right or just a *smidge* to the left.

ogle – to stare at, usually amorously or provocatively

> Half-time provided ample time to ogle the cheerleaders.

olfactory – relating to the sense of smell

> The fumes from the old factory disturbed his olfactory sense.

omen – a sign of a future event

> The ominous clap of thunder was an omen signaling the approaching storm.

omnipotent – unlimited authority or power

> He showed me how to cheat in the video game, making my character omnipotent.

omniscient – unlimited awareness or understanding

As an omniscient ruler of my people, I know all of their wants and desires.

onerous – burdensome

The onerous chemistry textbook weighed nearly 20 pounds.

opacity – the obscurity of a sense; not allowing light to pass through

You can tell how greasy your food is by rubbing it on paper and observing the opacity.

opulent – plentiful; rich

As an opulent ruler, I would give every citizen free candy bars.

ordnance – military equipment, such as guns and ammunition (not to be confused with *ordinance*, which is a law)

According to military ordinance, a soldier must always carry his or her ordnance.

orifice – an opening, such as a mouth or vent

Thermometers require an orifice.   Ew.

orthodox – conforming to the established norm; conventional

As we have told you, learning your Latin will help you understand many obscure words, so let's dissect this word together. "Ortho" implies "straight" (so an orthodontist makes your teeth straight) and "dox" implies "meaning" or "doctrine." Thus, if we combine the words, we have straight meaning. So imagine a religion where there are no alterations, and you would have an orthodox religion.

ostensible – intended to be seen; an appearance, usually false

The soft drink was advertised to ostensibly surround you with fun-loving friends.

ostentatious – showy; pretentious; vainglorious

Golden grills in your teeth are ostentatious.

ostracize – to exile or exclude; banish

> The cool kids ostracized their friend after it was discovered that he still plays action figures, even though, let's admit it, they're pretty cool.

overt – openly; in plain view

> Over-emotional people may overtly cry in public.

palatable – agreeable to taste; edible

> A painter's pallet is most likely not palatable, unless you like to eat paint.

palliate – to ease intensity without curing

> Cold medicine palliates: it treats symptoms, but not causes.

pallid – pale; wan; lacking liveliness

> A pallbearer aids in carrying a pallid corpse in a coffin to the cemetery.

palpable – tangible; easily perceptible

> After a few minutes of running hot water, the steam became palpable.

panacea – a cure-all; remedy for all ills

> Some people chew vitamin C thinking it is a panacea for their every ache and pain.

panache – spirit of zest or style; flamboyance

Sir Soufle's panache often caused him to dress and act a bit over the top, making him look foolish among the other superheroes.

paragon – an example or model of excellence or perfection

The Nobel Prize committee sifts through paragons when awarding the Peace Prize.

parch – to dry or shrivel due to heat

If a squeaky clean document were left outside in the desert, might it be called parch-mint paper?

parsimonious – frugal to the point of stinginess

My parsimonious friend filled his take out bag with hundreds of ketchup packets.

partisan – an adherence to a party; exhibiting blind allegiance

The cabinet maker leaned toward creativity, making her a partisan of the artisan party.

pathos – sympathetic pity, or a characteristic that provokes sympathetic pity

A pathetic character often invokes pathos from the viewer.

paucity – scarcity

My wallet seems to always have a paucity of bills.

peculate – to steal or embezzle

White collar crime sometimes involves peculating funds off shore.

pecuniary – relating to or measured by money

I looked at the stock market to make a pecuniary evaluation of the nation's wealth.

pedagogue – professor; dull, formal teacher

The most boring pedagogue of education is that of memorization.

pedant – boring person who flaunts his vast book smarts, but has little worldly knowledge; haughty, naïve bookworm

> Think of it this way. "Ped" means "child" or "childlike" (what do you think a *ped*iatrician treats?). Now picture an ant crawling up your leg as you are trying to take a nap in the grass. Then picture a rather annoying person who acts childlike.

> Even though the pedant often talked about his love of physics, he still proved worthless when it came to building bike ramps.

pedestrian – commonplace; unimaginative

> A pedestrian use of a chopstick is to pick up food; however, a much more interesting use is as a hairpiece.

penchant – inclination; liking

> I have a serious penchant for gel pens: they just come in so many colors!

pensive – deep and thoughtful, usually in a sad way

> After reading the poem, Josh became very pensive as he mused over what it's true meaning must be.

penurious – lacking resources, usually money; extremely stingy frugality

> After losing his job as an Elvis impersonator, Alvin found himself in a penurious position.

perfidious – treacherous; dishonest

> The perfidious car salesman put lots of used parts into what he said was a new car.

permeate – to diffuse or penetrate through

> A mutant perm ate through the scalp and ate the woman's brain. One might say it permeated through her head.

petulant – unreasonably impatient or insolent; ill-tempered

> My petulant boss asked, "Why haven't you cleaned the counters yet?" just as I arrived at work.

NOTES:

philanthropy – an act or gift intended to benefit others

> Bill Gates has used his wealth for philanthropy, such as trying to eradicate malaria.

pilfer – to steal, often repeatedly in small amounts

> The cashier would pilfer five dollars every night from the register. He didn't get caught until he started to steal $20 in one night.

pillage – to loot or plunder; rob

> The Vikings pillaged villages almost every time they touched land.

pithy – directly to the point

> My teacher wanted to be thorough, but since she was more eager about her blind date than my homework, the comments on my essay were short and pithy.

placid – serene; undisturbed

> The lake was so placid it looked like a piece of glass: not one ripple on it.

plaintive – melancholy; sad

> Following the death of her favorite actor, Ell's eyes took on a plaintive dullness.

platitude – a stale remark; dull

> His boring attitude was the cause of his never-ending platitude.

platitude

plethora – excess; abundance

> A plethora of pleather pants would self-nominate you for *What Not to Wear*.

plunder – to pillage; take by force; steal

> American settlers plundered the land from the Native Americans, causing Native Americans to be a minority in post-modern America.

politic – shrewd; tactful
A politician who plays hard ball is often politic.

NOTES:

polyglot – speaking or writing several languages; multilingual

> Poly means several (so a polygon has several sides). If you know your anatomy, perhaps you are familiar with the epiglottis (which is part of the digestive system and located near the tongue). So now you have many tongues, or many languages.

> Coming from a multiracial family, Jezzie was blessed to have grown up a polyglot; not only did she get great grades in English, but she passed Spanish with flying colors!

posthumous – occurring after death

> James Dean became the image of rebellion after he became post human. His fame is posthumous.

pragmatic – practical

> Thinking pragmatically, the city had to cancel a couple of art shows in order to pay for road repairs.

precarious – dangerous or perilous

> If you're wearing a bungee cord, jumping from a bridge isn't all that precarious.

precipice – cliff; a dangerous situation

> If you're unharnessed and sitting on a precipice, however, you're in danger!

precocious – unusually early development or occurrence

> A 30-year-old still living at home watching reality TV all day would be the antithesis of precocious.

prevalent – common; dominant

> Vampires are prevalent in American pop culture.

prevaricate – to lie

> Look into my eyes so I can tell that you're not prevaricating.

proboscis – long, flexible snout, generally hollow

> A honey bee will clean its proboscis on a flower to help fertilize the plant.

proclivity – inclination or predisposition

> I have a proclivity to use the Internet for unproductive tasks, such as looking at funny pictures of chubby animals.

profligate – extravagant

> How is it that every episode of "YAY I'M 16!!!" shows a girl with a profligate birthday party? Who pays for that?!

profuse – abundant; bountiful; extravagant

> I use profuse profanity when I have a short fuse.

proliferate – to grow, increase, or spread rapidly

> The weeds proliferated across my back yard and choked out every blade of grass.

prolific – fruitful; producing a lot of something

> Sociopaths are often prolific liars.

prosaic – dull; unimaginative

> This mosaic would be less prosaic if they used more than one color.

puffery – to promote with exaggerated praise; hype

> Cosmetic companies might utilize puffery to help calm puffy eyes.

puissant – powerful

> The president of the United States is one of the most puissant people in the world.

pulverize – to reduce to small pieces

> Putting an orange in a blender would pulverize it to pulp.

purloin – to steal; take dishonestly

> That little punk just purloined a coin out of my pocket!

pusillanimous – lacking courage; timid; cowardly

> Would the *Wizard of Oz* have been any different if Dorothy's companion had been called the Pusillanimous Lion?

putrid – having characteristics of something rotting, such as a foul smell

> Raw chicken left out in the Georgia summer sun for two weeks would produce a putrid smell.

quagmire – swamp; difficult, entrapping position

> Neglecting your vocabulary study will land you in a mental quagmire come exam day.

quail – to recoil in fear; cower

> The quiet puppy quailed from its evil owner.

qualitative – relating to quality

> The animal rescue squad took a qualitative assessment of the puppy's living conditions and decided it deserved a better home.

qualm – sudden doubt or fear, especially due to not following one's conscience; sudden onset of illness

> Don't have any qualms about staying calm for your exam.

quandary – state of doubt or uncertainty; predicament

> When offered chocolate or strawberry ice cream, I found myself in the most difficult quandary I'd faced since that one time I had to choose between a hard shell and a soft shell taco.

quantitative – relating to quantity

> To perform a quantitative analysis of the assembly line's production, we had to count every single marble the machine spit out.

quarantine – a period of isolation to contain pests or disease

NOTES:

> Sheldon was exposed to a deadly disease so he had to be in quarantine from his friends for two weeks.

queasy – nauseated; squeamish

> Greasy, cheesy pizza makes me queasy.

querulous – constantly complaining; fretful

> My querulous siblings are constantly fighting over stupid toys.

quip – a quick, clever remark

> Attracted to intelligent men, Della found herself enamored after Dale made a few cute quips.

quixotic – idealistic; foolish; impractical

> While I thought my idea for an umbrella, that also doubled as a pencil, seemed like a good idea, it proved to be quite quixotic when we tried to actually use it.

quotidian – commonplace; daily

> Brushing your teeth should be a quotidian practice.

rampage – to rush around wildly; violent or riotous action

> A ram, flipping through the pages of *Wuthering Heights*, went on a rampage because it found the book to be utterly boring.

rampant – unbridled growth or spread

> The beautiful building was covered in rampant vines that completely enveloped the west face of the store.

rampart – barricade or fort

If you know the lyrics to the "Star Spangled Banner" then you will be familiar with "O'er the ramparts we watched were so gallantly streaming." Just imagine a giant fort or barricade protecting the country while singing the song.

rancor – resentment; animosity

Due to the events of September 11, many Americans harbor rancor toward Middle Eastern people.

rapacious – ravenous; greedy

Upon being rescued from the life raft, the castaways ate with rapacious fervor.

rapprochement – reestablishment of a cordial relationship; reconciliation

It's always best to seek rapprochement with former friends: being enemies is good for no one!

ratiocination – pragmatic, exact thought

Prior to handing in her exam, she examined each of her answers with deep ratiocination.

ravage – devastate by plundering

Bearded and armored Vikings would often ravage through weaker villages like savages.

ravenous – hungry

The ravenous raven ate an entire turtle.

raze – to shave off or tear down; to destroy

Think of a razor. It could raze your face or legs if you are not careful.

After the earthquake took down half of the building, it was necessary to raze the rest and rebuild the library.

recalcitrant – defiant; stubborn

I became recalcitrant when my teacher tried to take away my notebook because she *thought* I was writing a note to my friend.

recapitulate – to summarize; repeat briefly

If you've been reading carefully, you should be able to recapitulate some of the previous words' definitions without hesitation.

recondite – hard to understand; obscure

Russian can be a recondite language even for native speakers.

recoup – to regain; to recover

Consuming hot soup will help a person recoup from the common cold.

rectify – to correct; remedy

I would ask you to rectify the statement "All rectangles are squares" to "All squares are rectangles" if I heard you say it. (Impromptu math lesson: rectangles are four-sided shapes with four, 90° angles; squares are a further defined as "rectangles with four equal sides." Bam!)

recumbent – reclining; lying down

After a long day at work, I couldn't *wait* to become a recumbent blob on the couch.

redolent – fragrant

Road kill can be described as redolent only to vultures.

redoubtable – evoking dread or fear; scary

The deadly car crash video was redoubtable and made us all think twice about texting while driving.

redress – to compensate; relieve; to set right

I made an effort to redress my wrongs after spilling coffee on Jen.

redundant – repetitious; superfluous; and unnecessary
redundant – repetitious; superfluous; and unnecessary
redundant – repetitious; superfluous; and unnecessary

refractory – defiant; disobedient

Regardless of how much conditioner and detangler I use, my hair remains a refractory mess.

reiterate – to repeat

> The best way to memorize these vocabulary words is to reiterate the definitions over and over!

remorse – distress arising from guilt; regret

> Even though there's like, a million calories in this cupcake, I have no remorse for slamming the whole thing in one bite.

renascent – to return into being; return with renewed vigor

> Standing behind a register for eight hours was fatiguing, but after a hearty dinner I was renascent and ready to go for a run.

repose – sleep; calmness

> Following a long day of hiking, we pitched our tents and lay down for a little repose.

reprove – admonish; opposite of approve

> Kelly is always being reproved for passing notes in class.

respite – a short rest

> In spite of the massive mound on his desk, Julius decided to take a respite before working anymore.

reticent – restrained or cautious

> Alan wasn't very confident, so he was rather reticent in large groups.

retrograde – moving backward, generally to an inferior position or state

> Retrograde motion occurs when an object moves in the opposite direction. So if Halley's Comet moves in the opposite direction of our star, the sun, then it would be in retrograde motion.

risqué – lewd or naughty

> It's unwise to take a risk and wear risqué clothing to school; you could face suspension.

rotund – round; fat

> Eric Cartman is a rotund boy.

ruddy – having a healthy, reddish complexion

> Her ruddy face turned to the color of rubies when her fiancé proposed to her.

ruminate – to ponder or consider; contemplate

> Before dedicating myself to a $500 purchase, I ruminated over the pros and cons of each laptop on the sales floor.

sabbatical – an extended break from a typical activity, usually employment

> Professors often take sabbaticals from the university, but most of the time it is to do research. An academic's work is never done.

sacrosanct – sacred or untouchable

> Muhammad is a sacrosanct figure to followers of Islam; even his image may not be depicted.

sagacious – insightful; wise

> The Dalai Lama is considered to be a very sagacious person.

salacious – arousing sexual imagery; lustful

> The *Playboy* centerfolds invoke salacious imagery for their readers.

salient – obviously important

> Having been underlined 15 times, we knew that this part of the notice was the most salient portion.

salubrious – healthy or nutritious

Baked tubers with a small amount of salt would be a salubrious meal.

sardonic – sarcastic

If a witty fish could talk, might it be a sardonic sardine?

scathe – to criticize sharply

Ben's mother-in-law was known for scathing him over every mistake he made.

scribe – a clerk or public writer

In ancient Egypt, scribes might have written down a prescription the doctor pre*scribe*d for you or they might have helped you sub*scribe* to a magazine by filling out your subscription information (pretending that these actually existed).

secede – formally withdraw or back out

The Civil War began, in part, when seven states seceded from the Union.

sedate – to make calm or tranquil

We were forced to sedate the poor pup so he wouldn't further hurt himself after he'd already ran into a wall and injured himself.

sedition – speech or action that provokes rebellion against authority, typically the government

The anarchists' sedition caused law-abiding citizens to riot and directly disobey the police.

segue – to transition smoothly from one thing to another

A good DJ knows how to segue from one song to another so as to keep the dance floor moving.

sequester – to separate; segregate

To get my beta fish to stop fighting to the death, I had to sequester them into different tanks.

servile – acting as a slave; submissive

> A good butler will be servile in his service without appearing resentful.

shiftless – lacking ambition; lazy

> A shiftless person may be considered too lazy to be employed.

simultaneous – concurrent; occurring at the same time

> I simultaneously drank hot coffee and jumped rope; it didn't end well.

sloth – laziness; idleness; a cute animal

> The animal 'sloth' is appropriately named because it is extremely slow moving and sleeps more than you'd believe.

slovenly – untidy; sloppy; unkempt

> A slovenly person might be forever single as people tend to be turned off by messes (whether it be a messy person or a hot mess).

sobriquet – nickname

> The obnoxious couple spent their entire dinner coming up with sobriquets for one another.

somber – dark; gloomy; melancholy

> A wake is a somber occasion.

sophist – one who argues deviously, usually an educated snob

> Sophie the studious social psychologist was such a notorious sophist that she was banned from Thanksgiving at her brother's house.

soporific – causing drowsiness

> The professor's monotone lecture about the intricacies of drying paint was soporific.

sparse – thinly scattered; scanty

> All the junior high school boys have sparse mustaches.

specious – apparently true, but actually without merit

> He imbued the rocking chair with specious history in order to make the antique dealer pay more money for it.

spurious – not genuine or true

> When the "diamond" cracked in half, I realized that it was a spurious piece of garbage!

stagnant – dull; inactive; lacking movement

> The stagnant swamp showed no signs of life.

stalwart – strong and determined; one who is stubborn

> The stalwart mother refused to leave the overcrowded mall until she had crossed off every item from her children's Christmas lists.

static – unmoving; stationary

> Even though they are just as alive as clownfish or sharks, coral is static. So it doesn't even move when "hunting", but rather allows the water current to filter food through its pores.

stigma – a mark of disgrace

> Penny's kindergarten accident is a stigma that follows her through middle school, where they call her "Peeing Penny."

stolid – not easily excited; showing little emotion

> While the rest of us cried like babies, Ray remained stolid.

subjective – relating to personal opinion or emotion

> Calling you an idiot for skipping your vocabulary study would be a subjective assessment (but it's true).

subvert – overthrow; ruin; pervert

> Teenagers often subvert their little siblings with the cold truths of life because they forget the joys of believing in Santa.

succulent – juicy; intriguing

> Cutting into a succulent cut of steak and watching the juices exude from the cut of meat would make a carnivore drool and an herbivore cry. (Water imagery)

suffrage – the right to vote

NOTES:

Women had to suffer to receive suffrage.

supercilious – pompous

The supercilious chef thought his food was so superior and so delicious compared to his peers' "attempts," as he haughtily referred to their dishes.

superfluous – exceeding what is necessary; surplus

Be careful to not get wordy and throw superfluous words into your essay!

superlative – extreme or unsurpassed

Ted was known for being superlative in his ability to be super late to class.

supersede – to replace; to take the place of (also spelled "supercede")

Our concern for clean drinking water supersedes our concern for more supermarkets.

surmise – to infer or accept with scanty or no evidence

Having never tasted sushi, Paul ignorantly surmised that raw fish is "naaaaaasty!"

surreptitious – done secretly or stealthily

Their heist was surreptitiously successful!

swindle – to steal by fraud, deceit, or cheating

The con artist could no longer proceed with his dirty tricks because the townspeople recognized his swindling ways.

sycophant – servile, fawning person, usually seeking to gain favor

A budding musician turned into a sycophant when he met his rock and roll idol.

sylvan – pertaining to a wooded or forested area

A sylvan fairy was known for playing jokes on anyone who hiked through her wooded home.

synergy – the combined effort of two things working together to create an effect greater than that attainable by one aspect alone

> Alone we are weak; but together we have great energy thanks to synergy!

synopsis – a condensation or summary

> Telling you the shortened version of the movie *Titanic* (the ship sinks in the Atlantic; tragedy ensues) would be a synopsis.

table – to postpone consideration of an option

> When we realized that building a plane out of balloons was not a viable option, we tabled the idea until we could perform further research and switched to a floating chair.

tableau – an expressive picture

> Art junkies everywhere were stunned by the monkey's ability to paint such an amazing tableau.

taciturn – not talkative; quiet; reserved

> Having been raised by a librarian who preferred her home to be as quiet as possible, Nelly grew up to be a rather taciturn woman.

tact – keen sense of how to act or speak to people in different social situations

> If you wish to be a politician, develop the ability to speak tactfully so as not to offend your diverse constituents.

tactile – relating to the sense of touch

Of the five senses, my favorite has to be touch because of the tactile experience of running my hand across silk.

talisman – an object used to ward off evil or bring good

A four-leaf clover is a talisman for good luck.

tangent – touching without intersecting; a digression from the main conversation

Talking about a tan gentleman while discussing the history of bowling would be going off on a tangent.

tangible – perceptible to touch; material

The professor tried to explain what a guinea pig looked like, but he found he had to literally bring one into class so the kids had something tangible, that they could see and touch, to understand how they differ from a hamster.

tautology – an unnecessary repetition of the same concept using different words

Even though Mr. Brass thought repetition was key to learning, his students found his tautology boring and ineffective.

tedious – boring; dull

Studying more than once may seem tedious, but it is incredibly beneficial.

temerity – daring; reckless

Adolescents pay higher car insurance rates because they exhibit much more temerity than adults.

temperate – moderate in indulgence

We know you've heard of a temperate climate. A temperate climate is marked by moderate conditions. Just remember that moderation bit and you're good to go!

tempestuous – explosive; stormy; turbulent

A tempestuous sea will make any unseasoned sailor nervous.

TOPIC / TANGENT

tenable – capable of being defended or maintained

> Thanks to the moat, King Rufus was confident that his castle was tenable from the invaders.

tenacity – difficult to pull apart; persistent

> Despite fierce opposition from the community, the Bully Club had the tenacity to push forward and fight against breed-specific legislation.

tenet – principle or doctrine

> A tenet of skepticism is always examining who would gain from a proposed truth.

tenuous – lacking substance or strength

> The drought turned our tomato plants into tenuous, shriveled vines.

tepid – lukewarm, either in temperature or spirit

> Tepid coffee will elicit tepid enjoyment from the drinker.

terrestrial – of the earth

> Therefore, an extraterrestrial is above (or over) the earth.

terse – brief; concise; to the point

> A terse essay, without all that superfluous fluff injected into it, will earn you high marks in school, on the SAT, and in college.

theocracy – government run by religious authority

> If the pope were to run all of Italy, his country would be a theocracy.

thermal – relating to heat

> Tanner's numbed fingers were warmed by a stranger's kind contribution of a pair of thermal gloves.

thwart – to successfully oppose; block; defeat

> Garlic naturally thwarts warts and vampires.

timber – wood

> Timber is like, you know, like, the stuff from trees.

timbre – the distinct quality of sound

> You can differentiate timber from timbre by remembering that timbre has a distinct sound (tam-burr), different from what you're used to, i.e., *timber* (tim-ber).

> I awoke from my nap to the timbre of firecrackers on a Fourth of July evening.

tirade – a long denunciation or irate lecture; rant

> Unhappy with the year's required curriculum, Ms. Crabapple went on a tirade of how disappointed she was at last night's school board meeting.

torrid – scorched; parched by the sun

> The Sahara Desert is one of the most torrid places on earth.

transcendent – above the material concerns; spiritual; beyond comprehension; universally significant

> True happiness often means transcending the need for copious amounts of material goods.

transitory – fleeting; existing briefly

> After all, material goods only provide a transitory feeling of joy.

travail – painful labor; toil

> Thanks to engineering genius, washing our laundry is no longer a day-long travail.

treachery – violation of allegiance; betrayal of trust

> A court of his peers found Earl guilty of treachery for selling state secrets to rival countries.

trenchant – clear and effective; caustic and cutting

> When she dressed up like her rival enemy for the school's Halloween party, Heather made a trenchant insult with how ugly she purposely made herself look.

NOTES:

trepidation – anguish caused by fear or intimidation; apprehension; anxiety

> Having seen all of these vocabulary words at least once before taking the SAT should help you with your feelings of trepidation.

tribute – gift or service meant to express gratitude or respect

> If you end up doing really well on the SAT, feel free to make a tribute to Test Prep Seminars for their contribution.

truncate – to shorten by cutting off the end

> If an elephant had a shortened trunk, it would be truncated (and that would be a very cruel thing to do to an elephant).

turbid – muddy; opaque; dense

> A SCUBA diver should avoid turbid waters if he wants to be able to see the beautiful aquatic life.

tutelage – instruction

> Attending free tutoring in college will do amazing things for your grades because they'll give you one-on-one tutelage, which isn't available in large classrooms.

ubiquitous – existing at all places at the same time; omnipresent

> These dreadful, ubiquitous advertisements are plastered on every surface!

ultimatum – final terms of an agreement delivered by a threat

> After years of poor communication, Beth gave Joe an ultimatum: learn how to communicate or find a new girlfriend!

NOTES:

unabridged – containing all the original text; uncut

> The unabridged version of a dictionary would be far too large, so editors usually cut out definitions of synonymous words and replace them with a reference to their counterpart.

unbidden – done without being asked

> Please mind your own business; your commentary is unbidden.

uncouth – awkward; clumsy; vulgar; unpolished

> The uncouth baby cougar had trouble catching fish with its mouth, so it used its claws instead.

undaunted – unafraid

> The brave little girl was undaunted by stories of the house being haunted, so she marched right up to the door and proudly rang the bell.

undulate – to wave, either in appearance or sound

> What you can't see underwater is that the ocean is constantly undulating.

unscrupulous – unprincipled; immoral; unethical

> Anyone who takes it upon himself to steal from charity is profoundly unscrupulous.

unwitting – unaware; inadvertent

> By not telling me their plan, my friends made me an unwitting accomplice in pranking our teacher.

upshot – aftermath; product; outcome; result

> I could tell you a long, detailed story, but the upshot of the whole fiasco was Fido was in serious need of a bath.

usurp – to take possession of something without the right to; to take by force

> I can't believe that someone usurped and slurped my entire bowl of soup!

usury – to lend money at a preposterously high interest rate

> Taking advantage of the applicant's desperation, the banker whipped up a loan offer with an interest rate so outrageous that it could only be called usury.

NOTES:

vacillate – to waver physically or in opinion

> Unsure of what his parents would think, Ned vacillated in his decision to join the Army.

vacuity – empty space, as in a vacuum; blankness; mindless

> After staying up too late cramming for the SAT, Dee faced a mental vacuity.

vainglorious – to be vain; conceited; boastful

> Jessica is so vainglorious: she seriously thinks she is God's gift to all of us!

valor – bravery; courage; heroism

> Sparky was given a medal for his valor in sniffing out and saving three children from the burning building.

vapid – dull; empty; boring

> My first blind date was the most vapid disaster of my life.

valediction – a farewell

> The valediction at our high school graduation inspired us to leave the school with high hopes for our futures.

vehement – impassioned; intensely emotional

> The Save the Whales activist vehemently shared her message.

venal – associated with corruption, especially bribery

> Any politician that is venal should be removed from office.

venerate – to honor

> Veterans Day is meant to venerate those who've fought for our country.

veracious (veracity) – truthful (ness)

> She was so veracious that she tattled on her best friend.

verbose – overly wordy; long-winded

> I really can't exactly determine whether or not this sentence might be purposefully verbose or if it is just something that we coincidentally can't help but do right now.

vernacular – the language or dialect of a particular region

> Calling a water fountain a bubbler is a vernacular idiom in parts of the Midwest.

vicarious – done in the place of another

> Tofu was used vicariously for meat when we hosted vegetarian taco Tuesday.

vigilant – alert to danger; watchful

> Unless you're prepared to be vigilant, don't go for a jog at night or you'll get yourself run over.

viceroy – one who rules by authority of royalty

> England is governed by a viceroy.

victuals – food prepared for a meal

> It has always been a ritual for my family to prepare victuals every Sunday evening.

vindicate – to exonerate; justify; avenge; assert

> Mack was vindicated from the crime of theft when Josh was discovered to be the culprit.

vindictive – spiteful; vengeful

> Realizing that Josh had stolen her MP3 player, Chelsea became extremely vindictive and began plotting her revenge.

visceral – instinctive or emotional

> Jen received a Mother's Day card so visceral that she cried for five minutes straight.

vitriolic – harsh or bitter

> After catching my boyfriend in a complex web of lies, I had some vitriolic words for him.

vivacious – lively; animated; energetic

> I knew that my party was a hit when I saw how vivacious everyone was!

vivify – to make vivid; give life to; animate

> Color television vivified Walt Disney's characters to a whole new level.

vociferous – blatant; clamorous; loud

> Maybe I'd like her if she'd keep her voice down and she'd stop being so vociferous!

voluble – fluent; smooth in speech; glib

> The politician had spent weeks in a speech class to become voluble.

voracious – extremely hungry; ravenous; eager

> Every Thanksgiving I find myself to be absolutely voracious.

vulgarism – a word used in poor taste

> All of those words that you're not supposed to say on television are vulgarisms.

waif – something found without an owner, especially by chance

> Walking along the beach, I stumbled across a waif: a note in a bottle.

wan – pale; sickly in appearance

> By the time we'd found the lost children, they'd become particularly wan and thin.

NOTES:

wanton – lewd; immoral; barbarous

> Burning ants with a magnifying glass is a wanton way to interact with nature.

wily – artful; crafty; cunning

> William was wily enough to trick us into buying him a stuffed animal.

wistful – showing a timid desire; yearning

> I'm not allowed to have pets in my apartment, so I do a lot of wistful volunteering at the animal shelter.

xenophobe – one who fears foreign people, items, and ideas

> If you're a xenophobe, traveling abroad is not for you.

yaw – to drift dramatically off course; alternate

> Caught up in a fantastic yawn, I stopped paying attention to the helm of the boat at it yawed away from my destination.

yielding – productive; flexible; obedient

> We knew that this puppy would be a true show champion when we realized how yielding he was to our every request.

zeal – enthusiasm; fervor

> Whenever I hear the ice cream truck, I jolt out of the house with an unnatural amount of zeal for someone my age.

Zen Master – what you must be to have made it here!

zenith – apex; peak; summit

> The sun reaches its zenith in the sky at noon.

zest – enhanced enjoyment

> Using a little bit of parsley to decorate the plates added more zest to the meal.

Usually Z signifies the end, but when it comes to the SAT, it signifies the beginning of another vocabulary list. (Sorry.)

Literary Terminology

allegory – an extended metaphor in which the figures, characters, or objects are representative of an idea outside of the narrative

> One classic example of an allegory is the mutants you see in comic magazines: they aren't meant to be viewed as monsters, but as outlying social and racial groups that are viewed as strange or threatening.

alliteration – the repetition of a sound, either at the beginning of or within each component of a word series

> The terrifying phrase "Purple nurple" is an alliteration of the "urple" sound and "Giddy, galloping giraffes" is an alliteration of the letter G.

allusion – the use of a reference to implant an idea in the reader that will affect how the literature is perceived

> Martin Luther King Jr, began "I Have a Dream" with the phrase "Five score years ago" which alluded to Abraham Lincoln's "Gettysburg Address," which began with "Four score and seven years ago." By using this literary technique, King's listeners would perceive his message with the same passion that they'd had for the abolishment of slavery: King's allusion paralleled the events and transposed a preexisting abhorrence of slavery onto the practice of segregation.

anecdote – a brief story, either extremely interesting or downright funny, that is told about a supposedly real person or event; while generally funny, anecdotes are not merely jokes, but examples of truths

> Last week, I was running late for an appointment and forgot to brush my teeth. I remembered once I was in the hallway, but since I'd already locked the door, I figured I would just chew on some gum. Unfortunately, that happened to be the day that I met the man of my dreams; doubly unfortunate was the fact that he was my new dentist, and when he saw the plaque on my teeth and smelled my breath, he nearly barfed. After watching him gag above my mouth, I couldn't imagine asking him out. Yes, funny; but more importantly, a lesson to always brush your teeth.

antagonist – opposition to the protagonist

apostrophe – a statement made to an absent person, an inanimate object, or an abstract idea, as if it were present

> Every time you scream obscenities at this book, you're making an apostrophe. We know, you hate the SAT— but hang in there, buddy, you'll make it. Now please stop punching the cover.

autobiography – a book written by an author about his or her own life

NOTES:

biography – a book written by an author about *someone else's* life

conflict – person vs. person
person vs. nature
person vs. self

denotation – the dictionary definition of a word

connotation – a set of emotions or ideas that are associated with a word

dialogue - a written exchange of speech between two or more characters

diction – the specific vocabulary chosen by the author in order to create a mood or tone for the literature

She *skipped* into the room.
She *stomped* into the room.
She *sauntered* into the room.

dramatic irony – an action that results in the *exact opposite* of what was intended

Jimmy really likes Susie. As far as Jimmy knows, punching girls is a way of saying, "You're pretty. Let's be best friends and hold hands." When Jimmy finally musters the courage to clock Susie in the shoulder, he knocks a devastating fear of boys into her at a young age. Susie never again steps near Jimmy.

epigraph – a quotation at the beginning of a piece of literature that functions as an introduction to a theme

NOTES:

> "The Winning Bunch" by Test Prep Seminars
> *Time flies like an arrow. Fruit flies like a banana.*
> — Groucho Marx
>
> Slippery, you are
> My foe, I slip
> Boom, I fall
> You win—temporarily
> See, when you bruise, you brown
> And are turned to bread
> But I, my butt, the bruise doth fade
> And I eat you
> And your bread
> So, slippery foe
> Human vs. Banana
> Who's the winning bunch?

epic – a *long* narrative that formally recounts a heroic journey

> Two words: Lord, Ring. Can you guess the epic?

fable – a short story with an explicit moral lesson

> Think *The Ant and the Grasshopper:* while the grasshopper has a grand ole time, the ant laboriously stows away food. When winter comes, the grasshopper starves as the ant hosts a dinner party.   Moral: sometimes you need to forego today's pleasures to prepare for tomorrow's necessities.

farce – comedy based on improbable or outlandish situations or characters; frequently uses slapstick humor

> If you've been lucky enough to have been assigned The Importance of Being Earnest for your English assignment, you will definitely enjoy this wonderful farce.

flashback – an interruption in a chronological story in order to reference an event that occurred prior to the main time frame

YAY!

NOTES:

foil – a character that provides contrast for another character, usually the protagonist, in order to highlight the foiled character's personality

> In *Monk*, Adrian Monk is the main character, i.e., the <u>protagonist</u>. As a keen detective with a phobia of germs and pretty much everything else, Monk's <u>antagonists</u> include germs, unorganized bookshelves, crooked picture frames, and criminals. His <u>foils</u> include brave officers and assistants who, though not debilitated by fear at every moment, are not nearly as brilliant as Monk.

imagery – use of description to construct a sensational image or setting

> If you've ever read Henry David Thoreau, you've been assaulted with imagery. He descriptively complains a lot about a train in one of his pieces. Here's a recap: "The steel train assumingly ripped through the earth, assaulting nature like a madman late for his afternoon appointment, and coughed out a thick cloud of vile fumes that suffocated the trees and blinded the birds." Does the imagery make you want to hold your breath until the train has passed, or step outside for some fresh air? Too bad, you're learning your vocabulary.

mood – the emotional tone or atmosphere established by the author

onomatopoeia – a word that imitates the very sound which it describes

> When a character gets punished in a comic book, you often see "POW" or "WHAM" then you know what an onomatopoeia is: written descriptions of the sounds you'd expect to hear in a scuffle.

paradox – a seemingly true statement or situation that appears to contradict itself or defy logic, but actually reveals a truth

> Perhaps you've heard the phrase, "You can save money by spending it." While it seems contradictory, you *could* spend money on investments such as savings bonds or items like gold that increase in value over time.

onomatopoeia

NOTES:

parallel structure – a series of items or sentences that share a pattern of words or phrases; shows that the parallel ideas have the same importance

> Let's revisit King's "I Have a Dream." He says, "I have a dream," and quotes the Declaration of Independence. He then repeats "I have a dream" as the opening to seven consecutive statements, thereby uniting each of his points to the Declaration of Independence. Consequently, King is able to equate the sentiment associated with the nation's freedom to the equality of the nation's people.

parody – a humorous imitation of an original piece of work

> If you've ever watched *Colbert Nation* or read *The Onion*, you've experienced news parodies. Specifically, Stephen Colbert parodies *The O'Reilly Factor's* "Talking Points Memo" with his segment "The W ø rd." If you don't know what we're talking about, crawl out from underneath your rock.

> SNL has been performing a parody of the news for years with their segment "Weekend Update." This segment is considered a parody because they take real stories and put a humorous spin on them.

point of view – perspective from which a story is being told; the narrator will say "I" if it is first person, "you" if it is second person, and "(s)he" if it is third person

> I said to her, "You're confusing second and third person. See, first you wrote, 'You open the door and a ghost jumps out at you,' but then you wrote 'She nearly soiled herself when the ghost spoke in the voice of her dead father.'" You know what she did? Instead of just learning the difference between second and third person, she threw the whole thing away right before my eyes!

> (This is a story being told in first person about a writer who begins with second person, but shifts to third person. Did you get all of that?)

protagonist – main character

pun – a play on words with similar or identical sounds

> Did you hear about the guy who had his entire left side cut off in an accident? He's "all right" now. Get it? No left side, so he's "all right?" Ok, we will stop trying so hard.

> You can tune a piano, but you can't tuna fish.

> Why did the hipster burn his mouth? He was eating pizza long before it was cool.

satire – literature that employs humor and wit to criticize its subject

soliloquy – an internal or spoken monologue that is made when the speaker is alone

symbolism – when a word, object, or person stands for something else

> Olive branches are offered as symbols of peace.

metaphor – compares two unlike things without using *like, as,* or *than*; eliminates the division between the identities of two things, thereby merging their characteristics

> She was an ocean: at times, tranquil; at times, tempestuous.

myth – a story passed from generation to generation that explains the creation or purpose of the world; typically contains supernatural explanation for natural phenomena that were not understood at the time of the myth's creation

parable – a brief, straightforward story that illustrates a moral or religious lesson

pastoral – a type of literature in which the author reflects nostalgically on the natural and wholesome characteristics of rural life, such as that of shepherds

saga – a lengthy narrative of a family that has been passed down through generations

NOTES:

simile – compares two things by using language such as *like, as,* and *than*; maintains the individual identities of the two things

> She was *like* a dragon: her nails were *like* talons, her skin *as* coarse as a reptile's, and her breath burned worse *than* a flame.

theme – the core idea of a piece of literature; typically, it won't be blatantly stated, but must be extracted by the reader by examining how the author constructs the story

tone – the attitude of the speaker

tragedy – a genre in which one bad thing after another happens to the protagonist until the end, when very little if anything at all is solved and the protagonist is ruthlessly abandoned by the author

verbal irony – something is conveyed by saying its exact opposite

> Taking the SAT is fabulous. You should wake up early and test every Saturday until your brain explodes!

figurative language – use of a word or phrase outside of its normal usage in order to make a point

> If someone were to say, "This cafeteria food tastes like a monkey's toe jam," the speaker doesn't necessarily need to know what a monkey's toe jam tastes like; she's using figurative language to tell you that the food is simply disgusting (and, unless you're a monkey, inedible).

Types of figurative language:

hyperbole – gross over-exaggerations

Have you ever been so hungry that you could "eat a horse"? Well, you were thinking hyperbolically, because while you were probably *quite* hungry, you wouldn't be able to actually eat a horse. We hope.

personification – where animals, objects, or ideas are endowed with human or living characteristics

Describing the SAT as a vicious, man-eating monster is a personification because, well, it's just a test. It isn't sentient, and it's inanimate, so the two of you aren't tangled in a vendetta, nor will it eat you when no one is looking.

understatement – gross devaluation (the exact opposite of a hyperbole)

It was simple! All I did was fly to Russia, denounce my allegiance to the United States, join their army, become a war hero, and get promoted to the elite spy division, specialize in advanced IT security systems, escape the country, infiltrate the College Board's grading center, intercept my bubble sheet, and replace it with one that has all correct answers. It was a piece of cake, really.

oxymoron – combination of two opposite terms

Lamb liver anyone? It's disgustingly delicious!

Lastly, we have the lifecycle of literature:

Everything You've Ever Read

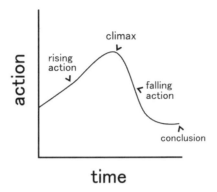

Key:

rising action – series of events, usually a conflict with the protagonist, that leads to the climax

climax – point of greatest action or tension

falling action – events that occur following the climax

conclusion – also called the resolution, the wrap-up or outcome of the preceding events of a story

If we made one of those graphs for this chapter, it would look like this:

This Chapter

CHAPTER 4

Mathematics

Mathematics

This section of the SAT is 70 minutes and contains 54 questions: 44 multiple choice and 10 grid-ins. It will be divvied up like this:

◇ One, 25-minute section, all multiple choice

◇ One, 25-minute section containing multiple choice *and* grid-ins, or "student-produced response," questions (don't worry just yet. Multiple choice questions are worth more than half of the math points, so these 10 questions won't be the death of you. Plus, later on we'll be pointing out some good stuff about them!)

◇ Another 20-minute multiple choice section

As with the majority of the SAT, each section starts off with easy questions that gradually increase in difficulty.

A few pointers on staying sane:

⭐ The College Board is notorious for crafting SAT Math questions that look more difficult than they are, so before you panic and painfully proceed to solve a complex problem, glance at the format of the answers. If you see a problem such as,

Solve $(x+2)^3 + 7 = 120$

and all of the answers have an x^3 in them, you're obviously not going to have to solve for each x so much as you need to multiply out the trinomial, i.e., $(x+2)(x+2)(x+2)$.

⭐ Remember to use your handy dandy annotations to mark the questions you've skipped (X) and the questions you're unsure of (?), and don't let a single question consume more than it's worth. Why? Because no one question… "Is worth more than another," we imagine you muttered. *You are absolutely correct!*

⭐ When it comes to doing work in your blank space, number the problems with a dark, circled number so you know where to look when revisiting your X's and ?'s.

⭐ Assess the question before you begin working. Do you know what your goal is? There's no point in running without knowing in which direction you'll find the finish line! Have your goal in sight before you take off.

⭐ Don't let the stress make you feel like a dunce! Always thoroughly read a question before blowing past it. Just because the accompanying figure is intimidating doesn't mean that the actual question isn't going to be super easy.

CALCULATORS

You went out and bought the most advanced, SAT-permissible graphing calculator. You're not exactly sure how to add or subtract using the super computer, but you're positive that it's a technological breakthrough and it's going to give you a leg up on the SAT. Not only will you be able to get your blood moving early in the A.M. by strapping this big boy to your back and hiking up two flights of stairs to your testing room, but it will work as a fantastic paper weight during the exam because, well, to be honest, that's all it really is to you since you've forgotten where the power button is located. And when you realize this in the middle of the SAT, you'll need a paper weight to hold down your exam as a typhoon of sobbing rages from your regret-ridden little head. Gee willikers, your new graphing calculator is doing wonders!

College Board

We suppose it would be helpful if you also brought along a less advanced and more user friendly scientific calculator. Or, better yet, a so-easy-a-Neanderthal-could-use-it four-function calculator. After all, those complex graphing calculators are designed for complex jobs, so why bring an astrophysicist to fix your clogged tub when you could just reach in with some rubber gloves and pull out the wad of Bigfoot hair? Sure, if you find a black hole lodged in your plumbing, grab your graphing calculator—err, astrophysicist—and let him work it out for you. But if it's a simple clog, either call in your local plumber (strangely named "Scientific Calculator" by his techie parents) or snap on your rubber gloves (brand name "Four-Function" for household cleaning, poking gross things, playing mad scientist, and changing the nastiest diapers you've ever seen) and dig out the hairball yourself.

Are we suggesting that you bring *three* calculators to the SAT? Not exactly, but one complex calculator and one simple calculator wouldn't be so bad! Just don't bother with a super-computer calculator, because those babies aren't allowed anyway. We also suggest that you ...

NOTES:

✪ ... know how to use your calculator long before test day. This means not going out and buying a new calculator just because you *assume* you'll be able to figure it out in a snap—plus, it will come equipped with fresh batteries! What!? That's a *terrible* idea! You have no idea how long that thing has been sitting on the shelf, or how many times it has been brought home, fumbled with, and returned woefully by students who couldn't get past the initial programming screen. Which reminds us to remind you to remember to ...

✪ ... bring a fresh set of batteries for your calculator and know how to get them in!

✪ ... know that all SAT questions can be solved without a calculator, so if you find yourself multiplying or dividing 6-digit numbers, you're either doing the problem entirely incorrectly or making it way more complicated than it is.

> Solve 23x × 12y for x=17 and y=6
> (A) 23460
> (B) 27581
> (C) 28512
> (D) 28618
> (E) 29706
>
> Since the last number in each set is different, we can work with only the last digits in our problem:
>
> $23(17) \times 12(6) = 3(7) \times 2(6) = 21 \times 12 = 1 \times 2 = 2$
>
> The last digit of the answer must end in a 2, so our answer must be (C).

NOTES:

⭐ Use your calculator for *all* grid-ins because, without options to choose from, a small mistake in your arithmetic won't be signaled by the lack of a corresponding answer. The best method is to use a calculator with a full operative read-out so that you can double-check your input before accepting the answer.

⭐ Even if you see a list of answers containing decimals and anticipate the need for a calculator, you don't necessarily need to use it for *every* aspect of the problem. Before getting carried away with the time-wasting process of punching buttons, let your brain do some work.

Solve for x. $3x^2 + 10 = 49$
    (A) 2.5
    (B) 3.6
    (C) 4.4
    (D) 5.1
    (E) 10.8

What can you do with your brain? Well, subtracting 10 is an easy task. So now we're at $3x^2 = 39$, and 39 is evenly divisible by 3, so we can get to $x^2 = 13$ without touching our calculator. Then, and only then, do we bother with the calculator because we're trying to solve $x^2 = 13$, and solving squares is a bit advanced when they're not perfect squares, like 1, 4, or 9. So we plug in 13, square root, and out pops our answer, (B). But what if you don't feel like using your calculator, because you're feeling extra awesome? Think about the perfect squares closest to 13: 9 and 16, for which the square roots are 3 and 4, respectively. Since squaring 4 is too high, we can knock out C through E. And since anything below 3 is going to be too low, we can knock out (A), leaving us with our answer of (B) 3.6!

★ Let's say you're looking at a tricky problem and feeling a little overwhelmed. You figure that your weary brain isn't nearly as sharp as a calculator, so you just begin mindlessly mashing keys, hoping for a correct answer to magically appear on your screen. Suddenly, an 800 appears on the screen and a calming wave of peace crashes over you because *that's exactly the score you wanted on this section!* Wait, none of this makes any sense. Why? Oh, that's right; because only *you*, not your calculator, can get you the score you need. Never tackle an SAT math problem with your calculator. Get a grip on it with your own mental faculties before calling in the calculator to *assist* you. (See how we italicized assist? That's because a calculator never solves problems: a calculator assists *you* in solving problems.)

⭐ Aside from not solving problems for us, a calculator isn't nearly as helpful as we'd like. It's just too dang eager to do what it's told, so it ignores everything you've ever learned in school about the order of operations—yes, even though it was sitting *right* there on the desk during the *whole* lecture—and it just calculates, calculates, calculates everything as it arrives. Like some kind of fool, it adds before multiplying and it divides before dealing with exponents. Only *you*, you intelligent little human, will remember, come the big day, that it is necessary to make a request:

Please Excuse My Dear Aunt Sally

Or, "Please execute my demands as so: parentheses, followed by exponents, then multiplication and division, and, lastly, addition and subtraction." But that's doubly dorky. Just use the original lame mnemonic since it's already been beaten into your brain and perform your arithmetic in the correct order.

Solve for when x = 4 $x^3 + 8(x+3) \div x + 3$

You could either grab your calculator and utilize parentheses

$4^3 + (8(4+3) \div 4) + 3$

Or you could do some math by hand

$64 + 14 + 3 = 81$
$64 + 8(7) \div 4 + 3$

Solve for when x = 4 $x^3 + 8(x+3) \div x + 3$

We happen to be firm believers in using our brains and doing some math by hand, but if you're astoundingly fast on your calculator, feel free to use those parentheses.

⭐ If the list of answers contains fractions, don't use your calculator *unless* it has an option to return answers in fraction form. Most calculators spit out answers as decimals, and converting a decimal to a fraction and then simplifying that fraction until it looks like one of your options can be a huge waste of time. Just do these questions using your noggin.

WHAT YOUR NOGGIN SHOULD KNOW

Squares and Square Roots

There's an *and* in there, but it's really only one set of information that can be read in two directions:

$$1^2 = 1 \quad \text{or} \quad \sqrt{1} = 1 \qquad\qquad 2^2 = 4 \quad \text{or} \quad \sqrt{4} = 2$$

$$3^2 = 9 \quad \text{or} \quad \sqrt{9} = 3 \qquad\qquad 4^2 = 16 \quad \text{or} \quad \sqrt{16} = 4$$

If you don't remember what square and roots are, think of them this way:

⭐ A number **squared** is that number times itself:

$$5^2 = 5 \times 5 = 25$$

⭐ The **square root** of a number is the opposite process: what number times itself equals the number under the square root sign?

$$\sqrt{16} = 4, \text{ because } 4 \times 4 = 16$$

You get the point. The rest that you should know before the big day are:

$5^2=25$	$6^2=36$	$7^2=49$
$8^2=64$	$9^2=81$	$10^2=100$
$11^2=121$	$12^2=144$	$13^2=169$
$14^2=196$	$15^2=225$	$16^2=256$
$17^2=289$	$18^2=324$	$19^2=361$

And now...to storm through four years of high school math!

FRACTIONS

Adding and Subtracting:

The sum or difference of two fractions can only be obtained when their denominators match. When the least common denominator (LCD) has been obtained, arithmetic can be performed across the numerator. For example,

$$\frac{a}{b} - \frac{b}{c} =$$

Has an LCD of bc, so we will multiply each fraction by its missing piece of the LCD over itself:

$$\left(\frac{c}{c}\right)\frac{a}{b} - \left(\frac{b}{b}\right)\frac{b}{c} = \frac{ac}{bc} - \frac{b^2}{bc}$$

Now that the denominators are the same, we perform the arithmetic across the numerator:

$$\frac{ac - b^2}{bc}$$

Since the terms in the numerator are not the same (e.g., ac versus b^2), we cannot simplify the fraction any further.

Dividing and Multiplying:

We begin with dividing fractions because the process *contains* the multiplication process. For example,

$$\frac{a}{b} \div \frac{c}{d} \quad or \quad \frac{\frac{a}{b}}{\frac{c}{d}}$$

is solved by taking the first (or top) fraction and multiplying it by the *reciprocal* of the second (or bottom) fraction, *reciprocal* being the number produced when the numerator and denominator are switched, as so:

$$\frac{\frac{a}{b}}{\frac{c}{d}} \quad becomes \quad \frac{a}{b} \times \frac{d}{c}$$

Lastly, we *multiply* straight across the numerator, followed by straight across the denominator:

$$\frac{a}{b} \times \frac{d}{c} = \frac{ad}{bc}$$

And you've seen both division and multiplication!

NOTES:

Manipulating units:

If you're given a problem with unit-containing fractions, be thankful. These can be some of the easiest problems to solve because all you need to do is arrange the fractions in a way that all of the extra units are eliminated and you're only left with the unit relevant to your answer. Eliminated how, you ask? Well, if you see something like

$$\frac{abc}{bcd}$$

you would immediately think, "Why, that can be simplified!" And your mathematic genius would recognize that both $\frac{b}{b}$ and $\frac{c}{c}$ cancel, leaving you with a much simpler $\frac{a}{d}$.

Guess what? Same thing goes for units! Do you see it happening in this problem?

Someone offers to pay you $12 per hour to study for the SAT. If you accept this offer, how long would you need to study before you could afford to cover your ridiculous $96 phone bill?

    a. 5 hours
    b. 6 hours
    c. 7 hours
    d. 8 hours
    e. Never, because I'm spending this money on a new phone!

$$\frac{12\ dollars}{\cancel{hour}} \times x\ \cancel{hours} = 96\ dollars$$

$$\frac{96\ \cancel{dollars}}{12\ \cancel{dollars}} = x = 8$$

NOTES:

Easy, and the answer is (D). And now you know that your phone bill is outrageous, get a better plan and then try this one:

Driving at 50mph, how long would it take to consume $96 worth of gas if your car burns it at a rate of 28 MPG? (Assume the current gas price is $3.84 per gallon, or 1.3 arms and .5 legs.)

    a. 6 hours
    b. 9 hours
    c. 10 hours
    d. 13 hours
    e. 14 hours

$$96 \ \cancel{dollars} \times \frac{\cancel{gallon}}{3.84 \ \cancel{dollars}} \times \frac{28 \ \cancel{miles}}{\cancel{gallon}} \times \frac{hour}{50 \ \cancel{miles}} = 14 \ hours$$

The answer is (E). (We're not sure what the market value of an arm or leg is, or how to get a fraction of an arm, and frankly we're afraid that searching for that information will put the FBI on our trail, so just leave the other option alone.)

It might take a moment to arrange the fractions correctly, but just remember that *when fractions contain units, the numerator and denominators* (making sure to include the units, of course) *may be switched.* Thus we were able to represent $\frac{3.84 \ dollars}{gallon}$ as $\frac{gallon}{3.84 \ dollars}$.

NOTES:

WORD PROBLEMS

Much of the SAT math section requires a special skill: the ability to translate normal language into math—and we're not just talking about two and 2, here. What we're referring to is the tricky business of turning a paragraph into a mathematical expression: restating everyday language into variables, relationships, and operations.

The trick is to know some **key words**, such as:

⭐ *Increases by, the sum of, x more than,* and *is greater than x by*, which all signify **addition**

  "y increased by 3" = y + 3

⭐ *Less than* and *# fewer than x,* which just means **subtraction**

  "y fewer than 8" = 8 − y

⭐ *Times, of,* and *the product of,* which indicate **multiplication**

  "the product of y and 9" = 9 × y

⭐ *Out of* and *per*, which translate to **division**

  "2 out of y" = 2/y

⭐ *Percent*, which means **per one hundred**

  "25% of y" = 0.25 × y

⭐ *Is*, which means **equals**

  "y is 3" = y = 3

You can then use these words as beacons in your journey to decipher a word problem, like so:

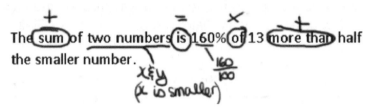

The sum of two numbers is 160% of 13 more than half the smaller number.

From here we could write the mathematical expression

$$x + y = \frac{160}{100}\left(\frac{x}{2} + 13\right)$$

But what if there's more than one variable involved? Try making a chart, like we have on the following page.

NOTES:

1,268 Snickerdoodles are sold at the annual Snickerdoodle State Fair. Anna sold eight times as many as Billy because Billy was caught picking his nose half-way through the bake-off, and twice as many as Claire (probably because Claire had foolishly advertised in the monthly *Snickerdoodle Review* that she was not, after all, a big fan of Snickerdoodles). If Dale consumed twice as many Snickerdoodles as anyone else at the fair, and Elizabeth sold 72 Snickerdoodles, all eaten by Dale, how many did each vendor sell?

First, we create a list of variables:

A = number sold by Anna

B = number sold by Billy

C = number sold by Claire

D = number eaten by Dale, but this has nothing to do with the equation, so ignore Dale's gluttonous ways

E = number sold by Elizabeth, 72

Now, we determine how they are related to the whole and to one another:

$A + B + C + E = \textbf{1,268}$

A = we know nothing about how many Anna sold, so we'll leave her as A.

$B = \frac{1}{8}A$

$C = \frac{1}{2}A$

$E = 72$

Plugging in the relationship of B and C to A, and inputting the value of E, we have:

$$A + \tfrac{1}{8}A + \tfrac{1}{2}A + 72 = 1{,}268$$

Which, simplified, is:
$$\tfrac{13}{8}A = 1{,}196 \ \text{ or } \ A = 736$$

Once we know what A is, or how many Snickerdoodles Anna sold, we can return to our list of variables and plug in A for all relationships to solve for Billy's and Claire's sales:

$$B = \tfrac{1}{8}(736) = 92 \qquad C = \tfrac{1}{2}(736) = 368$$

And now we know that Anna sold 736 Snickerdoodles, Billy sold 92 Snotterdoodles, Claire sold 368 Soullessdoodles, Dale is a pig, and Elizabeth sold 72 Dale-devoured-these-doodles for a grand total of 1,268 cookies.

Oh, hey! That's the number we're supposed to get!

And here's another that relies on an understanding of percentages:

Three people purchased new smart phones. If Sonja paid 30% more than John, and Kelsey paid 25% less than Sonja, who got the best deal?

    a. Sonja

    b. John

    c. Kelsey

    d. John and Kelsey

    e. Not enough information

To begin, we know *nothing* about the actual price, in which case we're tempted to choose e, "Not enough information." We do, however, know how each person's purchase related to the others'. Since we aren't told *anything* about John's purchase price, however, we'll declare his price to be x and write Sonja and Kelsey's prices in terms of x.

John = x

Sonja = x + .3x

Kelsey = S - .25S

    (and if we substitute in Sonja's equation for S....)
    = x + .25(x + .3x)

Simplified, John paid $x, Sonja paid $1.3x, and Kelsey paid $.975x—so whatever John paid, we still know that Kelsey paid less than he did, making our answer C.

If you're having a difficult time solving this one, try plugging in a random number for x. Why can we do this? Because all values are just relationships to x, and x itself really doesn't matter in order to answer this question. So let's try again using a random value (such as 10) for x:

Three people purchased new smart phones. If Sonja paid 30% more than John, and Kelsey paid 25% less than Sonja, who got the best deal?

John paid $10

Sonja paid 30% more than John,
so 10 + .3(10) = 13.33, or rounded to $13

Kelsey paid 25% less than Sonja,
so 13 − .25(13) = 13 − 3.25 = $9.75

And our winner, again, is Kelsey.

 PERCENTAGE SHORTCUT

Instead of calculating Sonja's price as 10 + .3(10), jump straight to the full sum of her price prior to multiplying:

100% + 30% = 130%,
so 1.3(10) = 13.

For Kelsey's price, 100% − 25% = 75%,
so .75(13) = 9.75.

You get the same answer, and since you can probably add/subtract whole numbers in your head lightning fast, this way is much faster.]

|ABSOLUTE VALUE|

Absolute value is defined as the distance of a number from 0. It is signified by two vertical bars, such as

|-1937285734896|

and is found by simply dropping the negative from the number— after all, you can't have a negative distance!

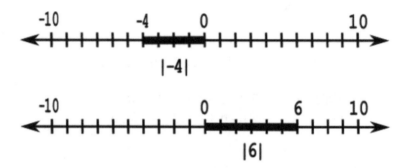

Solving equations with absolute values involves isolating the absolute value and then solving the resultant twice:

- ⮫ First, isolate the absolute value symbol.
- ⮫ Second, drop the absolute value bars and solve the equation as-is.
- ⮫ Third, distribute -1 throughout the content of | | prior to dropping them and solve.
- ⮫ If dealing with an inequality, remember that multiplying or dividing by a negative value switches the direction of the inequality, so always flip the direction of your inequality sign in the second step.
- ⮫ Last, report answers to equations as "and" statements and the solutions to inequalities as "or" statements.

Confused?

....................Totally normal!

The explanation tends to baffle students a bit, but with a little bit of practice, solving absolute value equations/inequalities are easy peasy. Starting on the next page, we're going to solve one equation and one inequality. Do yourself a favor and cover up the right-hand side of the page, try to perform each step on your own, and slowly uncover each step to see how you measure up. If you're not quite getting it, remember…your teachers are there to help!

NOTES:

Solve for x. 1 + 3|x − 2| = 28

(A) x = -7 and x = 11
(B) x = -7 and x = 14
(C) x = -5 and x = 9
(D) x = 11 and x =9
(E) x = 11 and x = 14

REMEMBER:
Cover the
answers on the
right, while you
do your work to
the left.

Step 1: Isolate | |

$$1 + 3|x - 2| = 28$$
$$-1 \qquad\qquad -1$$
$$\overline{}$$
$$3|x - 2| = 27$$

$$\frac{3|x - 2|}{3} = \frac{27}{3}$$

$$|x - 2| = 9$$

Step 2: Solve by dropping | |

$$x - 2 = 9$$
$$+2 \ +2$$
$$\overline{}$$
$$x = 11$$

Step 3: Solve by distributing -1 and dropping | |

$$-1(x - 2) = 9$$

$$-x + 2 = 9$$
$$\underline{-2 \quad -2}$$
$$-x = 7$$

$$\frac{-x}{-1} = \frac{7}{-1} \qquad x = -7$$

Answer: x = -7 and x = 11, or (A)

Now, let's do an inequality.

Solve for x. $-2|3x + 4| < 4$

(A) x > -2 or x > (-2)/3
(B) x > 2 or x > 2/3
(C) x < -2 and x < (-2)/3
(D) x < 2 and x > (-2)/3
(E) x > -2 or x < (-2)/3

Step 1: Isolate | |

$$\frac{-2|3x + 4|}{-2} > \frac{4}{-2}$$

$$|3x + 4| > -2$$

(Remember to switch
the inequality's direction)

Step 2: Solve by dropping | |

$$3x + 4 > -2$$
$$\underline{-4 \quad -4}$$
$$3x > -6$$

$$\frac{3x}{3} > \frac{-6}{3}$$

$$x > -2$$

Step 3: Distribute a -1, and then drop | | and solve

$$-1(3x + 4) < -2$$

$$-3x - 4 < -2$$

(Remember to switch the inequality's direction)

$$-3x - 4 < -2$$
$$\underline{+4 \quad +4}$$
$$\cdot \quad -3x < 2$$

$$\frac{-3x}{-3} < \frac{2}{-3}$$

$$x < \frac{-2}{3}$$

(Did you remember to switch the direction of the inequality?)

Answer: $x > -2$ or $x < \dfrac{-2}{3}$, or (E)

PROBABILITY

This stuff is way more useful than you'd even imagine. Not only will it help you get a good grade in your math class, thereby increasing the *probability* that you'll have a successful future, but it will help you avoid a long, dreadful road of regret paved in losing lottery tickets and overcast by hundreds of unredeemed free airline miles that could pretty much take you to your dream vacation spot *if only you weren't terrified of flying.* And right now, you are saying, "What??" KEEP READING.....

Wait, how does it help?

We're glad you asked! See, having an understanding of probability will make the odds printed on the back of your first lottery ticket *scream*, "You got like zero chance, dude!" And after that, if you're smart, you'll stop wasting your money.

And overcoming my dreadful fear of flying...?

Oh, right. Well, you've probably spent a lot of time in a car going to school, to work, to the mall, to the movie theater, to everywhere you could possibly need to go. *And* you have to drive home, as well. Agreed? Now, consider the statistics[23]: your lifetime odds of dying in a car accident are 1:244, but are only 1:4,975 in a plane! Now, understanding probability will teach you that the world truly is a dangerous place, but sometimes our fears blow the fear out of proportion and cause us to opt for more dangerous modes of transportation than safer modes simply because we've grown accustomed to the dangers of driving. Go on vacation.

---

23 http://www.purewatergazette.net/oddsofdying.htm - Data from 1999 study by National Safety Council

Phew! Now that we've gotten that one-to-one out of the way, the probability of an event (E) is

$$(P(E)) = \frac{\text{number of possibilities in which E is true}}{\text{total number of possibilities}}$$

The most common example of probability is in rolling a die, or (worse yet) tossing a coin. To keep you awake, we're going to look into the probability of you winning a *brand new scooter* on a game show!

One box has the key to your new scooter, and the others have SOMETHING else! Choose one!

$$(P(S)) = \frac{1 \text{ box with key}}{5 \text{ boxes total}} = \frac{1}{5}$$

But, what if you notice the flies buzzing around the second box and deduce that there absolutely must be a pair of stinky gym shoes in it, so you eliminate the second as a possibility? (Note: This whole fly-shoe connection is bulletproof. You're really on to something!) What would the probability be in this case?

$$(P(S_{\text{minus one shoe box}})) = \frac{1 \text{ box with key}}{4 \text{ boxes to choose from}} = \frac{1}{4}$$

Hey, looks like your odds are improving! You should ask if you can sniff the boxes before you choose.

RATIOS

Ratios just mean, "For every so many of this, there are this many of that." They're either written as fractions or as...

> This:That

All you need to know about ratios is that they can be manipulated by multiplying or dividing both sides by the same number, much like you could do to an equation.

> 2 cats:4 dogs
>
> reduces to
>
> 1 cat:2 dogs

> 3 friends:4 foes
>
> becomes a larger, albeit equally unbalanced, fight when it is
>
> 6 friends:8 foes

...And...that's it.

AVERAGE

An average is a number that represents a set of data. There are three different averages:

> ✐ *Arithmetic Mean*, the most commonly used average, is considered synonymous with "average" unless otherwise stated. The mean is the sum of all points of data divided by the number of items in the data set.

Median is the middle number in the set of data, found by eliminating the largest number in the set, followed by the smallest, then largest, and smallest, etc., until only one number remains. (Note: if the series contains an even number of items, the two middle numbers are averaged to produce the median.)

Mode is the most commonly occurring number in the set of data. (Note: it is possible to have *no* mode, and it is also possible to have more than one mode. In the case of {1, 2, 3, 4, 5}, there is no mode. In the case of a data set {1, 1, 2, 3, 3}, both 1 and 3 appear twice, so both 1 and 3 are modes.)

Example time!

Six men attend a concert with their girlfriends. Eight days later, each of them continues to be haunted by glitter. One man finds 9 sparkling points; two find 6; one finds 5; another finds 2; and the last poor soul finds 13 terrible, sparkling bits of glitter. What are the mean, median, and mode for those poor, haunted souls?

(A) 5.0, 6, 6
(B) 6.0, 9, none
(C) 6.8, 6, 6
(D) 6.8, 9, none
(E) 5.2, 6, none

Mean: $\dfrac{2+5+6+6+9+13}{6} = \dfrac{41}{6} \cong 6.8$

Median: 2̶ 5̶ 6 6 9̶ 1̶3̶   Find the mean of the two remaining numbers: $\dfrac{6+6}{2} = 6$

Mode: 6 appears twice and is thus the mode.

With 6.8, 6, and 6, our answer is c.

A Note on Weighted Averages

Problems involving weighted averages are an easy way for the College Board to trip up students because they require a simple and yet oh-so-easy-to-forget step. The most common question is something like this:

> What is the average varsity basketball team member's shoe size if half of the players wear a size 10, three wear a size 9, one wears a size 13 (he's really tall), and two wear a size 6 (twins, really short twins).
>
> (A) 8
> (B) 9
> (C) 10
> (D) 11
> (E) 12

Before you get all clumsy on us, you *can't* just average the shoe sizes since many more wear a size 10 than size 13. Rather, you need to account for the *weight* of each value. To do this, multiply each item by the number of times it is to be counted and *then* average the values.

$$\frac{(2\times6)+(1\times13)+(3\times9)+(6\times10)}{12} = 9.3$$

which rounds down to size nine, or answer (B).

If you're wondering how we figured out how many wear a size 10, or what the denominator should be, you need to start thinking logically! If we're asked to calculate an average, and "not enough information" isn't an option, we *must* have been given all players' shoe sizes. Since half wearing size 10 means half *don't*, and we're given non-10 sizes for six players, we must have 6×2 = 12 players.

Oh, and if you just average the shoe sizes without assigning them their appropriate weight, you would have gotten an answer of 9.5. Lo and behold, this rounds up to one of our options, 10! Don't fall for the trap!

SOLVING EQUATIONS

If you know basic arithmetic, you know how to solve an equation. The only reminder that we think you could possibly need is *whatever you do to one side of the equation must be repeated on the other side of the equation.* The only reason we're even reminding you of this is because the SAT includes questions that simply test your understanding of manipulating equations, AKA freebies!

Solve for x. $2x + 7 = 15$

$$\underline{\quad -7 \quad -7 \quad}$$
$$2x = 8$$

$$\frac{2x}{2} = \frac{8}{2}$$

$$x = 4$$

Solve for y. $3y + 6x = 48$

$$\underline{\quad -6x \quad -6x \quad}$$
$$3y = 48 - 6x$$

$$\frac{3y}{3} = \frac{48}{3} - \frac{6x}{3}$$

$$y = 16 - 2x$$

Solve for ♥. $3♥ + 3✎ = 15🎁$

$$\underline{\quad -3✎ \quad -3✎ \quad}$$
$$3♥ = 15🎁 - 3✎$$

$$\frac{3♥}{3} = \frac{15🎁}{3} - \frac{3✎}{3}$$

$$♥ = 5🎁 - ✎$$

EXPONENT RULES

When it comes to exponents, one of the most common mistakes made in math classes across the country involves something like this:

$f(x) = -x^2$ Solve for $f(1)$

The student drools away, dreaming of the perfect piece of cafeteria pizza plopping onto his tray and writes:

$f(1) = (-1)^2 = 1$

(this is wrong; hence, it is crossed out)

when, if he weren't daydreaming about lunch, he'd remember that

$f(1) = -(1)^2$

because *the exponent only belongs to the value of x, and the negative on the outside is a -1 that gets distributed after squaring x's value.*   Oh, now you remember!

$f(x) = -x^2$ vs. $g(x) = (-x)2$
$f(1) = -1$ $g(1) = 1$
$f(-1) = -1$ $g(-1) = 1$

Good job! Keep it up!

On to bigger things! There are a handful of rules that you've probably already memorized, but just in case you need a refresher, here they are:

Addition and Subtraction: $Ax^m + Bx^m = (A + B)x^m$

So long as the bases (x) and exponents (m) are the same, the sum or difference may be found by adding or subtracting the coefficients.

$$2x^2 + 4x^2 = (2 + 4)x^2 = 6x^2$$
$$7x^3 - 6x^3 = (7 - 6)x^3 = 1x^3$$

Multiplication: $Ax^m \times Bx^n = (A \times B)x^{m+n}$

So long as the bases (x) are the same, the product can be found by multiplying the coefficients and adding the exponents

$$5x^3 \times 6x^8 = (5 \times 6)x^{3+8} = 30x^{11}$$

Division: $Ax^m \div Bx^n = (A \div B)x^{m-n}$

So long as the bases (x) are the same, we can divide these values by dividing the coefficients (A÷B) and subtracting the exponents (m–n).

$$12x^{10} \div 4x^5 = (12 \div 4)x^{10-5} = 3x^5$$

Power to a Power: $(Ax^m)^n = A^n x^{(m \times n)}$

To calculate an exponent raised to a power of n, the exponent and n are multiplied. Remember to distribute the power to all values within the parentheses.

$(3x^4)^2 = 3^2 x^{(4 \times 2)} = 9x^8$

Multiplying Values with the Same Exponent: $A^n \times B^n = (A \times B)^n$

$9^2 \times 3^2 = (9 \times 3)^2 = 27^2 = 729$

Dividing Values with the Same Exponent: $A^n \div B^n = (A \div B)^n$

$22^4 \div 11^4 = (22 \div 11)^4 = 2^4 = 16$

Negative Exponents: $A^{-x} = (\frac{1}{A}^x)$

While they might look scary, a negative in an exponent just moves the value to which it belongs either into the denominator or into the numerator. So a negative exponent in the numerator moves the value into the denominator, and a negative exponent in the denominator moves that value into the numerator. For example:

$$\frac{A^2 B^{-3} C^7}{X^2 Y^{-4} Z^{-6}} = \frac{A^2 C^7 Y^4 Z^6}{X^2 B^3}$$

In addition, remember that if an exponent is outside of the parenthesis, distribute it to every value inside! For example:

$$(AB^2 C^{-4})^{-1} = \frac{1}{AB^2 C^{-4}} = \frac{C^4}{AB^2}$$

NOTES:

Fractional Exponents: $A^{\frac{m}{n}} = \sqrt[n]{A^m}$

More commonly known as *roots*, fractional exponents are another way of expressing a root. A fractional exponent is composed of a power (numerator) and a root (denominator).

$$2^{-2} = \frac{1^2}{2^2} = \frac{1}{4} \qquad 8^{\frac{2}{3}} = \sqrt[3]{8^2} = \sqrt[3]{64} = 4$$

Alternatively, you could solve this problem by replacing 8 with 2^3. (Go ahead and do the math. Ahh! Why it *does* equal 8!)

$$(2^3)^{\frac{2}{3}} = 2^{\frac{3\times2}{3}} = 2^2 = 4$$

(The 3 in the numerator cancels the 3 in the denominator.)

Speaking of roots, don't forget how to work with radicals!

Addition & Subtraction: When the radicands and roots are synonymous, treat the radicals as a variable and perform your arithmetic on the coefficients.

$$11\sqrt[2]{7} + 6\sqrt[2]{7} = (11+6)\sqrt[2]{7} = 17\sqrt[2]{7}$$
$$6\sqrt[3]{2} - 2\sqrt[3]{2} = (6-2)\sqrt[3]{2} = 4\sqrt[3]{2}$$

$11\sqrt[2]{7} - 2\sqrt[2]{2}$ cannot be simplified because the radicands are different

$\sqrt[3]{2} + \sqrt[2]{2}$ cannot be simplified because the roots are different

root

$^x\sqrt{y}$ radicand

Multiplication & Division: When the roots are synonymous, the coefficients and radicands are multiplied or divided separately.

$$4\sqrt[3]{7} \times 2\sqrt[3]{5} = (4 \times 2)\sqrt[3]{(7 \times 5)} = 8\sqrt[3]{35}$$

$$36\sqrt[2]{33} \div 9\sqrt[2]{11} = \frac{36}{9}\sqrt[2]{\frac{33}{11}} = 4\sqrt[2]{3}$$

$2\sqrt[3]{4} \div 7\sqrt[2]{2}$ cannot be simplified because the roots are different

FACTORING

You should know how to factor by now, but unless you've spent hours and hours factoring, and have thus developed an uncanny ability to "sense" the answer, you should still move through your factoring tool kit in an orderly fashion. We recommend:

1. Factor out commonalities (if there are any):

2xy + 4yz = 2y(x + 2z)

2. Determine if this is the difference of two perfect squares:

a² – b² = (a – b)(a + b)

3. Determine if the terms be grouped in a way that allows them to be factored:

2wy + 3xz + xy + 6wz → 2wy + 6wz + xy + 3xm↩
(2w + x)(y + 3z) ← 2w(y + 3z) + x(y + 3z)

NOTES:

4. Decide if this is the sum or difference of two perfect cubes:

$$a^3 + b^3 = (a + b)(a^2 - ab + b^2)$$
$$a^3 - b^3 = (a - b)(a^2 + ab + b^2)$$

And before you move on, check for #5.

5. Is this a quadratic equation?

$$x^2 + x - 2 = (x + 2)(x - 1)$$

(psst, the answer is yes!)

In Case You Forgot About Quadratic Equations

Quadratic equations can be factored many ways, but the most common methods are *guessing* and applying the *quadratic formula*. Before any method is sought, it is necessary to assure that you're working with an expression in *standard quadratic form*, meaning that it *must* be rearranged to look as so:

$$ax^2 + bx + c = 0$$

From there, you can choose your favorite method.

Guessing
This method involves, you got it, guessing which values go into the generic framework of

$$(qx + s)(rx + t)$$

where *q* and *r* are coefficients and *s* and *t* are constants. Luckily, the guessing method has a couple guidelines for

choosing the sign of each constant. From the standard quadratic form, $ax^2 + bx + c = 0$,

  +C: *s* and *t* have the same sign
     +B: both *s* and *t* are +
     -B: both *s* and *t* are −
  −C: *s* and *t* have opposite signs
     +B: larger of *s* and *t* is +
     -B: larger of *s* and *t* is −

With these rules, it's really just a matter of guessing which factors to use!

Let's try factoring $4x + 21x^2 - 3 = 5 + 2x$.

$$4x + 21x^2 - 3 = 5 + 2x$$
$$\underline{-2x \qquad\qquad\quad -\ 2x}$$
$$2x + 21x^2 - 3\ =\ 5$$
$$\underline{\qquad\qquad -\ 5\ \ -5}$$
$$2x + 21x^2 - 8 = 0 \qquad \text{rearrange}$$
$$21x^2 + 2x - 8 = 0$$

From −C and +B, we know that we'll have constants with different signs, the larger being negative.

One possibility is

$$(7x + 2)\,(3x - 4)$$

To check if we've guessed correctly, we *FOIL* it back out:

$$(7x + 2)\,(3x - 4)$$

$$\underset{\text{first}}{21x^2} \quad \underset{\text{outside}}{-\ 28x} \quad \underset{\text{inside}}{+\ 6x} \quad \underset{\text{last}}{-\ 8}$$

Which simplifies to:
$$21x^2 - 22x - 8$$

FOIL

First
Outside
Inside
Last

But, as you see, we end up with the wrong b value. So we guess again!

$$(7x - 4)(3x + 2)$$

And again, we check our work by FOILing it back out:

$$21x^2 + 14x - 12x - 8$$
$$21x^2 + 2x - 8$$

This time we get the original, so we've correctly factored this equation. Woo! But before you party, set each factor equal to zero and solve for x.

$$
\begin{array}{ll}
7x - 4 = 0 & 3x + 2 = 0 \\
\underline{+4 \ +4} & \underline{-2 \ -2} \\
7x = 4 & 3x = -2
\end{array}
$$

$$
\begin{array}{ll}
\dfrac{7x}{7} = \dfrac{4}{7} & \dfrac{3x}{3} = \dfrac{-2}{3}
\end{array}
$$

$$x = \tfrac{4}{7} \text{ and } x = \tfrac{-2}{3}$$

And initiate party.

Seems like a lot of work before partying, doesn't it?

Quadratic Formula

Recall the standard quadratic form. The generic expression contains number placeholders (a, b, and c) and represent the same values that are plugged into the quadratic formula:

$$x = \frac{-b \pm \sqrt{b^2 - 4ac}}{2a}$$

Notice the ± there? You calculate both the sum and the difference in the numerator in order to get two answers.

Let's try factoring $6x^2 + 5x = 4x^2 + 21 + 4x$ using the quadratic equation.

$$
\begin{array}{l}
6x^2 + 5x = 4x^2 + 21 + 4x \\
\underline{\quad -4x \qquad\qquad -4x} \\
6x^2 + x = 4x^2 + 21
\end{array}
$$

$$
\begin{array}{l}
6x^2 + x = 4x^2 + 21 \\
\underline{\quad -21 \qquad\quad -21} \\
6x^2 + x - 21 = 4x^2
\end{array}
$$

$$
\begin{array}{l}
6x^2 + x - 21 = 4x^2 \\
\underline{-4x^2 \qquad\qquad -4x^2} \\
2x^2 + x - 21 = 0
\end{array}
$$

NOTES:

Remembering the form Ax² + Bx + C, we plug in our values (A = 2, B=1, and C=-21) into the quadratic form:

$$\frac{-1 \pm \sqrt{1^2 - 4(2)(-21)}}{2(2)}$$

$$\frac{-1 \pm \sqrt{1 - (-168)}}{4}$$

$$\frac{-1 \pm \sqrt{169}}{4}$$

$$\frac{-1 \pm 13}{4}$$

x= 3 and x = (-14)/4

The best part of the quadratic formula is that it, unlike the guessing method, is capable of solving for imaginary x's. But don't worry! Imaginary numbers won't be on the SAT, so please don't hyperventilate just yet.

FUNCTIONS

A *function* is an equation of a line where each of its x-values has only one corresponding y-value. It is possible, however, for one y-value to have numerous x-values. Confused? Think of polygamous patriarchal societies: where each husband (y) may have many wives (x) as he'd like, but each wife (x) can only have one husband (y).

Functions are often written as f(x) = blah blah blah. But before you get nervous because you've never seen f(x), take a breath and listen: f(x) is synonymous with y, which means, for example, that f(x) = 2x and y = 2x are the same.

If an equation is graphed, you can test if it is a function by performing the *vertical line test*.

Vertical line test – a vertical line drawn anywhere across the graph will only touch the line at one point. Go ahead: take your pencil and drag it vertically across the graph. As you'll see, this is a function!

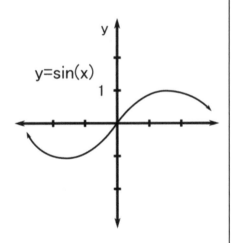

y=sin(x)

NOTES:

Special Functions

linear	$f(x) = mx + b$ m = slope b = y-intercept	
horizontal line	$f(x) = k$ k is any constant & x is always the same	
absolute value	$f(x) = |x|$	
quadratic	$f(x) = ax^2 + bx + c$	
polynomial	$f(x) = ax^n + bx^{n-1} + \ldots$	

(THINGS SURROUNDED IN PARENTHESES)

One such parenthetical information is a **relation**. A relation is an ordered pair (x, y) that represents an exact spot on a plane.

The other information you'll be reading in parentheses are **domain** and **range**. *Domain* and *range* are often reported as an ordered pair, but they mean something very different:

Domain: How far left and right a line goes on a plane, or *where x goes.*

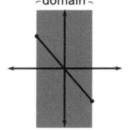
-domain-

Range: How far up and down a line goes on a plane, or *where y goes.*

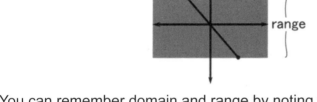
range

You can remember domain and range by noting that, the same way (**x, y**) is in alphabetical order, so is the corresponding (**domain, range**). Additionally, the brackets used practically tell you what they mean:

(An open bracket means that the line goes *around* this point; more specifically, the line *approaches* this point, but never actually reaches it.

[A closed bracket means that the line *stops* at this point; it does not simply approach it, but it closes in on the point and ends *exactly* at this point.

Lastly, you cannot ever actually *reach* infinity, right? That's why you see (-∞ and ∞), and *never* [-∞ or ∞]. (We crossed that one out for you. Don't get them confused.)

SYSTEM OF EQUATIONS

Solving a system of equations means *finding where two equations will intersect on a graph.*

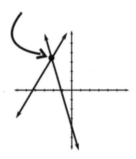

Yeah, like that!

And once again, since freedom entails a plethora of sweet, sweet options, you can choose how to solve a system of equations.

Before we show you how to do either method, we'd like to insist that you brush up on *both* methods since knowing how to do both will save you a *lot* of time.

⭐ *The Elimination Method* involves adding the two systems together in such a way that one of the variables is eliminated, thereby allowing you to solve for the remaining variable.

To solve the system $x - 17 + 3y = 0$ and $26 + 2x = 6y$ by the elimination method,

1. Arrange the equations in standard form
   (Ax + By = C) and write one above the other.

   $$x + 3y = 17$$
   $$2x - 6y = -26$$

2. Multiply one or both equations so that, when the
   system is summed, one variable is eliminated.

   We have a +3y and a -6y, so we're going to
   multiply the equation with +3y by 2 to achieve
   +6y. When added, -6y and +6y will cancel.

   (×2) x + 3y = 17 (×2)   2x + 6y = 34
     + 2x – 6y = -26   →   +2x – 6y = -26
                                        4x   = 8
                                            x = 2

3. After solving for one variable, plug it into *both*
   equations. This allows you to solve for the remaining
   variable *and* check your work.

   (2) + 3y = 17   2(2) – 6y = -26
   -2   -2   4 – 6y = -26
        3y = 15   -4   -4
         y = 5   -6y = -30
                              y = 5

Since both equations solve as x = 2 and y = 5, we
know that we have successfully solved this system
of equations. And what does x = 2 and y = 5 mean?
That's right—the lines cross one another at (2, 5).

⭐ Next, *the Substitution Method* involves solving one of the equations for a variable and plugging its value into the other equation wherever the solved variable appears.

To solve the system $3x - y = 3$ and $7x + 3y = 39$ by the substitution method,

1. Solve for a variable in one of either equation.

   Since the first equation has -1y, we're going to rearrange the equation to solve for *y*. We choose *y* because solving for *x* in the same equation would involve dividing both sides by 3—a total waste of time!

$$3x - y = 3$$
$$\underline{+y \quad +y}$$
$$3x = y + 3$$
$$\underline{-3 \qquad -3}$$
$$3x - 3 = y$$

2. Wherever this variable is seen in the *other* equation, replace it with the variable's value from the first equation.

   $y = 3x - 3$ plug $3x - 3$ in for y
   $7x + 3y = 39$ → $7x + 3(3x - 3) = 39$

3. Solve for the remaining variable.

$$7x + 9x - 9 = 39$$
$$16x = 48$$
$$x = 3$$

4. Plug this variable into both of the original equations to solve the system and verify your answer.

$$3(3) - y = 3 \qquad\qquad 7(3) + 3y = 39$$
$$9 - y = 3 \qquad\qquad\quad 21 + 3y = 39$$
$$\underline{-9 \qquad -9} \qquad\qquad \underline{-21 \qquad\quad -21}$$
$$-y = -6 \qquad\qquad\qquad 3y = 18$$
$$y = 6 \qquad\qquad\qquad\quad y = 6$$

Again, we have two matching answers of x = 3 and y = 6, so we know that these two lines intersect at (3, 6).

Do you see why *knowing both* is so very important? Depending on the equations, plugging one equation into another could result in huge numbers that take entirely too much time to multiply and divide, or *both* equations could be in need of multiplying, and that just makes more room for error.

NOTES:

SEEING THROUGH THE FoG

Or, dealing with composite functions! Composite functions list two different functions, quite often $f(x)$ and $g(x)$, and ask you to plug them into one another like some kind of weird mathematical get-together.

Given $f(x) = x^2 + 2$ & $g(x) = 2x + 3$, determine $f(g(2))$.

Begin at the center of the equation and solve your way out.

$$g(2) = 2(2) + 3 = 4 + 3 = 7$$

And plug this answer into the next layer:

$$f(7) = (7)^2 + 2$$
$$49 + 2 = 51$$

Using the same functions, determine $g(f(2))$.

$$f(2) = (2)^2 + 2$$
$$4 + 2 = 6$$

Now take your answer of 6 and plug that into g.

$$g(6) = 2(6) + 3$$
$$12 + 3 = 15$$

Notice how $f(g(2)) = 51$ and $g(f(2)) = 15$? Even though you're using the same two functions and the same x-value, the answers are very different, so be careful to begin in the center and work your way outward, because you can bet your lunch money that the answer for the *wrong* direction will be an option.

LOGARITHM RULES

Logarithms are the opposite of exponents and are thus easily interchangeable with an exponential expression:

$$\log_{\bigstar} = \square^{\triangle} \quad \leftrightarrow \quad \bigstar^{\triangle} = \square$$

And thus you can easily solve $\log_7 x = 2$. (Pssst, x is 49!)

Two common log bases are, as a matter of fact, so common that they have their own shorthand. They are *ln*, which stands for $\log_e$ (e being the "natural number"), and the seemingly baseless log, which is an understood $\log_{10}$. And here are the rules!

Rule	Example
$\log_a a^x = x$	$\log_6 6^{10} = 10$
$a^{\log_a x} = x$	$7^{\log_7 19} = 19$
$\log_a y^p = p \times \log_a y$	$\log_3 2^4 = 4 \times \log_3 2$
$\log_a x - \log_a y = \log_a(\frac{x}{y})$	$\log_4 10 - \log_4 2 = \log_4(\frac{10}{2})$ $\log_4 16 \quad$ rearrange $\rightarrow 4^? = 16$ $? = 2$, so $\log_4(4^2) = 2$
$\log_a x + \log_a y = \log_a(x \times y)$	$\log_6 9 + \log_6 4 = \log_6(9 \times 4)$ $\log_6(36) \quad$ rearrange $\rightarrow 6^? = 36$ $? = 2$, so $\log_6(6^2) = 2$

Important! For addition and subtraction, bases (a) must be the same!

NOTES:

SEQUENCES

Sequences are functions with a domain comprised of positive integers. Two types of sequences frequent the SAT: *arithmetic sequences* and *geometric sequences*.

⭐ *Arithmetic Sequences* are called such because each consecutive number is obtained arithmetically, i.e., by adding a constant.

> The set {1, 4, 7, 10 ...} is an arithmetic sequence because any term can be found by adding 3 to its previous term.

> To generate the equation of an arithmetic sequence, use the arithmetic sequence formula

$$a_n = a_1 + (n\text{-}1)d$$

> where a_n is the nth term, a_1 is the first term of the sequence, n is the variable into which you'd plug in the term number, and d is the common difference. (Don't worry about *why* the equation is this way—all you need to know is how to use it!)

> In the previous set {1, 4, 7, 10 ...} ...

> ☆ the first number in the sequence is 1, so a_1 = **1**
> ☆ the difference between 1 and 4 is 3, so **d = 3**

> If we plug these values into the arithmetic sequence formula

$$a_n = a_1 + (n\text{-}1)d \;\rightarrow\; a_n = 1 + (n\text{-}1)3$$
$$\text{or, simplified} \quad a_n = \text{-}2 + 3n$$

Try one on your own!

7 people each give you a dollar for helping them understand arithmetic sequences. You then realize that there is a strange amount of demand for assistance (probably because your math teacher contracted "senioritis" from her students), and that raising your fee to $2 would be *way* more profitable. How much dough would you earn by helping *n* number of people?

    (A) $a_n = 2n$
    (B) $a_n = 7 + 2n$
    (C) $a_n = 2 + 2n$
    (D) $a_n = 5 + 2n$
    (E) $a_n = 7 + 4n$

You start out with $7, so $a_1 = 7$. After helping one more person, you gain $2, and after helping another person, you'd gain another $2, so the difference is very clearly equal to 2.

So here's our equation: $a_n = a_1 + (n-1)d$, and with our values plugged in: $a_n = 7 + (n-1)2$

If we simplify our equation to $a_n = 5 + 2n$, we find our answer is D.

✪ *Geometric Sequences*, AKA "exponential growth sequences," change by a ratio rather than in arithmetic increments.

> The set {3, 1, $\frac{1}{3}$, $\frac{1}{9}$, ...} is a geometric sequence because each term is found by multiplying the previous term by a ratio of $\frac{1}{3}$.

To generate the equation of a geometric sequence, use the formula

$$a_n = a_1 r^{(n-1)}$$

where a_n is the nth term, a_1 is the first term, r is the ratio, and n is the variable into which you'd plug the term number.

In the previous set, the first number in the sequence was 3

($a_1 = 3$) and the ratio was $\frac{1}{3}$ ($r = \frac{1}{3}$). The equation to this sequence is therefore

$$a_n = 3 \times \tfrac{1}{3}^{(n-1)}$$

Here's another example:

> It is estimated that the average human brain contains 100 billion neurons. If nonexistent research that we're making up on the spot suggests that this number decreases by 2% every 10 hours spent playing *World of Warmaking*, how many neurons would Jebediah have after 87 hours of gaming?
>
> (A) None; he'd be brain-dead.
> (B) 83.7 billion
> (C) 85.6 billion
> (D) 92.8 billion
> (E) Who cares? Jeb is getting dumped for sure.

NOTES:

Assuming Jeb has never wasted his life away prior to this 87-hour binge, he begins with the average number of neurons (a_1 = 100, in billions). The ratio of change is a 2% loss, or a remaining 98% of the previous amount (r = 98%, or 0.98). *n* is determined by the number of times a 10-hour neural assault occurs ($\frac{1\text{ assault}}{10\text{ hours}} = \frac{n\text{ assaults}}{87\text{ hours}}$), which is determined to be 8.7. Plug and chug!

$$a_n = 100\times0.98^{(8.7-1)} = 85.6 \text{ billion, or answer (C)}.$$

(However, you could make a pretty good argument for answer (E).)

That's right—87 wasted hours later, Jeb is out almost 15% of his neurons (and probably a girlfriend). But if you still *really* want to play video games right now, in spite of all of this hard, non-scientific but mathematically sound evidence, go ahead. We're going to keep on keeping on with the math stuff.

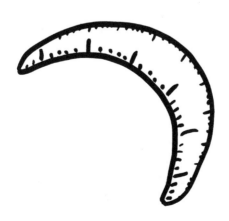

NOTES:

GEOMETRY

The best way to address the wonderful world of shapes is to revisit the language of geometry.

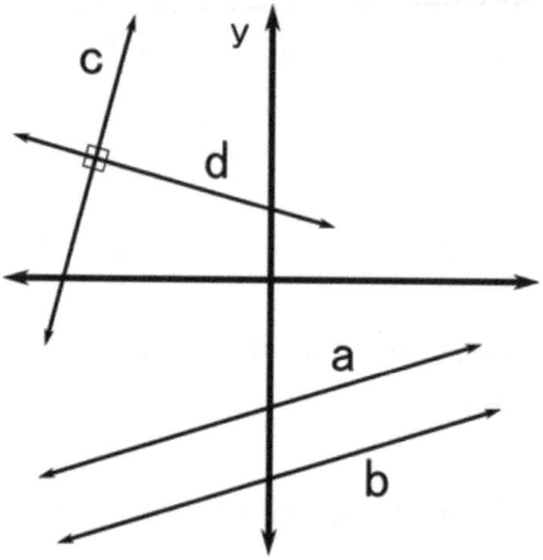

| | is the notation for *parallel*, which means "having the same slope so that no matter how far the lines are extended, they will never intersect."

AB| |CD means that line AB is parallel to line CD, or that no matter how far we extend and follow lines AB and CD, they will never intersect one another.

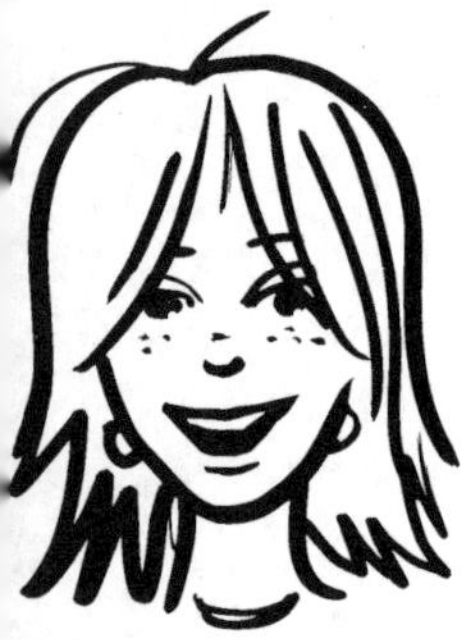

⊥ is the notation for *perpendicular*, which means "intersecting on a plane to create a 90° angle."

CD ⊥ EF means line CD is perpendicular to line EF, or that line CD intersects line EF to form a 90° angle (signified with ∟).

To determine if two lines are perpendicular, compare their slopes: the slopes of two perpendicular lines will be negative reciprocals (i.e., A and $-\frac{1}{A}$).

Are the following lines perpendicular?

y=3x+2 & y=-1/3 x+2

Since these equations are written in the handy-dandy point-slope form (y = mx+b), we can see right away that the slope of the first equation is 3 and the slope of the second is -⅓. Are 3 and -⅓ negative reciprocals? Why, yes—yes they are. And so we have perpendicular lines!

$\overleftrightarrow{AB}$ is the notation for a line that passes through points A and B.

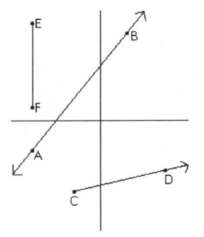

$\overrightarrow{CD}$ is the notation for a ray that starts at C and passes through D.

$\overline{EF}$ is the notation for a line segment with endpoints E and F.

Congruent Angles have equal measurements, i.e. if angle A and angle B are said to be congruent and we measure angle A at 47°, we know that angle B is also 47°.

Complementary Angles have a sum of 90°.

Supplementary Angles have a sum of 180°.

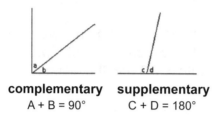

complementary	supplementary
A + B = 90°	C + D = 180°

Find yourself confusing complementary and supplementary? Just think alphabetically and numerically: "C and 90 come first; S and 180 come second."

A note on *angles not drawn to scale*: if you don't know the answer, see if the diagram "looks right." If not, try drawing it to scale, remembering that larger angles face larger legs and smaller angles face smaller legs. The only reason the College Board would be sloppy and *not* draw the images perfectly is because a perfect image would make the answer too obvious! So redraw the diagram and reap the benefits.

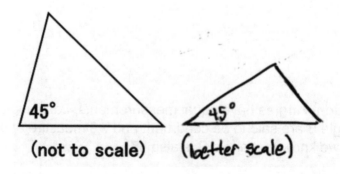

(not to scale)   (better scale)

Parallelograms are shapes made of two pairs of parallel lines. All parallelograms contain 2 pairs of congruent angles (congruent meaning *they have same measurement*, i.e., A/D, C/B) and 2 pairs of supplementary angles (supplementary meaning *they add up to 180°*, i.e., A/B, C/D).

Since the internal angles of a parallelogram add up to 360°, knowing a *single* angle allows you to determine *all* angles. If we're told that the measurement of angle A is 115°, we know that angle D must also be 115°. Since angles B and C are congruent, they must each account for half of the remaining (360 – 115 – 115) 130°, which means angles B and C are 65° each.

NOTES:

Similar Triangles have the angle measurements and *proportional* leg length. To say that the triangles below are similar, we use the notation $\triangle ABC \cong \triangle DEF$.

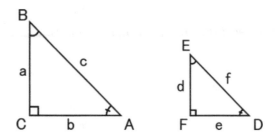

Since these triangles are similar, we know that side *a* is proportionate to side *d*, *b* to *e*, and *c* to *f*; and that angle *C* is equal to angle *F*, *B* to *E*, and *A* to *D*. As a matter of fact, without even being told that they're similar, we should know these things. Why? The curve along the inside of angles *B* and *E* tell us that they measure the same, and the curves with a single notch along angles *A* and *D* tell us that *those* angles are the same. The same would go for any angles or lengths with *three* notches.

Assuming that we're asked to find the dimensions of triangle DEF, given that side a = 3", side b = 2", and side d = 2", we would first solve for side *c*:

$$3^2 + 2^2 = c^2$$
$$9 + 4 = c^2$$
$$c = \sqrt{13}$$

Mind = Blown? Look to the right for a refresher on the *Pythagorean Theorem*.

We can then set up the generic ratios

$$\frac{a}{b} = \frac{d}{e} \quad \& \quad \frac{a}{c} = \frac{d}{f}$$

(or whichever ratios you'd like, so long as the numerators match positions on the triangle and the denominators match positions on the triangle, i.e., $\frac{b}{c} = \frac{e}{f}$ but not $\frac{b}{c} = \frac{f}{e}$.)

You then plug in the values you know and solve for the unknown:

$$\frac{3}{2} = \frac{2}{e} \qquad (3)e = (2)(2) \qquad e = \frac{4}{3}$$

$$\frac{3}{\sqrt{13}} = \frac{2}{f} \qquad (3)f = 2\sqrt{13} \qquad f = \frac{2\sqrt{13}}{3}$$

Speaking of the **Pythagorean Theorem**, Pythagoras made right triangles your favorite. Don't believe us? Check it out:

For any given right triangle, the sum of the square of its legs is equal to the square of its hypotenuse. *Or,*

$$a^2 + b^2 = c^2$$

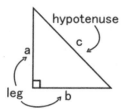

where C is the *hypotenuse*, the leg opposite of the right angle.

Still don't fancy Pythagoras? Without his theorem, you'd have to pull out your calculator and start punching in numbers to calculate the lengths with that whole "Soh-Cah-Toa" thing (yuck—we'll get to *that* later). So take a moment to thank Pythagoras.

NOTES:

Special Triangles

Why are they special? Because they're just so wonderfully predictable! These two triangles have consistent ratios, so no matter which side length you're given, you can swiftly calculate the others.

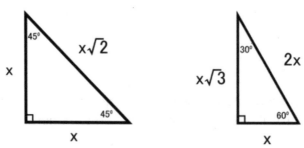

45-45-90 triangles are the easiest to remember: opposite of each 45° is x, and opposite of the hypotenuse is $x\sqrt{2}$.

30-60-90 triangles are easy if you remember the pieces. All you must do is think logically: the larger the angle, the longer the length: 30°:x, 60°:$x\sqrt{3}$, and 90°:2x.

Other Tidbits on Triangles

★ The sum of two legs' length must always supersede the hypotenuse.

★ The area of a triangle = ½ × base × height

★ The sum of all internal angles of a triangle is always equal to 180°, so knowing any two angles allows you to calculate the third.

★ For a triangle cut with a line parallel to another (such as that found on the right), the two triangles are similar

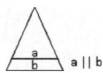

Conic Sections

The two conic sections that you'll see on the SAT are circles and parabolas—but *not* ellipses and hyperbolas, woo!

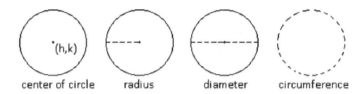

center of circle   radius   diameter   circumference

The *center of a circle* is denoted as the point (h,k).

Radius (r) is the length of a line that starts in the middle of a circle and ends on the edge of the circle.

Diameter is a line that starts on the edge of a circle, passes through the center of a circle, and ends on the edge of the circle.

Circle equations:

    ★ *Formula of a circle* = $(x - h)^2 + (y - k)^2 = r^2$
    ★ *Circumference,* aka the *perimeter* of a circle = $2 \times \pi \times r$
    ★ *Area of a circle* = $\pi \times r^2$

NOTES:

A *parabola* is a symmetrical curve composed of points that are equidistant from the *focus* and the *directrix*.

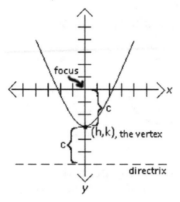

This parabola has a *directrix* of (0, -6),
a *focus* of (0,0), and a vertex of (0,-3).

The equation of a parabola depends on whether it opens...

Left or Right $(y-k)^2=4c(x-h)$ **-or-**   Up or Down $(x-h)^2=4c(y-k)$

In both cases, (h,k) is the *vertex* and c is the distance from the vertex to the directrix/focus.

Coordinate Geometry

The *distance formula* calculates the distance between two points on a graph.

$$d = \sqrt{(x_1 - x_2)^2 + (y_1 - y_2)^2}$$

For (3,5) and (-6, -2)

$$= \sqrt{(3 - -6)^2 + (5 - -2)^2}$$

$$= \sqrt{(9)^2 + (7)^2}$$

$$= \sqrt{81 + 49} = \sqrt{130}$$

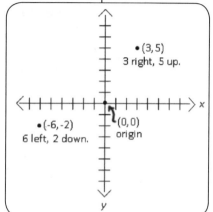

Slope (m) is the measurement of a line's "slant" or ratio of *rise* over *run*.

$$m = \frac{y_1 - y_2}{x_1 - x_2}$$

For (3,5) and (-6, -2)

$$m = \frac{5 - -2}{3 - -6}$$

$$= \frac{7}{9}$$

The *midpoint formula* is used to find coordinates of the middle of a line that connects two points.

$$\text{Midpoint} = (\frac{x_1 + x_2}{2}, \frac{y_1 + y_2}{2})$$

For (3,5) and (-6, -2)

$$\text{Midpoint} = \frac{3 + -6}{2}, \frac{5 + -2}{2} = \frac{-3}{2}, \frac{3}{2}$$

NOTES:

* In calculating the distance or slope for two points (x_1, y_1) and (x_2, y_2) are arbitrarily assigned. It is only important that you stay consistent throughout the calculation, i.e. not using $x_1 = 3$ and $y_1 = -2$.

Tangents are a little more complex than what we're going to get into here, and you probably don't want to hear about anything you're not going to need for the test, right? When it comes to the SAT, you're going to want to know this: a line is *tangent* to a circle if it passes through the circumference of the circle at only one point and forms a 90° angle (or, is *perpendicular*) to the radius.

The whole "perpendicular" part is easy to comprehend: the angle formed by the intersection of the tangent line and the radius must be negative reciprocals $\frac{a}{b} = -\frac{b}{a}$). But here's a picture of circumference-bit:

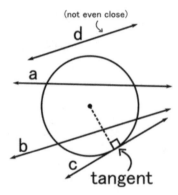

(not even close)

tangent

Only line *c* is tangent. Lines *a* and *b* touch the circumference twice and line *d* doesn't touch it at all.

Find the equation of a line that is tangent at (3,2) to a circle centered at (1,3).

(A) y = 2x - 5

(B) y = -²⁄₁x + 3

(C) y = -²⁄₁x + 8

(D) y = -2x + 4

(E) y = -2x + 8

Sometimes it's helpful to do a quick sketch and visualize your situation:

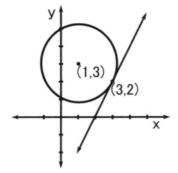

Ahh! Now we can see the relationship between those two points! Since a tangent line is perpendicular to the radius, we know that we'll need the slope of the radius:

$$\frac{3-2}{1-3} = \frac{1}{-2} = -\frac{1}{2}$$

From here we can calculate the slope of the tangent line to be $-\frac{2}{1}$, or -2. We then plug this slope and the point that is shared between the circle and the tangent line into the point-slope form:

$y-y_1=m(x-x_1)$
$y-2=-2(x-3)$
$y-2=-2x+6$
$y=-2x+8$

Sure enough, we have a match with answer (E).

SCATTERPLOTS

Scatterplots are graphs of data that seem to have no real semblance to a linear trend. They're often analyzed by "best fit lines," AKA a line that doesn't necessarily connect the dots, but passes through them in a way that minimizes how much each point deviates from the line. You're never going to be asked to draw a best fit line, and you'll never *see* a best fit line, but roughing one is sometimes helpful in making sense of a messy graph. Other times, a little bit of logical thinking is all you need to draw out a bit of information.

A major supplier of gag toys decided to eliminate the least profitable gadget from its line and pump the money into a new whoopee cushion design. The sales data for all products were graphed for analysis. According to the graph, which item should be eliminated?

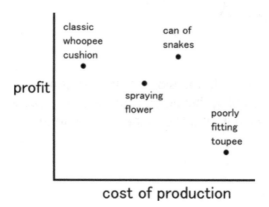

a. Whoopee Cushions
b. Spraying Flowers
c. Poorly Fitting Toupee
d. Can of Snakes
e. Disappearing Ink (no longer pictured)

Do we need to attempt a best fit line, or can we just think logically here? If a business wants to make the most profit at the lowest expense, we'd look for the item with the greatest slope. Lo and behold, it's the Classic Whoopee Cushion! Next it would be most reasonable for the company to eliminate the item with the smallest slope, which, with a little eyeballing, turns out to be the Poorly Fitting Toupee. (Big surprise. A poorly fitting toupee is really more of an embarrassment than a gag.)

GRAPH TRANSFORMATIONS

Once you know a handful of base graphs, you can transform them into any number of graphs without having to mess around with x-y tables and meticulously plotting the line. In the event that you did not formerly find base graphs to be worthy of your brain space, here they are again. Oh, and this time, you'll want to memorize them.

$$y = |x|$$

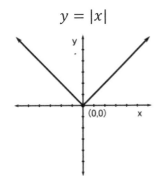

$$y = \sqrt{x}$$

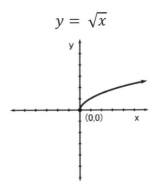

$$y = x^2$$

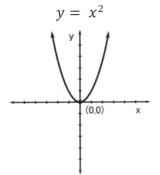

$$y = x^3$$

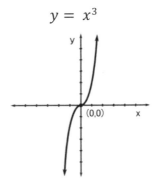

Transformations, or perhaps you've heard them called *translations*, involve sliding, reflecting, and stretching or condensing a base graph. And the rules are quite handy!

Given any base graph, consider y = (x) to be the function.

Transformations occur in the form of y = ±*(ax + b)* + c where *a* is a coefficient and *b* and *c* are constants.

★ *b* represents a shift left; if *b* is negative, the shift is to the right.

★ *c* represents a shift upward; if *c* is negative, the shift is down.

★ If |a| > 1, the base graph is horizontally condensed.

★ If |a| < 1, i.e., a fraction, the graph is stretched horizontally.

And lastly, *after* all other translations,

★ If the ± outside of the parentheses is negative, the base graph is reflected across the x-axis.

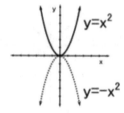

★ If a is negative, the base graph is reflected across the y-axis.

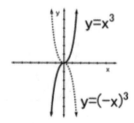

Confused? Probably. Look at these examples and refer to the list; once students can visualize what each translation means, they tend to find graph transformations to be one of the easiest things they've ever learned.

$$y = -\left|\frac{1}{2}x + 3\right| - 4$$

The base graph is y=|x|, which looks like so: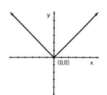

And the transformations include:

    −4 outside of function → move down 4:

    +3 inside function → move left 3:

    coefficient of ½ → apply a horizontal stretch:

    "−" outside of function → reflect across the x-axis:

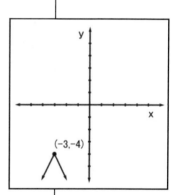

$$y = (-x - 1)^3$$

The base graph is $y = x^3$, which looks like so: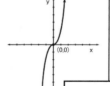

And the transformations include:

    −1 inside of function → move right 1

    − inside of function → reflect across y-axis

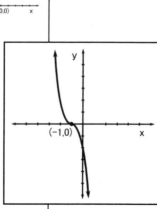

THIS DOESN'T LOOK LIKE MATH:

$x \blacksquare y = x^3 - 2y$. What is $2 \blacksquare 4$?

    a. -3
    b. 0
    c. 2
    d. 14
    e. What is $\blacksquare$?

No, this doesn't look like math at all! But you can solve it anyway. How? Just plug in 2 and 4 in place of x and y, respectively, and you'll get B.

And another!

$$\boxed{t} = (t^2 - 1) \div (t + 1). \text{ What is } \boxed{29}?$$

      f. purple
      g. 13
      h. 28
      i. 30
      j. giraffe

First of all, you can simplify the problem by factoring the numerator into (t-1) and (t+1) and canceling the (t+1)'s in the numerator and denominator. Then we'd be looking at the *slightly* less confusing

$$\boxed{t} = (t - 1). \text{ What is } \boxed{29}?$$

Once again, match the weird symbols and replace as necessary:

$$\boxed{29} = (29 - 1) = 28$$

This stuff is really just about your ability to think logically. Keep a calm head and remember that a couple wrong isn't such a big deal, especially when you're getting the same ones wrong as everyone else. Done panicking? Good! Now *try* them!

GRID-IN PROBLEMS

These guys are way cooler than you think for two reasons:

1. The College Board totally drops the ball in the directions and tells you to "grid" your answer. That's right: The College Board's proofreaders failed to catch their massive grammatical failure in which "grid," a word known only as a noun, was used as a verb. *Pfffft!*

2. You can only *gain* points in this section! With zero point deduction for incorrect responses, baby, this is a free-for-all educated guess extravaganza! Think you remember how to do some obscure math operation that you haven't seen in years? Go for it! If you're completely off base, that's A-OK—just "grid" your answer (bahahaha!) and move on to other points.

Dorks.

How to "Grid" Your Answers

There will be directions on the test. Yes, there will be lots of directions. But it's all one big time trap, 'cause here's all you'll need to know about "gridding" answers.

This is your grid.

This is where you "grid" in any necessary decimals or fractions. Only use one or the other per answer, and only use it once. →

← This is the top row where all who go by Nervous Pervous will write their answers. Since a computer will ultimately be grading your exam by reading the dots, anything written here is strictly for your waste of time—err, benefit. But really, unless you need to see the answers here to properly "grid" your answers, skip it.

These are all of the numbers. But we bet you already figured that out. Good job!

For training purposes, we're going to write and fill in answers: we don't want you wasting an hour translating the examples.

NOTES:

What you *may* "grid" are

> ★ Whole numbers (2!)
> ★ Fractions ($\frac{1}{2}$!)
> ★ Decimals (2.3!)

What you may *not* "grid" are

> ★ Variables (x, y, z)
> ★ Answers >9,999 (there are only 4 spaces!)
> ★ Commas (1020; not 1,020)
> ★ Mixed numbers (not $7\frac{1}{2}$, but $^{15}\!/_{2}$)

Oh, and did we mention that you *totally* get to express yourself in this section?

Consider a scenario in which your answer boils down to $\frac{1}{6}$. How will you choose to "grid" it?

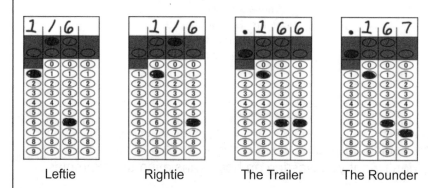

| Leftie | Rightie | The Trailer | The Rounder |

Doesn't matter! They're all A-OK! Just make sure you don't do

  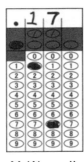 

Mr. McWrong   Mrs. McWrong   McWrong II   McWrong III

The Wrong family is wrong because they're lazy (genetically, apparently). Including another digit with their answer would make them more accurate, but being that they have terrible genetics, they fail to properly grid the answers and get it wrong. Moral of the story? Include as many digits as necessary!

Some Points on Being a Pro "Gridder":

★ "Grid" your answers as accurately (i.e., with as many digits) as possible.

★ When an answer is a fraction, stick to the fraction because it's probably less to "grid" anyway ($\frac{1}{6}$ is less work than .166, no?).

★ When an answer is a decimal, don't waste time converting it to a fraction to save on "gridding" time— the conversion will probably consume more time than it saves.

★ Don't waste lead adding a 0 before a decimal unless it is part of the number, such as 10.2.

★ Never "grid" a decimal point in the last column. Just pretend it doesn't exist, because it's a huge waste of time. "137" is just as good as "137."

So, what will you "grid" when the question boils down to ³⁄₂?

Lastly, before we bid you farewell and remind you to use the many resources at your disposal to practice, practice, practice the heck out of the math section, enjoy this complimentary list of formulas and numbers to remember:

FORMULAS AND NUMBERS TO REMEMBER

Cylinders
Surface area = $2 \times \pi \times r$
Volume = $\pi \times r^2 \times h$

Rectangles and Boxes
Area = $l \times w$
Volume = $l \times w \times h$
Surface Area = $2[(l \times w) + (l \times h) + (w \times h)]$

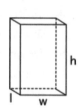

Trapezoids
Area = 1/2× height × (base1 + base2)

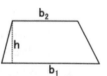

DRT: Distance = Rate × Time

TAN: Total = Average × Number

Helpful Numbers: $\pi \approx 3.14$ $e \approx 2.7$ $\sqrt{2} \approx 1.4$ $\sqrt{3} \approx 1.7$

If nothing else...Check these out!

The math section of the SAT calls on topics from arithmetic to geometry and algebra. Don't panic! We've got you covered, with 100 of the most tested concepts you'll see on the SAT.

Flip through this list to remind yourself of key topics you'll need to know. Pick five concepts a day, and you will be fully prepared in a month. Is there a concept that keeps tripping you up? Circle it, and refer to the page as you review your problems. You have probably learned this material in school already, so this review should be a nice refresher.

Definitions

1. Numbers

A **prime number** is a number that only can be divided evenly by itself and by the number 1. For example, 7 is prime, because it can only be divided by 7 and by 1. However, 8 is not prime, because it can be divided by 1, 2, 4, and 8. Since the SAT problems often are easier if you can recognize primes, look over this list of the primes from 2 to 100 every time you use this book: 2, 3, 5, 7, 11, 13, 17, 19, 23, 29, 31, 37, 41, 43, 47, 53, 59, 61, 71, 73, 79, 83, 89, 97. Note that 1 and 0 are not prime numbers.

The **whole numbers** are the counting numbers, and they include zero: 0, 1, 2, 3, and so on.

An **integer** includes all whole numbers, but also includes negative numbers. Integers do not include any decimal parts or fractions.

An **irrational number** can't be expressed by a fraction, terminating decimal, or repeating decimal. For the SAT, the most important irrational numbers are $\sqrt{2}$, $\sqrt{3}$, and π.

2. Addition and Subtraction of Signed Numbers

When adding a positive and a negative number, first find the difference between them as if they were both positive. Then look to see whether the positive or the negative number part was larger to begin with. That is the sign the answer will have. So to add 18 and –25, you first find the difference between 25 and 18. 25 – 18 = 7. Now go back to check which was the larger number part originally: It was –25. So the answer will be negative, –7.

3. Multiplication and Division of Signed Numbers

Often you will multiply or divide signed numbers on your calculator. But one wrong keystroke can make an incorrect answer. Instead of including negatives and positives in the multiplication, multiply and divide the numbers as if they all were positive. **The answer will be negative if there is an odd number of negative multipliers or divisors.** For example, to multiply –2 × –3 × –4, multiply the number parts: 2 × 3 × 4 = 24. Now count the negative signs in the original equation. There were three—an odd number—so the product is negative: (–2) × (–3) × (–4) = –24.

4. PEMDAS

Please Excuse My Dear Aunt Sally is the memory trick to remember the order of operations for simplifying a math expression. When you have multiple operations to do, follow the **PEMDAS** order: **Parentheses** first, then **Exponents**, followed by **Multiplication** and **Division** (from left to right), and finally **Addition** and **Subtraction** (from left to right).
To simplify the expression $3 \times (2 \times 5)^2 - 50 \times 4 + 200 \div 2$,
we start with the parentheses: $(2 \times 5) = 10$.
Then we do the exponent: $(10)^2 = 100$, which gives us
$3 \times 100 - 50 \times 4 + 200 \div 2$.
We do the multiplying and dividing next: $3 \times 100 = 300$,
$- 50 \times 4 = -200$, and $200 \div 2 = 100$.
At this point, the expression is: $300 - 200 + 100 = 200$

Number Operations

5. Arithmetic Sequences

A sequence that has a constant difference between the terms is an **arithmetic sequence**. The first term in the sequence is given as a_1, and each term that follows is a multiple of the constant difference. To find the nth term, use the formula $a_n = a_1 + (n-1)d$ where a_n is the nth term, d is the common difference, and n is the number of the term you want. An example of an arithmetic sequence would be 5, 8, 11, 14, 17. In this case, $a_1 = 5$, and $d = 3$.

6. Exponential Series

On the SAT, they sometimes give you a series of numbers and ask for the nth term. Here is how you solve this kind of problem. Let r be the ratio between consecutive terms, let a_1 be the first term and a_n be the nth term (the one you're looking for). Then $a_n = a_1 r^{n-1}$. Sometimes they ask for the sum of the first n terms, or S_n. The sum is $S_n = \dfrac{a_1 - a_1 r^n}{1 - r}$.

7. Union and Intersection of Sets

The **union** of two sets is the combination of items that are in either one set or the other. The union of Set A and Set B is written as $A \cup B$. If Set A = {5, 7, 8} and Set B = {2, 5} then $A \cup B$ = {2, 5, 7, 8}. The **intersection** of Set A and Set B, written as $A \cap B$, means the items that the sets have in common. In this case, $A \cap B$ = {5}.

Factoring

8. Factors

The **factors** of an integer n are the positive integers that divide evenly into n. For example, the factors of 24 are 1, 2, 3, 4, 6, 8, 12, and 24.

9. Prime Factors

Finding the prime factors of a number means breaking down all the factors until only primes are left. When you multiply all the prime factors together, you should get the original number. In prime factorization, it is OK to list a factor more than once. For example, here is how to find the prime factor of 24.
$24 = 8 \times 3 = 2 \times 2 \times 2 \times 3$.

10. Useful Squares

Knowing the values of the powers of 2 is a good way to solve problems. The value of $2^2 = 4$, and $2^3 = 8$. Can you quickly recognize that $2^4 = 16$, and $2^5 = 32$? These will come in handy for many different types of problems on the SAT.
Two more: $2^6 = 64$, and $2^7 = 128$.

11. Common Multiple

You sometimes will have to figure out the smallest common multiple of two numbers. This is also known as the least common denominator. Of course, two numbers multiplied together will give a product that both numbers divide into evenly. But we can make life easier by finding a smaller number that both of our numbers divide into evenly. For example, what is the smallest common multiple of 8 and 12? You could just multiply $8 \times 12 = 96$. To find the smallest common multiple, take multiples of the larger number until one is divisible by the smaller number. For our example, start with 12: 12 is not divisible by 8; 24 is divisible by 8, so it's the smallest common multiple.

12. Greatest Common Factor

The greatest common factor is the largest number that can divide evenly into two different numbers. A simple example is 8 and 12: The greatest common factor is 4. How do we determine this for larger numbers where the answer doesn't "jump out" at us? Break down each number using prime factorization, then multiply all the prime factors they have in common. For example, using 36 and 48: $36 = 2 \times 2 \times 3 \times 3$, and $48 = 2 \times 2 \times 2 \times 2 \times 3$. The common prime factors are two 2s and one 3. So, the greatest common factor is $2 \times 2 \times 3 = 12$.

13. Even and Odd Factors and Sums

For double-checking or just eliminating answers, figuring out whether the answer should be even or odd is a handy trick. For example, any odd number multiplied by an even number will have an even result. This is a little challenging to memorize. So, a better way is to try simple numbers such as 1 and 2 and see what happens. This is useful for predicting whether a sum, difference, or multiple should be even or odd.

14. Multiples of 2 and 4

Recognizing divisibility is a good way to turn a 3-minute problem into a 30-second problem. You know a number is divisible by 2 if the last digit is divisible by 2, or in other words, if the number is even. What about divisibility by 4? Just look at the last two digits. If the number formed by the last two digits is divisible by 4, then the entire number, no matter how many digits it has, is also divisible by 4. For example, the number 516 is even. So, it is divisible by 2. The last two digits, 16, form a number that is divisible by 4. So 516 is divisible by 4.

15. Multiples of 3 and 9

Finding out if a number is divisible by 3 or 9 is as easy as adding up the digits of the number. If the sum of the digits is divisible by 3, then the number is divisible by 3. If the sum of the digits is divisible by 9, then the number is divisible by 9. For example, the sum of the digits in 951 is 15, which is divisible by 3, but not divisible by 9; so 951 is divisible by 3, but not by 9.

16. Multiples of 5 and 10

Integers whose last digit is 5 or 0 are divisible by 5. Integers whose last digit is 0 are divisible by 10. For example, 755 is divisible by 5, but not by 10.

17. Remainder

The **remainder** is the number left over when one number does not divide into another number evenly. For example, 456 is 1 more than 455, which 5 divides into evenly; so, when 456 is divided by 5, the remainder is 1.

Fractions and Decimals

18. Reducing Fractions

To reduce a fraction, factor the top and bottom parts and cancel out all common factors.

$$\frac{40}{55} = \frac{5 \times 8}{5 \times 11} = \frac{8}{11}$$

19. Addition and Subtraction of Fractions

When adding or subtracting fractions, the first step is to find a common denominator. Next, add or subtract the numerators.

$$\frac{5}{8} - \frac{7}{12} = \frac{15}{24} - \frac{14}{24} = \frac{15 - 14}{24} = \frac{1}{24}$$

20. Multiplication of Fractions

When multiplying fractions, multiply the numerators together, and multiply the denominators together.

$$\frac{3}{7} \times \frac{5}{8} = \frac{3 \times 5}{7 \times 8} = \frac{15}{56}$$

21. Division of Fractions

When dividing fractions, invert the second fraction and then multiply.

$$\frac{2}{3} \div \frac{1}{2} = \frac{2}{3} \times \frac{2}{1} = \frac{2 \times 2}{3 \times 1} = \frac{4}{3}$$

22. Improper Fractions and Mixed Numbers

Answers on the ACT may be given as improper fractions (which give an amount larger than one, such as $\frac{4}{3}$) or as mixed numbers (such as $1\frac{1}{3}$). It is important to recognize when you have found the correct answer, but the answer choice is in another form. To convert an improper fraction to a mixed number, divide the numerator by the denominator to get a whole number with a remainder. The remainder is the new numerator for the fraction. For example, if you have

$$\frac{225}{8}$$

then to convert it to a mixed number, divide 225 by 8. The result is 28 with a remainder of 1. This gives a mixed number of

$$28\frac{1}{8}$$

To convert a mixed number to an improper fraction, multiply the whole number part by the denominator, and add that amount to the numerator. For example, to convert $5\frac{1}{3}$ to an improper fraction, first multiply 5 × 3 = 15 and add that to the 1 from the numerator. The improper fraction is then

$$\frac{16}{3}$$

23. Reciprocal

The reciprocal of a fraction is found by swapping the numerator and the denominator. The reciprocal of $\frac{2}{3}$ is $\frac{3}{2}$. The reciprocal of 7 is $\frac{1}{7}$. Multiplying a fraction by its reciprocal gives a value of 1.

24. Comparing Fractions

Sometimes it is necessary to determine which of two fractions is larger. This can be a challenge if the fractions are not ones we use every day. One solution is to express both fractions with a common denominator. For example, compare $\frac{3}{5}$ and $\frac{5}{7}$.

$$\frac{3}{5} = \frac{21}{35} \text{ and } \frac{5}{7} = \frac{25}{35}$$

So $\frac{5}{7}$ is bigger than $\frac{3}{5}$. Another way to compare is to convert both fractions to decimals. $\frac{3}{5}$ converts to 0.6, and $\frac{5}{7}$ converts to approximately 0.714.

25. Identifying Addition and Subtraction

Word problems count for one-third of all questions on the math portion of the SAT. Your job is to turn these "stories" into equations with knowns and unknowns. Words such as "increase," "sum," "exceeds," "more than," and "is greater than by" mean **addition**. Words such as "less than" indicate **subtraction**. For example, "The number of students in Homeroom 1 exceeds the number of students in Homeroom 2 by 5."

X = Homeroom 1 students $X + 5 = Y$ = Homeroom 2 students

26. Identifying Multiplication and Division

The words "product," "times," and "of" mean multiplication in word problems. The words "a ratio of" signify division. For example, "The product of two numbers is also equal to a ratio of 3 to 4." The word "product" tells us two numbers are going to be multiplied, and the word "ratio" means 3 will be divided by 4.

$$X \times Y = \frac{3}{4}$$

27. Identifying the Parts and the Whole

The SAT will give you word problems where it is your job to identify the **part** and the **whole**. Usually this will be given in a phrase such as "Half of the girls are eight years old," where the word associated with "of" is the whole; and the word associated with the verb "is" (or it could be "are") is the part. For this example, the whole is the girls ("*of* the girls") and the part is those who are eight years old ("*are* eight years old").

Percent

28. Percent Formula

You will encounter many problems involving percent on the SAT, but they all use the same formula:

$$\text{Percent} = \frac{\text{Part}}{\text{Whole}}$$

For example, "What is 5 percent of 80?"

$$0.05 = \frac{\text{Part}}{80}$$

And for another example, "15 is 10 percent of what number?"

$$0.10 = \frac{15}{\text{Whole}}$$

One last example, "6 is what percent of 50?"

$$\text{Percent} = \frac{6}{50}$$

29. Percent Increase and Percent Decrease

To increase a number by a percent, use this method. Add the percent increase to 100 percent, convert to a decimal, and multiply by the original number. For example, "Increase 30 by 25 percent." First, add 25 percent to 100 percent, to get 125 percent. Convert 125 percent to a decimal by dividing 125 by 100, $125 \div 100 = 1.25$. Now multiply 1.25 by the original number, 30, $1.25 \times 30 = 37.5$. The method is the same for a percent decrease, except that you subtract the percent change from 100 in the first step.

30. Find the Whole

In order to find the original whole, before a percent increase or decrease, use this method. Set up an equation where the variable you will find is the whole. For example, "After a 10 percent increase, the number of home runs for the team was 198 for the season. What was the number of home runs before the increase?" A 10 percent increase is the same as 1.1 times the whole. The equation to describe this situation is $1.1x = 198$.

31. Multiple Changes in Percent

When given a problem that asks you to increase and decrease "a number" by some percent or a chain of percents, use 100 as a starting point to figure out what will happen. The test writers expect you to add and subtract the percents, but this will give you the wrong answer. For example, "A number is increased by 80 percent and then decreased by 50 percent. What is the ratio of the new number to the original number?" Starting with 100 percent and adding 80 percent gives us 180 percent. Decreasing 180 percent by 50 percent gives us 90 percent. The new number is 90 percent, and the original number was 100 percent, so the ratio of new/original is 90/100.

Ratios, Proportions, and Rates

32. Setting Up a Ratio

In word problems, a ratio is often set up as "a ratio of x to y." To set up the ratio mathematically, set the number closest to the word "of" on the top, and set the number closest to the word "to" on the bottom. For example: "The ratio of 30 oranges to 40 apples." This is expressed as 30/40, which can be reduced to 3/4.

33. Part-to-Whole Ratios

Sometimes, an SAT math problem gives you a part-to-part ratio, and your job is to turn it into two part-to-whole ratios. This is possible—if the parts add up to the whole. To find a part-to-whole ratio, put one part in the top of the ratio, and put the sum of all the parts in the bottom of the ratio. For example, "The ratio of dogs to cats in the neighborhood is 2 to 3. What is the overall ratio of dogs to all pets?" Since there are 2 dogs, and the total of dogs plus cats is 2 + 3 = 5, the ratio of dogs to all pets is 2/5. In other words, 2/5 of all pets in the neighborhood are dogs.

34. Solving a Proportion

Solving proportions involves two steps: (1) write down the proportion based on the word problem; and (2) cross multiply to solve. For example, "There are 30.48 centimeters in 12 inches. How many centimeters are there in 20 inches?" The ratio is

$\frac{12}{30.48} = \frac{20}{x}$. Cross-multiplying gives us $12x = 20 \times 30.48$,

or $x = \dfrac{20 \times 30.48}{12}$.

35. Rates

Rate problems always use the formula $D = RT$ or Distance = Rate × Time. Use the units to double-check your answers. For example, "The butterfly flew across the lake at a rate of 20 feet per minute. The lake was 850 feet across. How long did it take for the butterfly to cross the lake?" Rearranged, the formula is $T = D/R$. Time = 850 feet / 20 feet per minute. The units cancel out and answer the problem in minutes for the time.

36. Average Rate

Never take two rates and take the average of them—this is an all-too-common mistake. To find an average rate, divide the total distance by the total time. For example, "What is the average speed for a trip where one leg went 60 miles at 30 miles per hour, and the second leg went 200 miles at 50 miles per hour?" The total distance is 60 miles + 200 miles = 260 miles. The total time is 2 hours + 4 hours = 6 hours. The average speed is 260 / 6 = 43.33 miles per hour.

Averages

37. Average Formula

The formula for the average is known as the TAN formula, Total = Average × Number. The total is the sum of the values, and the number is how many values there were. For example, "What is the average of the numbers 6, 17, 20, 21, and 21?" First, the total is $T = 6 + 17 + 20 + 21 + 21 = 85$. The number $N = 5$. $T = A \times N$, $85 = A \times 5$, $A = 17$.

38. Average of Evenly Spaced Numbers

To find the average of numbers that are evenly spaced, we can save time by averaging just the largest and smallest values. For example, "What is the average of all integers from 10 to 72?" From our TAN formula, Average = Total / Number $= 10 + 72 / 2 = 82/2 = 41$.

By the way, another math term for "average" is "mean"

39. Using the Average to Find the Total

Using the TAN formula, the total can be found by using the average and the number of terms. For example, "If the average of 5 numbers is 40, what is the total?" From the TAN formula, Total = Average × Number = $40 \times 5 = 200$.

40. Median

The median is the middle value of a set of numbers, when the numbers are in order. For example, "What is the median of the following five test scores: 72, 83, 92, 90, 81?" First, rearrange the numbers in increasing or decreasing order: 72, 81, 83, 90, 92. Now it is clear that the middle value is 83.

What if the number of items in the set is even? In that case, take the average of the two middle values.

41. Mode

The mode is the number in a set that occurs most frequently. For example, "What is the mode of the following set: 44, 46, 50, 44, 60, 88, 30? Since 44 occurs twice and all other numbers appear just once, the mode is 44.

Combinations and Probability

42. Combinations

To figure out how many combinations are possible, multiply the number of *m* ways for one event to happen by the number of *n* ways for the other event to happen. That gives us *m* × *n* ways for the two events to happen. For example, "John has 5 shirts and 3 pairs of pants. How many different combinations can he wear?" In this case, John has 5 × 3 = 15 different outfits.

43. Probability

Probability is a part-to-whole ratio. The top part is the number of desirable outcomes, and the bottom part is the total number of outcomes possible.

$$\text{Probability} = \frac{\text{Desirable Outcomes}}{\text{Total Possible Outcomes}}$$

For example, "There are 14 blue socks and 6 red socks in the drawer. What is the probability of picking a blue sock at random?" The desirable outcome is picking a blue sock, or 14. The total possible outcomes are 14 + 6 = 20. The probability is 14/20 = 7/10. This probability also can be expressed as 0.7 or 70 percent.

Exponents

44. Multiplying and Dividing Exponents

For exponents of the same base multiplied together, **add the exponents.**

$$x^2 \times x^5 = x^{2+5} = x^7$$

For exponents of the same base that are divided, **subtract the exponents.**

$$\frac{y^{10}}{y^3} = y^{10-3} = y^7$$

45. Exponents Raised to an Exponent

When an exponent is raised to an exponent power, multiply the exponents.

$$\left(x^3\right)^2 = x^{3\times2} = x^6$$

46. Simplifying Square Roots

Any perfect square that factors within a square root can be unsquared and removed from the square root sign.

$$\sqrt{50} = \sqrt{25\times2} = \sqrt{5\times5\times2} = \sqrt{5\times5}\times\sqrt{2} = 5\sqrt{2}$$

47. Adding and Subtracting Roots

If the value under the radical is the same, radical expressions can be added and subtracted.

$$4\sqrt{5} + 5\sqrt{5} = 9\sqrt{5}$$

However, if the value under the radical is not the same, then you can't simplify by adding and subtracting. The following expression can't be simplified:

$$6\sqrt{3} + 2\sqrt{5}$$

48. Multiplying and Dividing Roots

The square root of one value multiplied by the square root of another value may be combined as multiples under the same square root sign.

$$\sqrt{5} \times \sqrt{11} = \sqrt{5\times11} = \sqrt{55}$$

When both parts of a fraction are within a square root sign, each part may be set in its own square root sign.

$$\frac{\sqrt{6}}{\sqrt{2}} = \sqrt{\frac{6}{2}} = \sqrt{3}$$

You also can get the radical out of the bottom part of a fraction by multiplying both the top and bottom parts by the bottom radical. This is the same as multiplying a fraction by 1.

$$\frac{1}{\sqrt{2}} \times \frac{\sqrt{2}}{\sqrt{2}} = \frac{\sqrt{2}}{\sqrt{2 \times 2}} = \frac{\sqrt{2}}{2}$$

It will save you time if you memorize the value 0.7071 for the decimal value of this expression.

49. Negative Exponents and Fractional Exponents

Negative exponents indicate that the value can be thought of as the reciprocal of the positive exponent.

$$3^{-2} = \frac{1}{3^2} = \frac{1}{9}$$

Fractional exponents are the same as roots. A square root can also be written as a base raised to the 1/2 power. A cube root can also be written as a base raised to the 1/3 power.

$$\sqrt{2} = 2^{1/2}$$

An exponent in the form of $\frac{a}{b}$ means that the base is raised to the a power and also raised to the $\frac{1}{b}$ power, or in other words, to the b root.

$$4^{3/2} = 64^{1/2} = \sqrt{64} = 8$$

Absolute Value

50. Absolute Value

The absolute value of a number can be thought of as the distance from the number to zero on the number line. This distance is never negative. The absolute value of 5 is 5. Another way to put this is $|5| = 5$. The absolute value of –5 is also 5, $|-5| = 5$.

Algebraic Terms

51. Plug and Chug

Evaluating an algebraic expression can be done by plugging in the value for the variable, and chugging through the equation to find the value of the expression. For example, "What is the value of $2x^2 + x + 5$ if $x = -3$?" First, plug in the value of -3 for x.

$$2(-3)^2 + (-3) + 5 = 2(9) - 3 + 5 = 18 - 3 + 5 = 20$$

52. Adding and Subtracting Like Terms

Be careful when combining like terms. Make sure to add and subtract the coefficients of terms that are alike. For example, "What is the simplified way to show $3a + 2b - a + 5b$?" First, rewrite the expressions with the like terms grouped together.

$$3a + 2b - a + 5b = 3a - a + 2b + 5b$$
$$= 2a + 7b$$

53. Adding and Subtracting Polynomials

When adding and subtracting polynomials, there is more variety in what the variables may look like, but this is really just the same method: **group like terms, then add and subtract the coefficients**. For example, "What is a simplified view of the expression $(2x^2 - 3x + 14) - (x^2 + 7)$?" First, we rewrite the equation with the minus sign applied to the second parenthetic term.

$$(2x^2 - 3x + 14) - (x^2 + 7)$$
$$= 2x^2 - 3x + 14 - x^2 - 7$$
$$= 2x^2 - x^2 - 3x + 14 - 7$$
$$= x^2 - 3x + 7$$

54. Multiplying Monomials

To multiply monomials, multiply the coefficients together, and multiply the variables together. For example, "What is the simplified way to show $3x \times 4x$?" First multiply the coefficients (3×4). Then multiply the variables $(x \times x)$.

$$3x \times 4x = (3 \times 4)(x \times x) = 12x^2$$

55. FOIL—Multiplying Binomials

FOIL is another memory trick, this one for remembering how to multiply binomials. To multiply the binomial $(x + 2)$ by $(x + 5)$, use the FOIL method to multiply the **F**irst terms: $x \times x = x^2$. Next multiply the **O**uter terms: $x \times 5 = 5x$. Next, the **I**nner terms: $2 \times x = 2x$. Finally, multiply the **L**ast terms: $2 \times 5 = 10$. The last step is to combine like terms: $(x + 2)(x + 5) = x^2 + 5x + 2x + 10 = x^2 + 7x + 10$.

56. Multiplying Polynomials in General

FOIL is useful when multiplying binomials, but sometimes we have to multiply polynomials with more terms. Just multiply each term in the first polynomial by each term in the second polynomial, group like terms together, and simplify. For example, "What is the simplified way to show $(2x^2 + x - 3)(x + 4)$?"
$(2x^2 + x - 3)(x + 4) =$
$2x^2(x + 4) + x(x + 4) - 3(x + 4) =$
$2x^3 + 8x^2 + x^2 + 4x - 3x - 12 = 2x^3 + 9x^2 + x - 12$

Factoring Algebraic Expressions

57. Factoring Out a Common Factor

If there is a factor common to all terms, it can be factored out of a polynomial. For example, "Completely factor the following expression, $6x^3 + 12x^2 - 6x$." For this expression, each term has a common factor of $6x$ that can be factored out.
$6x^3 + 12x^2 - 6x = 6x(x^2 + 2x - 1)$.

58. Factoring the Difference of Squares

You can count on seeing a case of factoring the difference of squares in the math section.

$$a^2 - b^2 = (a + b)(a - b)$$

The important clue you will get is that both terms are squares, so be watchful of the perfect square numbers: 1, 4, 9, 16, 25, 36, 49, 72, 81, and 100, for the squares of the numbers 1 through 10. For example, "Factor $x^2 - 16$." $x^2 - 16 = (x + 4)(x - 4)$.

59. Factoring the Square of a Binomial

Learn to recognize polynomials that are the square of a binomial. With a little practice, you will be able to spot these.

$$(a + b)^2 = a^2 + 2ab + b^2$$
$$(a - b)^2 = a^2 - 2ab + b^2$$

For example, "Factor $4x^2 + 12xy + 9y^2$." The center term is positive, so we are looking for the $(a + b)^2$ type. Using the first formula, $4x^2 + 12xy + 9y^2$ factors to $(2x + 3y)^2$.

For another example, "Factor $z^2 - 10z + 25$." The negative sign in front of the second term tells us we are looking at the $(a - b)^2$ type. Using the second formula, $z^2 - 10z + 25$ factors to $(z - 5)^2$.

60. Factoring Binomials from Quadratic Expressions

With practice, you can recognize a quadratic expression that is really a multiple of binomials. Factoring out binomials is like doing the FOIL process in reverse. For example, "Factor the quadratic expression $2x^2 + 7x + 3$." What two **First** terms multiplied together could give the term $2x^2$? The first terms of the binomials will be $2x$ and x. What are the factors of the last term? The **Last** terms will be 3 and 1. Combine the first terms and last terms one way and another, until the combined **Outer** and **Inner** terms add up to $7x$, and you will see that $2x^2 + 7x + 3 = (x + 3)(2x + 1)$.

61. Simplifying Algebraic Fractions

Just like simplifying a fraction with only numbers, simplifying algebraic fractions follows the method of canceling out common factors from the numerator and the denominator. The first step will be to factor the expressions.

For example, "Simplify the following fraction."

$$\frac{x^2 - 3x - 4}{x^2 - 8x + 16}$$

First factor the numerator and the denominator.

$$\frac{x^2 - 3x - 4}{x^2 - 8x + 16} = \frac{(x + 1)(x - 4)}{(x - 4)^2}$$

Canceling the factor of $(x - 4)$ from the numerator and the denominator leaves the simplified

$$\frac{(x + 1)}{(x - 4)}$$

Solving Equations

62. Solving an Equation: One Variable

The math test may present you with an expression that includes an equals sign. To solve this type of problem, group the variable terms on one side of the equals sign, and the other terms on the other side. For example, "Find the value of x in the following equation $3x + 4 = x - 2$." First, rearrange the terms, $3x - x = -2 - 4$. Simplify both sides, $2x = -6$. Next, divide both sides by 2, $x = -3$.

63. Solving an Equation: Two Variables

When you have an equation with two different variables, the first step is to solve for one variable in terms of the other variable. This means separating the variables on either side of the equals sign. For example, "Solve the following equation for m in terms of t: $3m + 5t = t - 5m$." First, move the variables to opposite sides of the equals sign, $3m + 5m = t - 5t$, or $8m = -4t$. Divide both sides by 8: $m = -1/2t$.

64. Substituting Values into Linear Equations

Solving a pair of linear equations requires us to solve for one variable in terms of another. The next step is to substitute the value of the first variable from one equation into the second equation. This results in an equation that has gone from two variables down to one variable. For example, "Find the value of x in the expression $x = 3y + 2$, by substituting the value of $y = 4x - 1$."

$$x = 3y + 2 = 3(4x - 1) + 2 = 12x - 3 + 2$$
$$x - 12x = -3 + 2$$
$$-11x = -1$$
$$x = 1/11$$

65. Solving a Quadratic Equation

A quadratic equation should be set up in the form of $ax^2 + bx + c = 0$. By doing this, factoring the quadratic equation (if it is possible) can give us the two solutions of the quadratic equation. In this process, set each of the factors equal to zero and solve for x. For example, "Find the solutions of the quadratic equation $x^2 - 4x - 12 = 0$." Our first task is to factor the expression $x^2 - 4x - 12 = (x + 2)(x - 6)$. By setting each factored part to zero, we find the solutions, $x + 2 = 0$, and $x - 6 = 0$. The solutions are then $x = -2$ and $x = 6$.

66. Solving a System of Equations

A second way to solve a pair of linear equations is to add the two equations together in such a way that one variable is eliminated. To do this, the equations must be rearranged so that one variable matches up in both equations. For example, "Solve the following two equations, $5x + 3y = 4$ and $x + y = 6$." Multiply each side of the second equation by 5 to match the first equation. $5x + 5y = 30$.

$$\begin{aligned} 5x + 3y &= 4 \\ -(5x + 5y &= 30) \\ \hline -2y &= -26 \\ y &= 13 \end{aligned}$$

Finally, substitute the value of $y = 13$ into one of the equations to find a value of $x = -7$.

67. Solving an Inequality

Some expressions can use an inequality instead of an equals sign. To solve an inequality, just as with equations with an equals sign, isolate the variable on one side. The only difference to note is that **any time both sides are multiplied or divided by a negative number, the inequality must be reversed**. For example, "Solve the inequality $-3x + 2 \leq -7$ for x." First, isolate the variable on one side. $-3x \leq -7 - 2$, which is equivalent to $-3x \leq -9$. The final step is to divide both sides by -3. Since you have divided both sides by a negative number, remember to reverse the sign: $x \geq 3$.

68. Equations with Radical Terms

A variable in a radical can seem intimidating, but just treat it as you would any variable: isolate it, and square both sides to spring the variable out of the radical. For example, "Solve $5\sqrt{x} + 4 = 24$ for x." Isolating the variable on one side gives $5\sqrt{x} = 20$; dividing both sides by 5 gives us $\sqrt{x} = 4$. Squaring both sides solves the equation: $x = 16$.

Functions

69. Evaluating Functions

Function notation is written as $f(x)$, which is read as "function of x" or simply "f of x." To evaluate the function $f(x) = 3x + 5$ for $f(2)$, substitute x with 2 and simplify, $f(2) = 3(2) + 5 = 6 + 5 = 11$.

70. Direct Variation and Inverse Variation

In a direct variation, one term increases as another term increases. The general form of a direct variation is $y = kx$, where k is a constant that does not equal zero. For example, if a phone plan gives 50 minutes for every dollar paid, this can be expressed as $D = 50m$. If the number of minutes used were to double, then the amount of dollars will double also.

In an inverse relationship, as one term increases, the other term decreases proportionally. For example, the DRT formula, Distance = Rate × Time, shows an inverse relationship between rate and time if distance is constant. As the rate is doubled, the time is divided by two.

71. Domain and Range of a Function

The domain of a function is the allowed inputs to a function, and the range of the function is the set of all values that may be outputs of a function. When asked to give the domain for a function, it is important to look into what values will not allow it to be evaluated. For example, "What is the domain of the function $f(x) = 1/(1 - x)$?" The denominator of a fraction is not allowed to equal zero. So, a value of x that would make the denominator be zero is not in the range. $1 - x = 0$ when $x = 1$. Therefore, the domain of the function is all numbers not equal to 1.

The range of a function such as $f(x) = x^2 + 1$ is all numbers greater than or equal to 1, because x^2 cannot have a negative value.

Coordinate Geometry

72. Distance Between Two Points in the Coordinate Plane

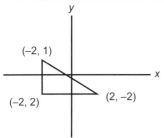

There are two ways to find the distance between two points in the coordinate plane. One way is to use the **Pythagorean Theorem**, and the other is to use the **distance formula**. The triangle can be drawn in the coordinate plane by dropping a vertical leg showing the y distance between the points, and drawing a horizontal line showing the x distance between the points. For example, "Find the distance between the points $(-2, 1)$ and $(2, -2)$." Drawing these points on the coordinate axis, as shown in the figure, shows that the vertical leg is 3 and the horizontal leg is 4. Just knowing this, we can recognize it is a 3-4-5 triangle, and the distance between the two points is 5. Even without this insight, we can use the Pythagorean Theorem to find the third leg, $3^2 + 4^2 = x^2$ to again find that $x = 5$.

The distance formula can also be used

$$d = \sqrt{(x_1 - x_2)^2 + (y_1 - y_2)^2}$$

To find the distance between points $(-2, 1)$ and $(2, -2)$,

$$d = \sqrt{(-2 - 2)^2 + (-2 - 1)^2} = \sqrt{16 + 9} = \sqrt{25} = 5$$

73. Finding the Slope by Using Two Points

The slope is equal to the rise divided by the run, or the change in y divided by the change in x. For example, "Find the slope of a line that includes the points $(1, 4)$ and $(-3, 0)$." The change in y is given by $4 - 0 = 4$. The change in x is given by $1 - (-3) = 4$. The rise divided by the run is 4/4 or 1.

74. Finding the Slope by Using the Equation of a Line

The equation describing a line is given in slope-intercept form as $y = mx + b$. The slope is m and the intercept is b. For example, "What is the slope of the line defined by the equation $2y - 6x - 10 = 0$?" First, rearrange the equation into $y = mx + b$ form.

$$2y - 6x - 10 = 0$$
$$y - 3x - 5 = 0$$
$$y = 3x + 5$$

The slope is 3.

75. Finding an Intercept by Using the Equation of a Line

The y-intercept is the place where a line crosses the y-axis. Using the slope-intercept form of a line, $y = mx + b$, the b is the y-intercept. Note that the y-intercept is the point where $x = 0$. This suggests another way to find the y-intercept is to set $x = 0$ and solve the equation for y. If you have to find the x-intercept, just set $y = 0$ and solve the equation for x.

Lines and Angles

76. Intersecting Lines

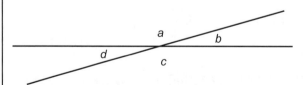

When two lines intersect, as in the figure, angles $\angle a$ and $\angle b$ are **supplementary angles**, which means that $\angle a + \angle b = 180°$. Angles $\angle a$ and $\angle c$ are **vertical angles**, which means that $\angle a = \angle c$. From these two facts, if you know one of the angles $\angle a$, $\angle b$, $\angle c$, or $\angle d$, then you can figure out the values of the other three angles. For example, "If $\angle b = 20°$, what are the values of $\angle c$ and $\angle d$?" Since $\angle b$ and $\angle d$ are vertical angles, then they are equal. So $\angle b = \angle d = 20°$. Since $\angle b$ and $\angle c$ are supplementary angles, $\angle b$ and $\angle c = 180°$, $= \angle c + 20° = 180°$, so $\angle c = 160°$.

77. Parallel Lines and Transversals

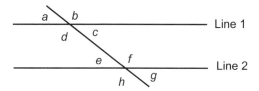

A transversal is a line that crosses two parallel lines, as in the figure. Once you know any one angle of the angles formed, you can figure out the others. The acute (less than 90°) angles are all equal, and the obtuse (greater than 90°) angles are all equal. In fact, any of the acute angles is supplementary to any of the obtuse angles. For example, "Which angles are supplementary to $\angle a$?" Angles $\angle b$, $\angle d$, $\angle f$, and $\angle h$ are supplementary to $\angle a$. Corresponding angles are angles that are in the same relative position to the transversal and the parallel lines. For example, in the figure above, $\angle a$ and $\angle e$ are corresponding angles. So are $\angle d$ and $\angle h$, $\angle b$ and $\angle f$, and $\angle c$ and $\angle g$. By definition, corresponding angles are equal.

Triangles

78. Exterior and Interior Angles of a Triangle

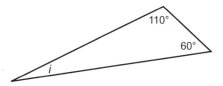

The sum of the angles of any triangle is 180°. In the figure, $\angle i$ is unknown, but the other two angles are given. So we know that $\angle i + 110° + 60° = 180°$. This means that $\angle i = 10°$.

What else adds up to 180°? Supplementary angles! If we extend one line of the triangle, it forms an exterior angle of the triangle, shown as $\angle j$ in the figure. The exterior angle of a triangle is equal to the sum of the remote interior angles. In the figure, $\angle j$ is equal to the sum of the remote angles, or $\angle j = 110° + 60° = 170°$.

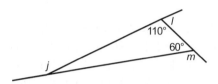

Another exterior angle tip is that the sum of all three exterior angles of any triangle is 360°. In the figure, $\angle j + \angle l + \angle m = 360°$.

79. Similar Triangles

Two triangles that have the same shape are similar triangles. For similar triangles, the corresponding angles are equal. Also, the corresponding sides are proportional to each other.

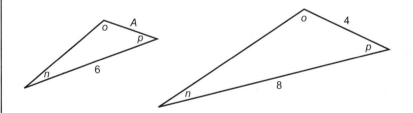

The triangles in the figure are similar because their angles measure the same. The sides are proportional. So to figure out the length of side A, we set up the proportion

$$\frac{A}{4} = \frac{6}{8}$$

$$A = 3.$$

80. Area of a Triangle

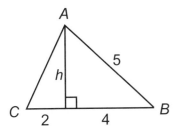

The formula for the area of a triangle is $A = 1/2bh$. That is, the area = 1/2 (base)(height). The height of a triangle is the length from the base to the opposite vertex. For example, "What is the area of triangle ABC?" In the figure, the base of triangle ABC is side CB, or 6. Since triangle ABC is not a right triangle, we need to draw a perpendicular line from side CB to point A. From the figure, the height of side h is 3. The area of the triangle is

$$A = \frac{1}{2}bh = \frac{1}{2} \times 6 \times 3 = 9$$

81. Triangle Properties

The sum of two sides must be greater than the length of the third side. Also, the difference of two sides must be less than the third side. If you are figuring out the third side of a triangle, you can use these checks to see if your answer is reasonable. For example, if two sides of a triangle are 8 and 11, the third side must be greater than 11 − 8, and less than 11 + 8.

82. Isosceles and Equilateral Triangles

An isosceles triangle is one with two equal sides. The angles opposite these sides are also equal. These angles are called the base angles.

Equilateral triangles have three equal sides and three equal angles. In fact, the three angles are all 60° angles.

Right Triangles

83. Pythagorean Theorem

Right triangles are triangles that have a right angle, or a 90°
angle. The Pythagorean Theorem states that, for all right
triangles, the length of the sides is given as $A^2 + B^2 = C^2$,
where A and B are the two legs, and C is the hypotenuse. For
example, "Find the length of the hypotenuse if the legs are
$A = 5$ and $B = 12$." From the Pythagorean Theorem,
$A^2 + B^2 = C^2$, so $5^2 + 12^2 = 25 + 144 = 169$. This means that
$C^2 = 169$. Taking the square root of both sides gives us $C = 13$.

84. The 3-4-5 Triangle

Any right triangle with two legs that are 3 and 4 will have
a hypotenuse of 5. If a right triangle has a leg of 4 and a
hypotenuse of 5, then the other leg is 3. The 3-4-5 triangle can
also show up on the SAT as any multiple of those sides, such as
6-8-10 (sides multiplied by two), or 9-12-15 (sides multiplied by
three).

85. Turning Equilateral Triangles into Two Right Triangles

Since equilateral triangles have three 60° angles, they can be
turned into two 30-60-90 triangles by drawing a perpendicular
line from one side to the opposite vertex.

86. The 30-60-90 Triangle

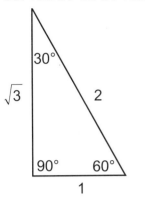

If you have a triangle with angles of 30°, 60°, and 90°, there are some shorthand ways to remember the leg lengths. The short leg is half of the hypotenuse. The hypotenuse is the short leg multiplied by 2. From the figure, you can also think of a 30-60-90 triangle as a $1 : \sqrt{3} : 2$ triangle. For example, if you have a right triangle where one base is half the hypotenuse, you know that it is a 30-60-90 triangle and that the second leg is $\sqrt{3}$ times the first leg.

87. The 45-45-90 Triangle

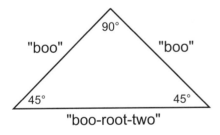

The isosceles right triangle, or the 45-45-90 triangle, is one to remember. If you know one of the leg lengths, then of course you know both leg lengths (because all isosceles triangles, even right ones, have equal leg lengths). The hypotenuse of this triangle equals the leg length multiplied by $\sqrt{2}$. The rounded off decimal of $\sqrt{2}$ is 1.414, for a quick calculation. The easy way to remember this is the saying, "boo, boo, boo-root-two," which means that if the leg length is "boo" then multiply the "boo" by "root two" ($\sqrt{2}$) to find the hypotenuse.

Other Polygons

88. Rectangle Properties

A rectangle is a four-sided figure with right angles. The lengths of the diagonals are equal. The long sides are equal and the short sides are equal. The perimeter of a rectangle is equal to the sum of the four sides, or 2(length) + 2(width).

In the figure, *ABCD* is shown to have three right angles. Therefore, the fourth angle, at point *C*, is also a right angle, and *ABCD* is a rectangle.

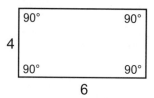

The area of a rectangle is equal to the length times the width.

From the figure,

$$A = 4 \times 6 = 24.$$

89. Parallelogram Properties

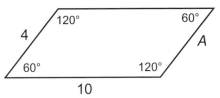

A parallelogram is a four-sided figure with two pairs of parallel sides. The opposite sides have equal length, and the angles opposite each other are equal. For example, "The figure shows a parallelogram. What is the length of side A?" Since the side opposite side A has length 4, therefore $A = 4$.

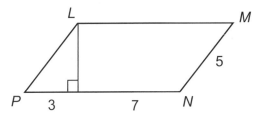

The area of a parallelogram is equal to the base times the height. For example, "What is the area of parallelogram $LMNP$?" First of all, the height of a parallelogram is not the same as the side of the parallelogram. The side $MN = 5$, and therefore the side $LP = 5$ also. Now we are ready to figure out the height, because we have two legs of a right triangle formed by a line from point L perpendicular to the base. Since we know one leg of the triangle is 3, and the hypotenuse is 5, then this is a 3-4-5 triangle. The height is 4, and the base is 7 + 3 = 10, so the area = base × height = 10 × 4 = 40.

90. Square Properties

A square is a rectangle that has four equal sides. The perimeter of a square is equal to four times the length of one side. The perimeter of square $RSTU = 4 \times 5 = 20$. The area of a square is the length of one side squared. The area of square $RSTU = 5^2 = 25$.

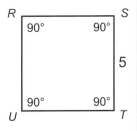

NOTES:

91. Polygon Properties

Triangles (three sides), squares (four sides), and pentagons (five sides) are all examples of polygons. The sum of the interior angles of every polygon conform to the formula:

$$\text{Sum of interior angles} = (n - 2) \times 180°$$

where n is the number of sides. Triangles, having three sides, work out to

$$(3 - 2) \times 180° = (1) \times 180° = 180°$$

Pentagons, having five sides, work out to

$$(5 - 2) \times 180° = (3) \times 180° = 540°$$

Circles

92. Circumference of a Circle

The circumference of a circle is given by the formula

$$\text{Circumference} = 2\pi r$$

For example, "What is the circumference of the circle in the figure?" Since the radius is 4,

$$\text{Circumference} = 2\pi(4) = 8\pi$$

93. Length of an Arc

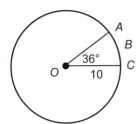

An arc is a portion of the circumference of a circle. The formula for the length of an arc uses n as the angle of the arc in degrees

$$\text{Length of an Arc} = \frac{n°}{360°} 2\pi r$$

For example, "What is the length of arc ABC?" The angle of the arc $n = 36°$, so

$$\text{Length of the Arc} = \frac{36°}{360°} 2\pi(10) = \frac{1}{10} 2\pi(10) = 2\pi$$

94. Area of a Circle

The area of a circle is given by the formula

$$A = \pi r^2$$

For example, "What is the area of the circle in the figure?" Since the radius of the circle is 7, then the area is

$$A = \pi(7^2) = 49\pi$$

95. Squares and Circles

The SAT testers like to have you figure out what a radius or a diameter is before you are able to determine the area or perimeter they are asking you about in the problem. One common theme is to combine a circle and a square in a diagram.

For example, "What is the diameter of the circle in the figure?" Since the side of the square = 5, and all sides of a square are equal, then the radius = 5. The formula for the diameter is $D = 2r = 2(5) = 10$.

For another example, "What is the radius of the circle in the figure?" The square in this figure is on the outside of the circle. The side with length 5 is parallel to a diameter of the circle. Therefore, the diameter is $D = 5 = 2r$. The radius, which is what the question asked for, is $r = 5/2$.

And yet another example, "What is the diameter of the circle in the figure?" This time, the square is drawn inside the circle, and there is no diameter or radius of the circle to refer to. However, if we draw a diagonal of the square, it is also the base of a 45-45-90 triangle. Both legs of that triangle have length = 5, and therefore the hypotenuse is $5\sqrt{2}$. Therefore, $D = 5\sqrt{2}$.

96. Tangency

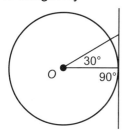

A line tangent to a circle is perpendicular from the radius of the line at that point. In other words, the radius and the tangent form a 90° angle. For example, "In the figure, the radius is 5, and a line tangent to the circle extends to meet another line that extends from the center of the circle, and forms a 30° angle with the original radius. What is the angle formed by the new line and the tangent?" Since the tangent is at a 90° angle from the radius, and the angle between the two lines extending from the center of the circle is 30°, this must be a 30-60-90 triangle. The unknown angle equals 60°.

Solids

97. Surface Area of a Rectangular Solid

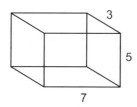

A rectangular solid has six faces, but each face is the same as its opposite face. For a rectangular solid with length $l = 7$, height $h = 5$, and width $w = 3$, the surface area is given as

$$\text{Surface Area} = 2lw + 2wh + 2lh$$

The surface area of the rectangular solid in the figure
$= 2(7)(3) + 2(3)(5) + 2(7)(5) = 42 + 30 + 70 = 142$.

98. Volume of a Rectangular Solid

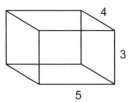

The volume of a rectangular solid is the length times the width times the height.

Volume of a Rectangular solid = *lwh*

For example, "What is the volume of the rectangular solid in the figure above?"

The volume = *lwh* = (5)(4)(3) = 60.

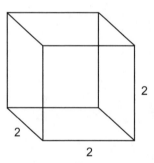

A special case is the volume of a cube, for which the formula is

Volume of a Cube = (side)^3

For example, "What is the volume of the cube in the figure?"

Volume = (side)^3 = (2)^3 = 8.

99. Volume of a Cylinder

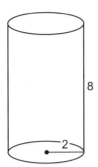

You can think of the volume of a cylinder as the area of the circle at the base times the height of the cylinder. The formula is

Volume of a Cylinder = $\pi r^2 h$

For example, "What is the volume of the cylinder in the figure?" The radius of the circle at the base is 2, and the height of the cylinder is 8.

$V = \pi(2^2)(8) = 32\pi$

NOTES:

Symmetry

100. Flips and Rotations

The SAT will test you on whether a figure is symmetrical about an axis. In other words, if you held a mirror at the axis, would the reflection match the missing half of the original figure? The choices may rotate a correct answer, so you have to rotate it in your mind before asking yourself if it is symmetrical.

For example "What is the mirror image of the figure? The image may be rotated." You will have to look at several choices and match the correct one. Can you tell that the correct answer image was flipped and rotated? Practice flipping and rotating the image in your mind to see if it fits the original image.

CHAPTER 5

Writing

Writing

After reviewing the SAT in March of 1994, The College Board realized they were ignoring a potent source of torture. A bit of monkeying later, the SAT II Writing Test was brought into the world, and after generous hyping, it became a standard necessity for college admission. Students everywhere wept.

After students had thoroughly cried themselves into shriveled-up raisins, the University of California reckoned that they could produce even *more* SAT-induced raisins just by whining that the writing test wasn't "sufficient." *Correcting poor writing isn't enough*, they said. *Make those raisins write*, they demanded. *Oh, and make them do it after bearing through the other two sections,* they plotted, *just so their spirits are nice and broken.*

Pleased with their new partner in crime's request, The College Board tacked on an essay and told parents, "We just want to make sure your kids can communicate their fabulous thoughts!" Impressed with the College Board's interest in little Billy's and little Sally's radical ideas, parents everywhere held the SAT in high regard and forced it *lovingly* upon their children to an even greater extent.

And here we are today. Since there's no point in fighting the inevitable, let's just grin and bear the writing section—and by bear, we mean maul it like a cranky mama grizzly mauls a badger with the gall to meander too close to her cubs.

For 60 minutes, you'll be mauling on a scale of 200 to 800 in two separate sections: 25 minutes in which you'll compose an original essay, and 35 minutes in which you'll answer 49 multiple choice questions. Your multiple choice questions break down into 18 sentence error identification questions, 25 sentence improvement questions, and 6 paragraph improvement questions. But fret your little head not, for TPS has developed a state of the art navigation system for each question type. Presented in ascending order of difficulty:

USAGE QUESTIONS

These questions require you to identify sentence errors and are presented as so:

> The <u>stapler</u> viciously <u>attacked</u> the pages of her
>   (A)   (B)
>
> crummy thesis paper and <u>permanently</u> bound <u>it</u>
>   (C)   (D)
>
> together. <u>No Error</u>.
>   (E)

Now, treating the portions of the sentence that aren't underlined as an unchangeable skeleton, try to determine which underlined portion, if any, contains a usage error.

    1.) Read the entire sentence slowly.
    2.) If you see the error, mark it and move on.
    3.) If you don't notice an error, re-read the sentence, keeping in mind the common writing errors (discussed later).
    4.) If you still don't see an error, mark "E" and move on.
    5.) If you have any extra time at the end, return to all questions marked "E" and re-read them in case you missed the error the first time through.

The answer to our sample is (D). Object switches from plural (pages) to singular (it).

SENTENCE CORRECTION QUESTIONS

These questions require you to ponder how, if possible, sentences could be improved and are presented as so:

> Unaware of the irresponsibly discarded banana peel lying on the ground, <u>it were the case that Joe slipped</u> in a comical fashion and, rather sadly, broke his arm.

> (A) it were the case that Joe slipped
> (B) it was the case that Joe slipped
> (C) the case were that Joe slipped
> (D) the case was that Joe slipped
> (E) Joe slipped

Once again, proceed under the assumption that only underlined portions may be changed: anything not underlined is set in stone and mentally revising any of it will only confuse you. Now,

1.) Read the *entire* sentence as-is. Avoid the temptation to only read the underlined bit as it might be grammatically correct in an isolated universe, but totally nonsensical in context.
2.) Answer A will always be the equivalent of "No Change"; it is the original underlined portion, verbatim. Since you've already read it once, *don't bother re-reading it.*
3.) Even if you think the original was groovy, proceed to read options B through E because one of them might be even *better*. After all, you're looking for the *best* answer, not the only grammatically correct answer.
4.) In the event of finding two grammatically correct answers and being unable to determine which is better, go with the shorter answer. Why? Brevity is the mark of quality writing.

The answer to our sample is (E). Even though (B) is also grammatically correct, (E) gets the point across in fewer words.

REVISION IN CONTEXT QUESTIONS

These questions are the love child of Usage and Sentence Correction Questions. You'll need to read through a passage meant to mimic the rough draft of an essay and correct a few of the indicated mistakes. Your goal in reading the essay—while turning a blind eye to the grammatical abuse occurring on the pages before you—is to *try* to get a general idea of what the essay is attempting (miserably) to convey. Since the questions will indicate the location of each error, don't waste your time marking up the booklet during your first read-through. Here is an example essay:

1. America is facing an epidemic. 2. Children cannot any longer read analog clocks. 3. They rely now mainly on digital watches and cellphones. 4. Sometimes they also use television shows to gauge the hour. 5. This trend is disturbing.

6. Some critics have made the suggestion that this issue is an indicator of other problems. 7. Perhaps it means the educational system is failing. 8. Maybe it is a sign that analog clocks are going out of style faster than a sundial at sunset. 9. Or, maybe, the analog clock needs an update, such as utilizing two different colored lasers instead of long and short arms which, let's face it, are way boring. 10. Whatever the case, critics agree that something must be done.

11. Test Prep Seminars agrees that we have a problem, but for a different reason. 12. TPS is concerned for the subtle communication of ideas in the cafeteria, such as "Hottie at 3 o'clock." 13. How will Mary tell Jessica that she digs the guy eating six bowls of pudding yonder, to her right? 14. Will our youth be forced to wear and learn to read compasses? 15. If we want to maintain the tradition of discreetly communicating who is hot and who is not, we must save the knowledge of the analog clock.

The questions that follow include combining sentences, revising sentences, and questions similar to the critical reading questions seen earlier.

1. Which is the best way to combine sentences 2, 3, and 4?

   (A) Children rely mainly on digital watches because they cannot read analog clocks, and sometimes they even use TV shows to gauge the hour.
   (B) Sometimes children use TV shows to gauge the hour or read digital watches because they can't read analog clocks.
   (C) Unable to read analog clocks, children rely on digital watches and TV shows to tell the time.
   (D) TV shows and digital watches are replacing analog clocks.
   (E) TV shows and digital watches, not analog clocks, are used by children to tell time because they can't read analog clocks.

Answer: (C). (C) is the most to-the-point version to fully encompass all three sentences.

2. Which of the following is the best revision of the underlined portion of sentence 13 below?

   How will Mary tell Jessica that she digs the guy eating six bowls of pudding <u>yonder, to her right</u>?

   (A) to the right-hand yonder
   (B) over Mary's right, but Jessica's left, shoulder
   (C) sitting over to Mary's right
   (D) yonder in the right-hand direction
   (E) to her right

Answer: (E). Even though (C) includes to *whose* right, the sentence structure already indicates the subject.

Note: Unlike sentence correction questions from earlier, answer (A) isn't equivalent to "No Change." That rule only applies to single sentence corrections outside of a passage.

3. Considering the content of the entire passage, what function does the third paragraph serve?

    (A) to neatly summarize the passage
    (B) to show the horrific implications of the issue
    (C) to expand on the second paragraph
    (D) to argue that analog clocks are useless (Get over it.)
    (E) to suggest that analog clocks should be placed in museums on top of large towers

    Answer: (B). The third paragraph doesn't do anything other than (B). We hope you figured this one out.

Looks pretty easy, doesn't it? Or at least manageable! As long as you know how to read, which you probably do... you know... if you're reading this... you should be able to avoid an awful crash and burn. And if you're a good reader, prepare yourself for success!

The Vocabulary of Vocabulary

Before we get on with all of the rules you'll need to know for this section, let's go over some basic vocabulary:

Noun – a person, place, thing, concept, quality, or act

> The *girl* picked up a jump *rope* from the corner *store*; she anticipated great *joy* to be found in the *carelessness* of *skipping*.

Pronoun – a stand-in for a noun {him, her, he, she, we, me, you, they, us, etc.}

> Even though *he* hadn't studied, Jake was horrified to find that *he* hadn't procured a perfect SAT score.

Adjective – a modifier of a noun or pronoun that gives a
   description of the (pro)noun

   The *rotund* man looks like an *over-stuffed* teddy bear.

Verb – an action

   Your nervous laugh *tells* me that I'll *be* highly
   disappointed when I *bite* into these cupcakes.

Adverb – a word that describes a verb, adjective, or
   another verb

   My pencil *rudely* broke as I *very carefully* crafted my
   argument on how *rather swiftly* the permanent marker
   became an important form of expression.

Subject – the performer (a noun) of the action

   Freddy freaked when he realized that his shampoo had
   been spiked with green hair dye.

Object – the recipient (a noun) of a subject's action

   The green-haired Freddy hunted down the *culprit*.

Preposition – a word or phrase that is used to link (pro)nouns
   and phrases to the object {at, in, to, up, under, over, after, of}

   He then got revenge by breaking a carton of eggs *over*
   the jokester's head.

Speaking of prepositions, English (the Standard American
version, at least) has a *ton* of prepositional idioms (idioms:
groups of words that are considered the standard expression
for no logical reason). These guys exist only because they
have been established over time. We've listed the most
common prepositional phrases, but since there are so many,
and because different regions adhere to certain ones and break

the rules for others, we recommend that *you* remake the list with *only* the ones that you don't already know. Prepositional idioms will be tested on the SAT, so from your condensed list, study away!

according to
accountable for [action]
accountable to [person]
adapt to [situation]
adhere to
anxious about
apologize for [thing]
apologize to [person]
approve of [thing]
ashamed of
aware of *(not that)*
composed of
concerned with
congratulate on
conscious of
consist of
consistent with
corresponding to [thing]
correspond with [person]
engaged to [person]
engaged in [activity]
equal to *(not with)*
except for
full of *(not with)*
glance at [thing]
glance through [thing]
grateful for [thing]
grateful to [person]
in accordance with
in the habit of
incapable of
inconsistent with

NOTES:

independent of
inferior to
insist (up)on
interest in
in accordance with
in contrast to *(not with)*
in comparison with *(not to)*
in the habit of
is sufficient for
knowledge of
next to
occupied by [thing]
occupied with [action]
opposite of *(not to)*
part with [thing]
preoccupation with
prior to
proceed to [action]
proceed with [thing]
regard to
related to
rely (up)on
satisfied with
similar to
surrounded by [people]
surrounded with [things]
wait at [place]
wait for [thing]
with regard to
with respect to

Seriously, you should remake this list. Do you really think it'll help if you're looking for the couple that you don't know among the many that you already do?

Now, on to the…

Rules of the Writing Test!

1. Subject-Verb Agreement

In short, singular subjects require singular verbs, and plural subjects require plural verbs.

For starters, you need to know a few pronouns that are singular subjects: **anyone, anybody, somebody, everybody, nobody, no one**[24]**, someone, everyone, one, neither, either, each,** and **every**. This list is important for this very reason:

> **Everybody** who completed the exam without mid-test mental breakdown *is* welcome to my post-SAT party on the beach!

Indeed, if you want some company in the sand, you better not confuse *everybody* as a plural subject!

Now, on to the major tricks!

---

24 Not *noone,* because for the last time, *noone* isn't a word.

⇨ The SAT *always* contains at least a couple instances of this mistake:

> Even though we can agree that the Internet is an amazing resource, there is still many parents who aren't comfortable allowing their children to get familiar with this helpful technology.

What they're hoping you'll miss is the subject-verb disagreement. The subject isn't *there*, but *parents*. Since *parents* is plural, our verb (*is*) should be *are*.

> Even though we can agree that the internet is an amazing resource, there *are* still many parents who aren't comfortable allowing their children to get familiar with this helpful technology.

The same goes for this one:

> Just beyond the mall's food court lays the giant laser tag battlefields.

Trick? While mall court is singular, it isn't the subject! The subject of our sentence is the plural *battlefields*, so *lays* should be *lay*.

Speaking of lay, let's have a quick lesson in lie versus lay! *Lie* means to *recline*, as in, "Feel free to lie down and take a nap." *Lay* means *to put or place*, as in, "You can lay your jacket on the banister."

Present Tense	**Lie**	**Lay***
Past Tense	**Lay**	**Laid**
Past Tense	**Lain**	**Laid**

*Remember, the present tense *lay* requires an object, as in the jacket in our second example.

⇨ Another way to hide subject-verb disagreement is by throwing a bunch of stuff between them:

A couple's argument, especially over one of many serious issues, are the most uncomfortable things to experience.

The problem here is that our subject is *argument*, but our verb is *are,* when it should read *is.* Throwing in the extra information makes you forget the singularity of the subject focusing on the *subjects.* Similarly,

The package of mismatched socks are a top seller among the indifferent.

has a singular subject, *package*, and a plural verb, *are.* The correct verb would be *is.*

The package of mismatched socks is a top seller among the indifferent.

⇨ Lastly, you're likely to see sentence construction which *suggests* a plural subject even though it's singular.

Take, for example, the very incorrect

White chocolate mocha, in addition to cappuccino, are delicious treats that should be savored sparingly.

Since the singular subject phrase "_____ in addition to _____" is used, we know that our verb should *not* be *are*, but *is,* as in,

White chocolate mocha, in addition to cappuccino, is a delicious treat that should be savored sparingly.

You'll want to memorize the following *singular subject* phrases, phrases that *contain* two singular nouns that function as a single subject by becoming a group:

- ✔ either _____ or _____
- ✔ neither _____ nor _____
- ✔ _____ in addition to _____
- ✔ _____ along with _____
- ✔ _____ as well as _____

What do we mean by singular nouns? Well, plural nouns, such as in *either hamburgers or hotdogs*, your choices are plural and this is no longer a singular subject phrase. On the other hand, if you *do* have singular nouns, as in *either a hamburger or hotdog*, you're in singular subject phrase territory.

↬ **Pro tip:** Check the agreement of a sentence's subject and verb by simply <u>underlining</u> each and comparing the number value.

    <u>Each</u> of the chickens <u>clucks</u> incessantly when poked.

"Each clucks" sounds correct, so our subject and verb agree.

    The distraught <u>look</u> on the students' faces <u>are</u> inspiration for The College Board.

If you think the plural *students'* was the subject, then you've fallen for the trap! The subject is truly the singular *look*, so we'd check "look are." Since this sounds off, we know that our subject and verb are in disagreement and our verb should be *is*.

2. Subject-Pronoun Agreement

Once again we're talking about number values, but this time for the subject and the pronoun. The most common error occurs when "their" is used as a pronoun for a singular subject, as in the case of:

> Whoever left their undies on the bathroom floor should pick them up before we put them on display!

Since *whoever* is singular, *their* is an inappropriate pronoun (almost as inappropriate as turning someone's underoos into a flag). The sentence could be corrected by replacing *their* with *his* or *her*.

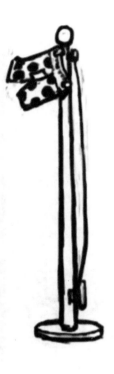

Here is another fine example, this time broken down by the way of our **pro tip**:

<u>Each</u> of the old ladies was startled to find that <u>their</u> chair had been rigged with a whoopee cushion.

Subject: Each, singular.

Pronoun: Their, plural.

Correction: to find that *her* chair

3. Pronoun: Subjects versus Objects

Students rarely *use* the wrong one because they know what sounds right, but when they *hear* or *read* the wrong one—for whatever unidentifiable reason—just seem to *completely* miss the error! Strange, but maybe it has something to do with simply not reading carefully enough. Keeping in mind the role of subjects (actors) and objects (acted upon), remember these lists:

> subjects: I, he, she, they, we, who
> objects: me, him, her, them, us, whom

The most complex trick the College Board could use is making the subject or object consist of more than one person. All you need to do is simplify the sentence by removing the second noun:

> ~~Mal and me~~ slipped on the spilled detergent.

Me slipped? Sounds wrong, and rightly so. The actor in this instance is identified as the object *me* instead of the subject. The corrected sentence would read, "Mal and I .... "

> Us ~~and the teachers~~ were amazed by Magic Matt's disappearing rabbit.

Us were amazed? Once again, we're using an object where we're supposed to be using a subject, so the correction would be "We and the teachers ... ."

Sentences are *generally*—but not *always*!—written in the order of subject-object, so as long as you can remember which pronouns are subjects (actors) and which are objects (acted upon), you should be able to identify problematic pronouns.

4. Pronoun Consistency

Staying consistent in your pronoun choice is extremely important. It is the difference between an obvious first draft and something that wouldn't make your teacher rage until his head simply popped off. Watching your pronouns is as easy as underlining them and making sure pronouns that refer to the same thing are the same.

So if you like your teacher's head affixed to his or her body, do not write:

> It's extremely important that when **one** is looking for a first car, **you** bring along someone with experience with vehicles or **you** might get stuck with a lemon.

Instead, be consistent with your pronouns and write:

> It's extremely important that when **you** are looking for a first car, **you** bring along someone with experience with vehicles or **you** might get stuck with a lemon.

A pronoun inconsistency is a small, small error, but it could ruin a reader's trust in your voice as an authority. Next thing you know, everyone is out buying lemons and it's entirely your fault! You don't want to be responsible for all of your friends' cars exploding for no reason, do you?

5. Ambiguous Pronoun

> Julie and Meg have a pronoun ambiguity problem—*especially* her!

Wait, *her*? Who is her? Confusion! And hence we understand the dangers of ambiguous pronouns.

Lesson: Don't go crazy with pronouns. It's better to repeat a noun than to confuse your reader with an ambiguous pronoun.

> Julie and Meg have a pronoun ambiguity problem—*especially* Meg (which is why Julie was kind enough to correct her pal without judging her).

6. Tense Consistency

Even though writers have the freedom to fly through time with a simple phrase, they must maintain tense consistency. While they may discuss the present and the past in the same sentence, their *voice* must stay in one or the other. So when you see:

> After the time traveler moved from 17th Century England to 21st Century America, the people of America will judge his bow tie as "not cool."

you need to clean up a bit of tense mess. Since we begin with the past tense (traveled), we need to end in past tense (~~will~~ judged). So it should say:

> After the time traveler moved from 17th Century England to 21st Century America, the people of America **judged** his bow tie as "not cool."

---

7. Adjectives versus Adverbs

A common error that students make is confusing adjectives and adverbs. Adjectives describe nouns (nouns, such as a *beautiful* pickle) and adverbs describe verbs and tend to end with -ly (such as to *loudly* sneeze)—and they are in no way interchangeable.

Not comfortable discerning adjective from adverb? Figure it out by seeing which of the following sentences works best:

> Adjective: This _____ test smells.
> Adverb: This test _____ smells.

Here are some sample texts:

Please put down that box careful.

What is being described? The verb *put*.

How is it being described? *Careful*.

Is careful an adverb or adjective? "This careful test smells" makes sense, so it's an adjective.

Since we're trying to describe a verb, it should be the *adverb* carefully. So the correct sentence would be: Please put down that box carefully.

Seriously, if you break my limited edition *Star Fighters* mugs because you're too slowly to understand the word "fragile," I'll cry for a week.

What is being described? The pronoun *you*.

How is it being described? *Slowly*.

Once again we have adverb-adjective confusion. To correctly express the seriousness of this situation, slowly should be changed to the adjective *slow*. So the correct sentence would be:

Seriously, if you break my limited edition *Star Fighters* mugs, it must because you're too slow to understand the word "fragile", I'll cry for a week.

8. Parallelism

No... it doesn't mean writing in perfectly straight lines so that your words don't overlap.... Parallel structure simply means that related ideas are presented in a similar fashion. For example, this list is parallel:

> to slide, to skip, to slip

Why? All items are infinitives ("to" verbs).

This list, however, is *not* parallel:

> biked, ran, swum

Even though all of these items are part of a triathlon, they aren't parallel because there are two past tense verbs followed by one past participle. To remedy this list, *swum* would become *swam*.

9. Run-Ons and Fragments

We're quite positive that you're familiar with run-on sentences because everyone, and we mean *everyone*, has been handed back an essay plagued with red ink declaring "run-on" over and over again, then you realize in horror that some of your sentences are, like, *ten* lines long but you somehow missed it when you were proofreading because your thoughts were otherwise grammatically correct and, let's face it, this was the best idea you've ever enunciated. Phew!

And then fragments. Almost-sentences that are missing just. They're almost.

Run-ons and fragments are a natural occurrence when we write: they're a testament to the writer's passion or distraction and often we just can't help but slip them into our first draft. When they're present in final drafts, however, they're a testament to sloppy editing.

Run-on sentences are usually caused by the nasty comma splice. Comma splices create a Frankenstein out of two complete sentences by merging them together without proper use of a semicolon or coordinating conjunction. Take, for example,

> Power in the United States has very low voltage compared to the rest of the world, it is primitive compared to more recently industrialized countries, which have significantly better power supplies that run cleaner and can deliver more voltage.

We have two complete sentences:

> Power in the United States has very low voltage compared to the rest of the world.

&

> It is primitive compared to more recently industrialized countries, which have significantly better power supplies that run cleaner and can deliver more voltage.

Splicing them together with a comma creates a run-on. How can we fix a run-on? Let's use a tasty example:

> I like cheese pizza it is great.

A. Use a period. Just let the two complete sentences be two separate sentences.

> I like cheese pizza. It is great!

B. Use a semicolon. As long as the two complete sentences are closely related and, together, express one idea, a semicolon can be used to join them.

> I like cheese pizza; it is great!

C. Use a coordinating conjunction after the comma. Coordinating conjunctions can be remembered by the mnemonic **FANBOYS**: for, and, nor, but, or, yet, so.

> I like cheese pizza, for it is great!

The best way to spot a fragment is to remember what constitutes a complete sentence: a subject performing an action in such a way that a complete idea is expressed. What do we mean by a complete idea? Compare the following two examples.

The dog jumped.   &   The dog jumped over.

The first sentence is complete because it has a subject (dog) and an action (jumped), but once we add in a preposition (over) to the second sentence, our thought becomes incomplete: over *what* is the dog jumping? To create a complete idea, we would have to add an object, such as "The dog jumped over *the moon*."

10. Spot the Typo Questions

Also known as "Are you kidding me?!?!" questions, these have nothing to do with your knowledge of the English language and everything to do with your ability to spot a typo.

No <u>matter</u> how hard <u>they</u> tried, the Punk Rock Polka
     (A)   (B)
<u>band</u> just couldn't <u>seam</u> to book a single show.
 (C)   (D)
<u>No Error</u>.
   (E)

If you noticed it right away, congratulations! If not, the answer is D. That's right. If you didn't spot *seam* in lieu of *seem*, you would've lost ¼ a point. Lame!

Advice? We have none. It's bogus, but the College Board does that. Deal with it.

11. Dangling and Misplaced Modifiers

A modifier is a word or phrase that provides extra detail for a noun or verb, such as "having been thrown into the air" in the example below. Since modifiers alter the nearest noun or verb, they should be placed as closely as possible to the intended recipient of the modification. If they're not, you end up with funky sentences like:

> Having been thrown in the air, the dog caught the stick,

So, tell us, what was thrown? As written, some poor dog is being flung into the air. To remedy this modifier misplacement, we need to move the modifier and modified closer together:

> The dog caught the stick that had been thrown into the air.

As with all sentences in the format of:

> Blah-*ing*, blah blah blah.

the intended recipient of the modification should come immediately after the comma. These will pop up in the sentence correction portion of the exam, so be conscious of modifier usage.

Here are a couple other misplaced modifiers mixed in with correctly used modifiers. Can you identify the errors?

1. Indifferent to the children's whining, the babysitter casually flipped through the television channels.

2. We kept an eye out for signs of paranormal activity as we walked across the desert in green jumpsuits.

3. Not understanding misplaced modifiers, the errors in this list could go unnoticed by students.

4. Careful to keep his fingerprints off the paperwork, Jack swapped out his bubble sheet for that of the nerd sitting next to him.

5. Fanciful of Picasso's artwork, Cubism inspired Aster's senior project, "The Renaissance, Cubed" in which she remade some of the greatest artworks from the 16th Century.

Reread #2 and ask yourself, who or what is in a green jump suit? As written, it's the desert! We could remedy it with a little movement:

> Wearing green jumpsuits, we kept an eye out for signs of paranormal activity as we walked across the desert.

Now the modifier "wearing green jumpsuits" is right next to the intended recipient, "we."

Next, reread #3 and try not to miss that this example says that *the errors* don't understand misplaced modifiers. See it? Fix it up with a little rearrangement:

> Not understanding misplaced modifiers, students could miss the errors in this list.

And now the modified, "students", is directly next to the modifier, "not understanding misplaced modifiers."

Lastly, you should notice the error in #5, for it suggests that Cubism, not Aster, was fanciful of Picasso's work. To correct this sentence, get to shifting!

> Fanciful of Picasso's artwork, Aster's senior project was inspired by Cubism. The installation was "The Renaissance, Cubed" in which she remade some of the greatest artworks from the 16th Century.

12. A Lapse in Logic

Usually revolving around a bad choice of coordinating conjunctions, these sentences just don't make very much sense. They're not grammatically incorrect in any sense, but if you think about what they're saying, you'll notice that they either come to strange conclusions or contradict themselves.

We try very hard to <u>write well, and sometimes</u> our best efforts fail miserably to convey our thoughts.

    (A)   write well, and sometimes
    (B)   write well, for sometimes
    (C)   write well, but sometimes
    (D)   write well, so sometimes
    (E)   write well however

The correct answer is (C). The two pieces of the sentence contradict one another, and the only way to join them logically is to use a coordinating conjunction that joins two opposite ideas. (Remember how (A) is always the same as the original? Don't forget! It's a huge time-saver.)

NOTES:

The same lapse in logic occurs when a coordinating conjunction comes at the beginning of the sentence but fails to connect the two pieces of the sentence.

> <u>Because I don't like vanilla ice cream, Neapolitan</u> is my favorite because it delivers delicious strawberry and chocolate that somehow make that boring vanilla delicious!

> (A)   Because I don't like vanilla ice cream, Neapolitan
> (B)   Because I love vanilla ice cream, Neapolitan
> (C)   While I like vanilla ice cream, Neapolitan
> (D)   Even though I don't like vanilla ice cream, Neapolitan
> (E)   Because I don't like ice cream, Neapolitan

The correct answer is (D) because it sets up the sentence in a way that the two pieces of the sentence agree: even though vanilla doesn't fit the speaker's pallet, Neapolitan comes with two other delicious flavors that bring out the subtleties of vanilla (or just mask it, whatever!).

13. Comparing Apples and Oranges

… should be avoided. That's why you need to be on the lookout for odd comparisons, such as:

> "My basketball skills are better than you."

> What is said: My basketball skills are superior to you, a person.

> What is intended: My basketball skills are better than your basketball skills.

> What is correct: My basketball skills are better than yours. And there's nothing wrong with that statement.

14. Past and Present Participle: Irregular Verbs

Almost always seen in the sentence error section, these questions confuse the simple past and past participle forms of a verb. For example:

> Some jerk taken the whiteboard Emily had affixed to her locker.

Here we have taken the past participle form of *take*, but no helping verb (such as *be*, *have*, and *do*). Thus the sentence must be corrected by turning "taken" into the simple past verb form "took," or by adding a helping verb, as in "has taken."

This is a problem that you'll only run into with irregular verbs since normal verbs have identical simple past and past participle forms, both ending in –ed (i.e., *laugh*: "She laughed at me!" and "She has laughed at me!"). We've compiled a list of some of the most common irregular verbs we've seen tested on the SAT. The key is to be on the lookout for these specific words when reading sentence error questions and to *study*!

Infinitive	Simple Past (can stand alone)	Past Participle (requires helping verb)
arise	arose	arisen
become	became	become
begin	began	begun
blow	blew	blown
break	broke	broken
come	came	come
draw	drew	drawn
drink	drank	drunk
drive	drove	driven
do	did	done
eat	ate	eaten
fall	fell	fallen
forget	forgot	forgotten
freeze	froze	frozen
fly	flew	flown
give	gave	given
get	got	gotten
go	went	gone
grow	grew	grown
know	knew	known
ride	rode	ridden
ring	rang	rung
rise	rose	risen
run	ran	run
see	saw	seen
shake	shook	shaken
shrink	shrank	shrunk
sing	sang	sung
sink	sank	sunk
speak	spoke	spoken
swim	swam	swum
take	took	taken
throw	threw	thrown
write	wrote	written

15. Homophones & Near-Homophones

Homophones are two words that sound the same (homo: same, phone: sound). The College Board will introduce at least two of these sneaky guys into the test, so be on the lookout for something like

We would like to <u>adapt</u> a healthier <u>lifestyle, but</u>
          (A)   (B)
McBurgerBox makes it <u>difficult; it's</u> just so darn
                                  (C)
delicious <u>and</u> convenient. <u>No Error</u>.
          (D)   (E)

We feel your pain, America, but *adapt* should be *adopt*, making our error (A). Didn't catch it? There's still hope! We've created this handy, dandy list of commonly encountered homophones.

Accept & Except

  Accept is to receive something, like an A on your test.

  Except means to exclude something, like your ex from your birthday party.

Adapt & Adopt

  Adapt is to adjust to a new condition, like a rat does to avoid a new housecat.

  Adopt is take up as one's own, like the cat that was saved from the shelter (and couldn't quite catch the adaptive rat).

Affect & Effect

Affect is to have an influence on something, as in "We would like to affect your feeling for the SAT."

Effect (*v*) is to bring about a change <u>and</u> (*n*) is the result of an affect, as in "We would like to effect a positive change on your SAT score."

*Note that affect comes before effect, both alphabetically and chronologically.

Afflict & Inflict

Afflict is generally used as a passive verb, meaning *to distress*, such as in, "I am afflicted with looking *too* good."

Inflict means to impose punishment, such as in, "God, why would you inflict me with such dashing good looks!?"

Allusion & Illusion

Allusion is a reference to something without explicitly saying it, like how we sneakily allude to what we'd like for our birthday without explicitly saying, "Buy me a new computer."

Illusion is a deception, like when you pretend to be ill so you can stay home from school and play video games. (We're onto you. Stop it.)

Anyway & Any Way

Anyway means *in any case* or *regardless*, as in, "Adverbs such as *anyway* can only be singular, but silly people end up adding a useless s to the end of them, anyway."

Any way means to do something by whatever means, such as, "We will drill the difference between *anyway* and *any way* any way that we can."

Climactic & Climatic

Climactic (with 3 C's) is the peak of intensity, as in "The climactic point of the film was when the crazy, crabby, cruel old lady got a pie in the face."

Climatic (with 2 C's) refers to environmental conditions, such as "We have found the perfect climatic conditions: cool and cozy."

Elicit & Illicit

Elicit is to draw out or evoke (Remember: **E**licit-**E**voke).

Illicit means *disallowed*, as in, "Serving spoiled foods is an illicit act because it could make the recipients ill."

Emigrate & Immigrate

Emigrate is to **e**xit one's native country.

Immigrate is to *insert* oneself into a new country.

Eminent & Imminent

Eminent is outstanding or prominent, as in "Emily is an eminent member of the *VIP Club*."

Imminent is *impending* or about to happen, as in "Animals are put on the endangered species list when their extinction is imminent."

Lay & Lie

(We already touched on these, but since they're so often confused, we thought we'd remind you!)

Lay usually comes with a direct object and means to put something somewhere, as in "Lay the jacket on the couch" (direct object: jacket). Past tense for lay is *laid*, as in "Good job; you laid the jacket on the couch."

Lie never comes with a direct object and means to recline or be at rest, as in "I'm going to lie in a recliner and get some rest." Lie is an irregular verb with a simple past form of *lay*, as in "I lay in the recliner all day," and a past participle form of *lain*, as in "I had lain so long that I began to get bed sores." Gross.

Principal & Principle

Principal is a leader, a *person*, a noun that can be your *pal* (after all, it has "pal" right in it).

Principle is a fundamental law or truth, such as the princi*ple* of gravity discovered when an ap*ple* fell on Newton's head[25].

*Principal can also refer to the amount borrowed via loan; it is the amount that gains interest as the loan ages.

Than & Then

Than is used in comparative statements, such as in, "Apples are tastier than apricots."

Then is used to indicate time, such as in, "Exit the elevator, and then enter the escalator."

---

25 Not true, but a cute story, nonetheless.

16. Idiomatic Verb-Preposition Combos

Yeah, there's even *more* idiomatic garbage to regurgitate. Idiomatic verb-preposition combination questions look like so:

<u>Even though</u> Steve and Coral <u>make</u> a great couple,
     (A)   (B)
<u>they</u> always seem to <u>argue over</u> the weekend movie
 (C)   (D)
choice. <u>No error</u>.
        (E)

The correct answer is (D) because the idiomatic verb-preposition combination is *argue about*, not *over*.

And so here comes another list to study! Lucky you! Once again, we highly recommend remaking this list with only the ones you need to study. If you try to study from the whole list, you'll probably just keep focusing on the ones that you do know because it makes you feel better. But really, that's not going to help you on the test when you come across one from the list that you *don't* know. Got it? Dive in and enjoy.

abide by/in	cover with	participate in
accuse of	decide (up)on	pray for
agree on/to/with	depend (up)on	prevent from
apologize for	differ from	prohibit from
apply for/to	distinguish from	recover from
approve of	dream about/of	rely (up)on
argue about/with	escape from	rescue from
arrive in	excel in	respond to
believe in	excuse for	stare at
blame for	forget about	stop from
care about/for	forgive for	subscribe to
charge for/with	hide from	substitute for
compare to/with	hope for	succeed in
complain about	insist (up)on	thank for
contribute to	object to	wait for[26]/on[27]
count (up)on	protect from	work with
discriminate against	provide for/with	worry about

Now that we've covered everything that you'll need to fix on the SAT Writing Section, are you prepared to start from scratch? It's a lot easier than you probably expect! Whereas pre-written material forces you to sift through other people's mess, beginning from scratch means that you don't have to worry about hidden traps!

---

26 "Wait for" is used in the sense of expecting. "We had to wait for the bus."
27 "Wait on" is used as to act as a servant.   "Since she's ill, he has pledged to wait on her, hand and foot."

The Essay

The essay is your chance to express your creativity. You get to run free—but prance carefully. The SAT essay is like a yard surrounded by an electric fence: you get the illusion of being able to do *whatever you want*, but if you wander too far, you'll get zapped.

The SAT essay is worth about 30% of your total Writing Section score (240 of the 800 points) and is all about showing the College Board that you're eloquent and that you're capable of taking a stance and persuading anyone to join your side of the debate. You get to use all of that knowledge you've gathered from school, from your life experiences, from your extracurricular activities, and even from your fascination with alien abduction (seriously, we'll show you in a bit).

Fortunately for your cramped hand, the SAT essay is *also* all about being concise. You must understand: the SAT evaluator readers read thousands of essays. Many of these essays are best described as panicked ramblings of high school students. The most thoughtful thing that you can do for the readers is to remember the phrase

It's not about writing a long, verbose essay: it's about using your words to create a clear, strongly-supported argument. If you're writing for quantity, you'll surely end up filling the paper with fluff—so instead of writing for quantity, write for quality.

Since you'll only have 25 minutes to plan your essay, write your essay, *and* proofread your essay, keeping it short shouldn't be too difficult. (Plus, you're pretty much forced to keep it short; there's no such thing as "an extra sheet of paper" on the essay section.) The most difficult part of the process is going to be budgeting your time, so practice is going to be key to your success.

Let's start by introducing your assignment. The essay section begins a little something like this:

> **Directions:** Think carefully about the issue presented in the following excerpt and the assignment below.
>
> Quote.
>
> **Assignment:** Blah blah blah. Write some stuff.

The quote functions as a bit of inspiration. You don't necessarily need to focus on the quote or even refer to the quote; it's merely there to help you get started. (We suspect this is done for the sake of the essay readers' sanity. Can you imagine how terrible the essays would be if they didn't throw students a bone? Eesh!)

The assignment is always some *extremely* vague prompt, like "… using examples from literature, current affairs, history, or personal observation …," *which is awesome* because it means that you can talk about your love of alien abduction conspiracy! Skeptical? (No pun intended.)

NOTES:

Let's say that you're a proud Eagle Scout, you've collected over 100 books on alien abductions, and your dad has a fascination with trains that has naturally rubbed off on you. How could you apply your knowledge—all obtained outside your standard high school curriculum—to the following essay questions?

1. **Directions:** Think carefully about the issue presented in the following excerpt and the assignment below.

   "That you may retain your self-respect, it is better to displease the people by doing what you know is right, than to temporarily please them by doing what you know is wrong." – William J. H. Boetcker

   Assignment: Are widely held views often wrong, or are such views more likely to be correct? Plan and write an essay in which you develop your point of view on this issue. Support your position with reasoning and examples taken from your reading, studies, experience, or observations.

   Here's a great place to talk about your fascination with alien abduction conspiracies. You could argue that what is popular is not always what is right. After all, we used to think that the Earth was the center of the universe, but we now know that's entirely wrong. As a matter of fact we now know that we live in one of many galaxies, so who's to say that we're the only form of life in the vast, infinite number of galaxies out there? And if you've read half of those books, you could probably regurgitate Carl Sagan's quote in which he says that everything we have ever been, felt, or believed has merely been a "mote of dust, suspended in a sunbeam."

2. Directions: Think carefully about the issue presented in the following excerpt and the assignment below.

> "History calls those men the greatest who have ennobled themselves by working for the common good; experience acclaims as happiest the man who has made the greatest number of people happy."
>
> – Karl Marx

Assignment: Does the good of the whole outweigh the good of the individual? Plan and write an essay in which you develop your point of view on this issue. Support your position with reasoning and by using examples from literature, current affairs, history, or personal observation.

Having spent plenty of time by your father's side as he marveled over the construction of the first transcontinental railroad, you learned all about the great sacrifices of the Chinese immigrants. He thoroughly bored you with how they worked in dangerous conditions, through the worst of weather, and managed to lay rail at the pace of man's casual stride—and they did it for a meager $28 per month. With the completion of the railroad, the United States was able to industrialize on a larger scale, giving the country a boost in the global market. Clearly, without the sacrifice of the Chinese, America would never have known such a level of prosperity. End of surprisingly helpful knowledge. Thanks, Dad!

NOTES:

3. **Directions:** Think carefully about the issue presented in the following excerpt and the assignment below.

> "We receive three educations: one from our parents, one from our schoolmasters, and one from the world. The third contradicts all that the first two teach us." – Charles-Louis de Secondat

Assignment: What form of learning is more valuable: learning from a book, or learning from experience? Plan and write an essay in which you develop your point of view on this issue. Support your position with reasoning and examples taken from your reading, studies, experience, or observations.

> You've survived being a Boy Scout, a Tenderfoot, and you've filled every requirement to become an Eagle Scout. How many fires have you started by rubbing two sticks together? Do you think you could have learned to do that by reading about it in a book? No way! You also couldn't learn how to cut off the blood flow to someone's arm to save him from bleeding to death without, at some point, picking up a tourniquet and actually trying it. Even though books grant us access to the abstract, some of the most important things that you've ever learned can only be taught through hands-on experience. Tell them all about it!

Keep in mind that there is no right or wrong "side" of the argument. The essay isn't a test of your beliefs or your ability to deal with a moral dilemma. You just need to take one side of the argument and stick to it, so make sure you take the side with which you're most comfortable. Oh, and don't you *dare* flip-flop! Wavering won't make you sound reasonable and sympathetic; it'll make you sound indifferent and wimpy. Make a choice and stick to it!

Speaking of choices, you can opt to write about something from literature, current affairs, history, or personal observation, right? Take notice of the "or" bit: you need to choose one subject and *stick to it*. Don't write about how the Roswell incident is proof that aliens have visited our planet and then bounce to the story of that super creepy night when you could have sworn you witnessed a UFO abduct your neighbor's dog.

The best way to stay on topic is to develop a strong thesis statement from the very beginning. If you're cringing at the word *thesis*, you're not alone. Strong theses can be extremely difficult to develop, but the cool thing about them is that once they're nailed down, the rest of the essay just flows organically. Before you begin writing your essay, determine the following:

☆ What topic will you be discussing? What is the main point that you would like to make?

☆ Can you get any more specific?

☆ Does your thesis directly address the question?

These questions help combat what we like to call the thesis-to-end-all-theses claims, such as "Sugar is not good for your health." What's wrong with this thesis statement? Well, your topic is sugar, your main point is that it's not good for you, and you *really* could be *much* more specific. Perhaps you could say, "Sugar is bad for your teeth" or "Sugar is addictive and causes unhealthy weight gain."

Wondering how to write a better thesis? It's all part of taking a BOW. Not, like, bow and expect your essay readers to yell "Bravo!", but take a BOW as in…

BRAINSTORM (2 – 4 minutes)

Carefully read your assignment and reflect on your pre-written essays. Do any of them apply to the assignment in any way? Say you developed a super solid essay that argues how aliens *totally* exist. You've even come up with a list of proofs that support your argument. But how do you apply this to the question, "Are widely held views often wrong, or are such views more likely to be correct?"?

Begin by drafting a rough thesis. You'll be improving it, so don't fret over how eloquent it is or if it fully makes your point. Getting something out is what's important.

Just because a lot of people believe something doesn't mean it's true.

Rough, but that's OK. Let's start refining.

What topic are you discussing? What is the main point that you'd like to make? Alien abduction is your main topic, but it seems that we've skipped that part. Let's work it in.

Looking at alien abduction theories is a great way to show that popular opinion does not equate to truth.

Can you get any more specific? What about alien abductions makes you think that popular opinion is not necessarily related to truth?

Considering the prevalence of alien abduction stories and recent advances in our understanding of the vastness of the universe, it is easy to see that popular opinion, such as Earth's uniqueness in its ability to sustain life, is not always correct.

Does this point directly address the question? Sort of, but it falls a little short. The question is whether widely held views are usually *right* or *wrong*, not if *all* views are right. Perhaps we could talk about the limits of knowledge and what role it plays in the rightness or wrongness of a belief.

Considering the prevalence of alien abduction stories and recent advances in our understanding of the vastness of the universe, it is easy to see that popular opinion, such as Earth's uniqueness in its ability to sustain life, tends to be naïve in its simplicity.

Unless you have a knack for writing, you probably couldn't come up with the final thesis without going through a refinement process. *But that's OK!* It doesn't take very long and it's a necessary process that will make the writing process much easier.

NOTES:

So, remember how the rest is supposed to flow organically? You've set yourself up to write about quite a bit!

- 💡 Alien abductions are generally considered delusions caused by Hollywood.

- 💡 Recent advances in our understanding of the vastness of the universe change how we view the world and physics is debunking many of our basic beliefs. Imagine, we used to think that Earth was flat and the center of the universe!

- 💡 If popular opinion holds that alien abductions are figments of overactive imagination, it stands to reason that popular opinion holds that Earth is the only planet capable of supporting life.

- 💡 This belief is naïve and egocentric because it doesn't consider how many other galaxies may have planets with conditions similar to Earth's.

- 💡 This is an example of a popular belief being wrong. Popular opinion tends to be too simple to encompass the truth.

Not too shabby for a single sentence, eh?

ORGANIZE (3 – 5 minutes)

Next, you need to organize your essay. The organization process should pretty much always follow the same fool-proof outline. And don't you *dare* write without first constructing your outline or you'll end up rambling out a spineless, unorganized essay that says a whole lot of nothing.

A typical SAT essay is composed of five paragraphs, as so:

1. Introduction
   a. Introduce your stance, including your awesome thesis statement
   b. Briefly introduce example 1
   c. Present counter example and note that it is incorrect OR briefly introduce example 2
   d. Briefly introduce example 3 (*strongest example*)

2. Discuss 1b, including how it pertains to your thesis

3. Discuss 1c, including how it pertains to your thesis

4. Discuss 1d, including how it pertains to your thesis

5. Conclusion
   a. Rephrase your position
   b. Revisit examples
   c. Restate how examples apply
   d. Go out with a bang: answer the "So what?" question

Seems like a significantly less daunting task when it's broken down this way, doesn't it? Another great thing about starting with an outline is that you'll have something to anchor you to the heart of your essay and yank you back in if you wander off topic.

WRITE (16 – 20 minutes)

If you paid attention to the thesis discussion earlier, 1a and 1b are pretty self-explanatory. So, let's talk about 1c, where you introduce a counter example. 1c is your opportunity to say, "Hey, look, I get what the other guy is saying, but he's wrong because he hasn't considered this other thing." So, in your case, if someone is claiming that we haven't found any other forms of life, even though we've been looking for so long, you could point out that this argument is a logical fallacy (specifically, an appeal to ignorance: "Since we haven't proven that aliens exist, they must not exist."). You could then point out that it is simply impossible, with the current technology, to contact or examine planets in distant galaxies. We're just not equipped to use any data as reliable proof!

Now, 1d is your third example. We recommend that it be your strongest example because it will be the last thing your essay readers read before you serve up a conclusion. Authors of books and movie scripts use this same building effect: they introduce you to the subject and build on it, making the material stronger and stronger until the climax. It's a time-tested way to pull in your reader, so use it!

Parts 5a through c—rephrasing your position, revisiting examples, and restating how your examples apply—are super helpful for reminding the readers how all the pieces relate. What do these recent advances in physics tell us about the nature of our beliefs? Why is it important that the widely held view assumes that Earth is alone in its ability to sustain life? What's wrong with an egocentric assessment of the world? Use this opportunity to reinforce the connection between your supportive points and your thesis.

Regarding 5d, you're probably like, "Whaaaaaat are you even talking about?" And it's such a shame! For some unfortunate reason, answering the "So what?" question isn't emphasized in high school classrooms. It is the key to making your essay "jump off the page," so to speak. It's where a writer says, "This

is why what I'm saying is important; this is why everything I've said was worth your time." It prompts the reader to think differently or to act differently, or even to *take* action. It animates otherwise flat, lifeless scribbles.

In our sample, this could be a prompt for your readers to stop over-simplifying the unknown; to make it *more* known by getting involved in the discussion or even just reading up on what the fringe movement is discovering. Why? Because the universe is a beautiful, mysterious place and we shouldn't rely on the general populace's beliefs to limit our exploration. After all, widely held views are limited to widely comprehended knowledge, and what percent of the general population has eased up on their skepticism—or, is even *capable* of fathoming just how vast our universe is?

So what about 5d, the "going out with a bang," the answer to the "so what" question? Not only have you shown that you know your stuff, but you've also shown that this knowledge doesn't exist in a vacuum; not accepting the public's opinion allows you to view more beauty in the natural world and enjoy the unknown. If the readers do the same, their lives will be made all the richer!

Feeling inspired readers? Inspired enough to dish out six points? Score!

ESSAY SCORING

Speaking of getting a six, you're probably wondering how the essays are scored. Here's the gist:

Two people will read your essay. Each person will grade your essay on a range of 1 (severely flawed) to 6 (fabulous!) based on an overall impression of your essay. (While this shouldn't happen because you're such a smarty pants, a score of 0 can also be given if an essay is horrendously illegible or written off topic.) The final score is the sum of your readers' individual assessments, so your final score will be from 0 to 12.

Note: The College Board throws you another bone here. Say one reader gives you a 5, but the other reader, one with a burning hatred for alien abduction conspiracies, gives you a 2. Since the two scores differ by more than one point, a third reader will come in to score your essay and resolve the discrepancy. This only happens to about 3% of the essays, but it's assuring to know that one person isn't going to destroy your score, isn't it?

Readers are fully aware that the essays they're grading are written by high school students under time constraints, so they're not going to expect perfection. They don't pay attention to your handwriting and they're not expecting a novel. As long as they can read it, and as long as it makes a good argument, you're golden.

You're not going to be grading essays, so you don't need to know *exactly* what they're looking for. As a matter of fact, knowing what they grade on isn't going to help you become a better writer; *practicing* your writing is going to help you become a better writer. What we're trying to say is that we're not going to waste your precious gray matter with the scoring scheme. Instead, we're going to infuse your brain bits with some more useful information. So prepare yourself for...

TPS's Essay Writing Tips and Tricks

🖊 Some 50 – 70% of students make a critical error from the get-go: they think about their 25-minute task and panic. Instead of remembering to take a BOW, they dive in and write something that is disorganized, poorly argued, poorly written, and straight up appalling to the readers' senses. *Do not start writing immediately. Take the time to plan your essay and you will produce a significantly better essay.*

🖊 If you're going to write about your personal observations, make sure you don't choose a recent event. If you're still mulling over your feelings about the event, you'll have a harder time defining how you feel about the occurrence or how it affected you. Instead, choose something that happened in the more distant past so that you can talk about it in a more rational, objective manner. You'll also be able to talk about the long-term implications and how you've grown since it happened.

🖊 Another bit on personal observations: it's OK to make stuff up or exaggerate your story. No one is going to fact-check your essay, so feel free to take the opportunity to make up a scenario (creative writers, this is where your short stories will shine!) or embellish the truth (fishermen, you're pros at this). Just be careful that your story doesn't get outrageous or you'll lose all credibility.

🖊 A portion of your writing time—at least two minutes— should be dedicated to proofreading your essay. This is your opportunity to catch run-on sentences, fragments, sneaky homophones, and the like.

NOTES:

✎ When making corrections, be it in the middle of writing or during your proofreading, don't waste time erasing text. Instead, simply ~~cross bad bits out~~ and use an arrow

to point to the updated, better version of what you meant to say.

✎ Avoid non-words, such as the very popular but still *oh*-so-not-legit

    ✓ Oughta
    ✓ Gonna
    ✓ Wanna
    ✓ Ain't[28]
    ✓ Could of [29]

✎ Don't split infinitives. As mentioned earlier, infinitives are the "to (verb)" form of a word. If you're writing about how you'd like to treat the College Board for ruining a perfectly good Saturday, *don't* write, "I would like to mightily smack them." but, "I would like to smack them with all my might."

✎ Either/or and neither/nor are the correct pairs. Just keep the N's together!

    ✓ You can either have a good night's rest, or you can spend the entire evening fidgeting.
    ✓ Neither a super-duper sized slush drink, nor a very mega venti sized coffee should be consumed prior to testing.

---

28 No one in academia cares that this non-word has somehow forced its way into the dictionary. As a matter of fact, using "ain't" will likely provoke disdain from your essay readers and have a negative effect on your score.

29 It's *could've*.

A country is a place, not a group of people. Thus a country should not be referred to as "they," but as "it."

Use very specific details or quotes (like that Carl Sagan one from the first example essay question), or point out an obscure fact. New and interesting bits of information can be used to "wow" your essay readers.

Avoid needlessly long prepositional phrases. They're a waste of time and space and add zero meat to your essay. So, instead of … ➔ Use …

At the present time ➔ Now

In order that ➔ So

In reference ➔ Regarding

In the interim ➔ Meanwhile

In the near future ➔ Soon

In the event that ➔ If

In the course of ➔ During

In the process of ➔ During or In

Take into consideration ➔ Consider

With the exception of ➔ Except for

Remember how to use your apostrophe!

NOTES:

It's vs. Its: With an apostrophe, *it's* is the contraction of "it is"; without an apostrophe, *its* is the possessive form of it.

It's imperative that you study hard so you can free yourself from the College Board and its evil test.

Whose vs. Who's: *Whose* is the possessive form of who; *who's*, with an apostrophe, is the contraction of "who is." (Helpful reminder: if you know it's versus its, just follow the same apostrophe means contraction rule.)

Whose smelly shoes are these!? Who's responsible for this travesty!

Dogs' vs. Dog's: When the apostrophe comes after the possessive S, multiple dogs are in possession. When the apostrophe comes before the possessive S, only one dog is in possession.

Two dogs' leashes wrapped around the walker's legs and caused her to trip.

2 dogs = dogs'

1 walker = walker's

NOTES:

✎ Avoid ambiguity: employ the Oxford Comma.

> In a list containing flour, sugar, vanilla extract, chocolate, and eggs, the comma between chocolate and eggs is called an Oxford Comma.

Even though it is completely optional, TPS recommends that you *always* use it. Occasionally, the lack of this comma produces a sentence that can be interpreted two different ways, such as

> I would like to dedicate this next song to my parents, Cleopatra and Franklin D. Roosevelt.

What is meant? Is the speaker the love child of Cleopatra and a time-traveling FDR?

Or does the speaker want to dedicate the song to his parents, Cleopatra, and FDR?

Since the writer opted to not use the Oxford Comma, we'll never know. Avoid such a disaster and always use an Oxford Comma.

NOTES:

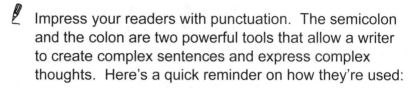 Impress your readers with punctuation. The semicolon and the colon are two powerful tools that allow a writer to create complex sentences and express complex thoughts. Here's a quick reminder on how they're used:

> ✓ Semicolon – separates two independent clauses that, together, create a single idea: may also be used to manage large lists.

> ✓ Colon – only used after an independent clause, a colon can introduce a list, introduce a quote, or signify the elaboration of a preceding idea.

When it comes to semicolons, "two independent clauses" means two complete sentences, i.e.,

> Complete sentence; complete sentence.

The purpose of using a semicolon is largely to develop a complex idea; it allows you to signify that more information is on its way to build up this one idea. When it comes to managing large lists, semicolons allow items to contain descriptions that require commas, such as

> Our Halloween decorations included dancing skeletons; pumpkins, all carved by our guests during the party; creepy, sticky spider webs carefully stretched across doorways to snag any passerby; and plenty of flashing, disorienting lights.

Colons, likewise, are only used after an independent clause, i.e., a complete sentence. The first two uses, introducing material, are the easiest to command.

> If you're going to properly carve a pumpkin, you should obtain the following items: a pencil or permanent marker, a kitchen knife, a spoon to scoop the guts, and a small knife to carve the pumpkin.

> The homicidal clown had some good advice: "Run."

A little more advanced use of the colon is to elaborate on an idea.

> When enjoying a haunted house, it's always a good idea to be prepared: to be ready to leave your best friend behind while you run for your life.

Regardless of how you go about constructing your sentences, it'll only help if you can incorporate various structures into your essay.

Each supportive paragraph should end with a direct connection to your thesis. Even if you think the connection is perfectly obvious, take a moment to explain how your examples are relevant.

NOTES:

Use a variety of transitional phrases to keep your essay fresh. Instead of saying, "For instance" over and over and over and over… pull from the following list of transitional phrases.

Relationship	Transitional Expression
additional support	also, as well, besides, equally important, further, furthermore, in addition, moreover
cause & effect	accordingly, consequently, hence, so, therefore, thus
emphasis	even, indeed, in fact, of course, truly
example	for instance, namely, specifically, to illustrate
exception/contrast	conversely, however, in spite of, on the contrary, nevertheless, nonetheless, notwithstanding, on the other hand, still, yet
similarly	also, likewise, similarly

Personal observations are great for essays, but don't overuse "me" or "I." Instead, focus on the ideas. After all, the proverb goes

Great people talk about great ideas;
average people talk about average ideas;
small people talk about other people.

NOTES:

✎ Don't be satisfied with a *short* essay. Even though the College Board claims that they don't focus on the length of essays, a noticeably short essay might negatively influence your score. If you're a concise writer, use the extra space to provide more information. We don't want you to ramble, but we don't want you to barely be heard.

✎ Finally, *practice writing.* No one becomes a strong writer without many hours of practice. Keep a journal or write weekly essays on any topic of your choice. Be sure to go back and proofread your work so you can learn where you usually make mistakes and, with that information, strive to become a better writer. Do you always find yourself creating comma splices? Pay closer attention to every comma you use. Do you tend to create non-parallel lists? Be conscious of the way you itemize lists. Whatever mistake you can train yourself away from is a mistake that won't ruin your wonderful SAT essay.

Now that we have told you how to plan out your essay using the BOW method, we've given you the 5 paragraph layout, and we've thrown a bunch of tips your way, you may be asking, "But what does the essay actually look like? How can I tell if I've written a 2-worthy essay or a 6-worthy essay?" We're glad you asked because here are 3 examples!

ESSAY A (SCORES 1/2)

Many people scoff at the idea that aliens have visited our little planet, but just because a lot of people hold that view don't necessarily make it true.

When most of us think of aliens, we picture little green men, but that idea may not represent what is out there in the vast distances of space. Microbial life is

NOTES:

far more abundant on the earth than large mammals so scientists have even scoured the red sand of Mars searching for evidence of microscopic life among traces of past liquid water.

But that is life another planet, not traveling to our own. The clues to how microscopic life travels to our planet may begin with the first life on earth. We don't know how life started here, but one theory is that bacteria may have hitched an interstellar ride on an asteroid. There are bacteria called extremophiles that live in very extreme environments, so we know that such a microbial journey is feasible.

We could expand our search for aliens even further. Even though what we know as life is based off of cells that is simply based on pour experience. Life in the cosmos may follow some entirely different paradigm that we struggle to comprehended, for example: organisms based on particles of light.

In the end, there are no clear answers to the question of whether we have been visited by entities from another planet. If something can survive here, it may become a part of our ecosystem without us even knowing it. It's also possible that something from here is able to survive elsewhere, so why is it not possible for microbial life disappeared into space following some prehistoric asteroid collision? Just because common knowledge focuses on our lack of experience with alien life doesn't mean that aliens don't exist, so we can't count the popularity of an opinion as the truthfulness of an opinion.

ESSAY B (SCORES 3/4)

Just because many people believe something does not necessarily make it correct. For example, consider the prevalence of alien abduction stories and recent advances in our understanding of the vastness of the universe. When you are open to these difficult ideas, it is easy to see that the belief that Earth is alone in its ability to create and sustain life may be wrong.

For instance, most people treat an interest in extraterrestrial life like a hobby for 12 year-olds. They don't take the thought seriously because Hollywood has created such a stereotypical image that no one ever considers what alien life might realistically be like, but default to the stereotype of little green men and declare, "impossible!" Most people find it too difficult to consider alternatives to little green men because they don't want to be labeled a loon or easily manipulated by television.

The problem with this way of thinking is that it never considers how large the universe is and how very little of it mankind has experienced. It never reaches beyond the self-centered view of reality. With science debunking many of mankind's core beliefs, such as Earth being the center of the universe, it wouldn't be surprising to find that we are not the only planet to create or support life.

As a matter of fact, recent discovery has proven that we aren't the only planet in our galaxy capable of supporting life! A planet wad discovered some 600 light years away: Kepler-22b, an "Earth-like" planet that is suspected to have oceans and continents. Could a place like this not offer the same conditions for life as Earth? And if it could, have we completely debunked our long-standing belief that we are alone in this universe—or even on a smaller scale, in this galaxy?

If other planets are capable of supporting life, then we must consider the possibility that life does indeed exist elsewhere (though not necessarily that is has visited us), and that the popular belief that we are unique is simply wrong. This is just one example of a popular opinion being wrong; if we also consider the many "common sense" ideas that have been debunked by science, we can see that the general view has a propensity to be far from right.

ESSAY C (SCORES 5/6)

Many people scoff at the suggestion that alien life forms inhabit the unknown, but this is an example of a commonly held view having no tangible truth to it. Considering the prevalence of alien abduction stories and recent advances in our understanding of the mechanics and vastness of the universe, it is easy to see that widely held views, such as Earth's uniqueness in its ability to sustain life, tends to be naive in its simplicity.

Alien abductions are generally considered to be delusions caused by Hollywood. If popular opinion holds that alien abductions are merely figments of overactive imaginations, it stands to reason that popular opinion holds that Earth is the only planet capable of supporting life. The issue with this belief is that it is limited by our technology. We have only been able to examine the conditions of a few planets in our galaxy, and based on images from the Hubble telescope we know that there are likely to be thousands more planets in other galaxies! We cannot know what we cannot examine.

Those who rely on a lack of alien contact as proof of a lack of alien life rely on the fallacy of ignorance, i.e. "We haven't found any yet, so there must not be any." Unfortunately, these oversimplifications tend to be the way that many popular beliefs are formed and understood. Consequently, we cannot count on frequently fallible "common sense" to steer us toward truth.

What we can rely on to expose the truth is scientific discovery. Unfortunately, the majority of people outside of the scientific community either have trouble understanding new information because of its ecclesiastic nature, or they have a hard time accepting it because it debunks what they used to "know to be true." The examination of subatomic particles is a perfect example because it uses jargon like "quarks" and "strings", and because it shows that all of the rules that apply to matter as we know it fall apart once you look inside an atom. Thus incorrect, commonly held beliefs are difficult to remedy when faced with new, dissonant information.

The problem with widely held views as a whole is that they are limited to common knowledge and common knowledge tends to be naive and oversimplified. If we wish to get to the heart of any matter, we must not merely accept common beliefs; rather, we must get involved in the discussion and do some of our own exploring. After all, as the late astronomer Carl Sagan said, everything we have ever been, felt, or believed has merely been a "mote of dust, suspended in a sunbeam."

Do you see how a little refining makes the essay a little better each time? Do your refining at home while you write practice essays! As part of your practice for the essay, try writing a number of essays on the same two or three subjects. Make sure the foci of the essays are vastly different so that you can get used to applying these ideas in many different ways. Then, when it comes to the real deal, you'll be so used to talking about the implications of alien abductions and the building

of America's railroad tracks that you'll have zero trouble showing that the possible existence of aliens is the reason that competition, not cooperation, results in more success (the race to space, anyone?).

Now, if you're having a hard time getting yourself to prewrite essays, consider this: when you apply to the University of Prestige, they'll be able to request a copy of your SAT essay at *no charge*. The only thing going against this practice is the shortness of admissions officers' time. But, of course, this doesn't mean that they *won't* use it in the event that they're trying to decide between admitting you and another seemingly identical student.

What we're saying here is that you need to try. Don't go in on the test day and just assume you'll be able to "wing it." It doesn't take a lot to prepare yourself, so don't throw away the opportunity to prewrite and practice. It will do wonders!
Not sure what to practice writing about? Well, here's a handy list of generic SAT topics. If you can prewrite a stellar essay on these (which includes proofreading and, ideally, chatting with your English teacher about it), you'll be *so* prepared for that essay!

- 💡 *Beauty*. Is there a universal standard of beauty? Should people be influenced by other people's perceptions of beauty?

- 💡 *Ethics*. Does being ethical make it more difficult to achieve success?

- 💡 *Experience*. What is more valuable in education: hands-on experience, or reading textbooks?

- *Hard Work.* Are successful people more accomplished because they expect more from themselves?

- *Nature vs. nurture.* How much of each person is attributed to nature? How much is contributed to how we were nurtured? Can we really say that *we* define who we are, or are we products of genetics and environment?

- *Popular Views.* Are we more likely to accept the opinions of others, or are we more likely to challenge them? Why?

- *Technology.* Have modern advances truly improved our lives? Are there aspects of our lives that suffer because of technology?

- *Success.* What is it and where does the definition come from? Can we ever truly achieve it?

Yeah, yeah, we know, "It seems like soooo much work!" But can you somehow think of a topic that covers two or more of these prompts? Can your sample essay be easily adapted to answer two or more of these essays? Because that's your goal: to create two or three well-written essays—not one for each and every one of these topics—that can be easily adapted to answer any prompt thrown your way. And remember, refine your prewritten essays; the more times you read and rewrite them, the easier they'll come to you while you're sitting at your desk staring down the SAT.

CHAPTER 6

Conclusion

The Last Chapter!

Well, hello! Didn't think you'd make it this far! Kidding, of course, you studious stud, you. Unfortunately, this means you're on your own for the rest of the journey—but only in the sense that you're entirely responsible for the outcome from this point. Remember how we told you that you should

Well, if you're lucky enough to have been part of our seminar—or were dedicated enough to buy our practice book—you'll have 26 workouts with detailed explanations of the answers. But it's up to you how this stuff gets used!

Ideally, you should create the study schedule on page 29 with times allotted for practice tests. During this time, your cell phone needs to be turned off; you should be in a rather silent room; you should limit yourself to your mental faculties, your pencils and erasers, your calculator, a watch, and a glass of water. (Why the water? So you have fewer excuses to get out of your seat and break concentration, duh!) Be sure to follow time limits and abide by the rules. Then, once you've completed a practice test, you can score yourself to figure out not only where you currently stand, but you can also read the reasoning behind each answer and learn how The College Board thinks. The more you know about how they think, the better you'll be able to evade their tricks—so get all up in their heads and learn how they tick!

"But what if I don't understand why I got a question wrong, even with the explanation?"

Remember how we said that teachers teach because they love to help students learn? Go ask your writing teacher to help you improve your practice essays, go humbly to your math teacher and ask him/her to review graph translations with you, skip into your chemistry room and ask Mr. Explosions to help you understand how to read graphic representations of data! (As an added bonus to getting the help you need, you're going to make the teacher feel good and make yourself *look* good— brownie points, anyone?).

"OK, I get that practicing is important. But why bother with the PSAT?"

The PSAT is written and scored by the same people who produce and grade the SAT. More importantly, it is given to students in the same environment as the SAT, so those who have experience with the PSAT are less likely to be overwhelmed by the process of the SAT. Look: we told you that you're going to take it in an oddly quiet room that amplifies every sniffle and sneeze by your peers, that your desk will probably be uncomfortable, that the temperature is bound to make you shiver or sweat (or both, Clammy Hands McGee), that the time limits can create a sense of urgency that spirals into anxiety... and this all probably makes you nervous! Why not ease yourself into the conditions of the SAT *before* you ever take it? Plus, there are scholarship opportunities in the event that you do really well on the PSAT! No loss for you!

"And what if I'm already feeling pretty confident just from reading everything here? I mean, I knew what you were going to say before you even said it! I know how to FOIL like a boss!"

To this we say, *fantastic*! That means the practice test will be a *breeze*. Why not prove to yourself that you really are as learned as you think and go take one of the practice tests? If you realize that you're not scoring where you'd like, you can save yourself some money and practice *before* the big day (you know, the one that costs a bunch of money?) and work out all of those silly little mistakes you made. And if you realize you really are prepared for the SAT? Heck, practice a little bit to improve your score a couple points (hello, scholarships!) and increase your confidence. Being positive is just as important as being prepared!

"Does it really matter when I take the test? There's this band coming into town on the first weekend, and I want to go with my best friend to a waterpark on the second weekend; then, after that, I really should pick up an extra shift to pay for the festival that is held on the fourth weekend...."

Look... You're going to have to make sacrifices here. The SAT is a once in a lifetime challenge to which you'll need to dedicate time and effort. If that means that you need to not go to a concert or *put off* that waterpark visit to a later date, then it means you're going to be a little bored a couple weekends for the sake of your future success. Equally important in determining when you'll be taking your test: what happens if you catch a wicked cold on Thursday and wake up on Friday with the cold of the century? Do you really want to be forced to take the exam on Saturday with the added stress of a million germs bouncing around in your sinuses and tickling the back of your throat? Or would you rather cancel your test date and reschedule for the next weekend? The point is... taking the test earlier gives you more opportunities to reschedule it or, in the event of catastrophic failure (e.g., your breakfast decides that it doesn't agree with your stomach and demands a divorce), retake it.

All joking about barfing aside, we really think that if you've made it this far, you're dedicated enough to do what's right. Before we send you off on your own, however, we'd like to remind you of a couple things. After all, your dedication to mastering the SAT means you've covered a *lot* of territory (kudos!).

Critical Reading Highlights

 Remember your plan of attack for one-blank and two-blank sentence completions. Don't forget the TPS Sentence Completion Method!

 Each passage will be prefaced with an italicized introduction. Always read it! It could contain valuable information that determines whether or not you have *any* idea what the passage is talking about.

 You will read a few short passages, each approximately 100 words, and answer two or three questions for each. You will also be reading five long passages, each between 450 and 850 words, and these will contain significantly more questions. Be prepared to read and don't let anxiety make you rush faster than you can comprehend the material!

 Do not—we repeat—do *not* get bogged down with taking notes and underlining things while you read. Questions contain line indicators so that you don't *have* to be like the search function on a computer. It's important that every one of your tiny marks means something, otherwise you'll take a bunch of time writing and underlining and even more time searching for that *one* thing you really should have underlined. So save your pencil for the stuff that *really* jumps out at you.

Revisit the **Question Key Words and Phrases** chart: almost every question related to a passage falls into one of these categories.

 Most importantly: remember that there may be multiple correct answers; however, your goal is to find the *best* answer.

Vocabulary Highlights

Study those prefixes, suffixes, and roots so you can disassemble words that you've forgotten. It's better than guessing from thin air!

Your notecards (which you most definitely have made or are close to completing, we're sure) don't need to be created as we've presented them. If you have a way of remembering a word that we didn't list—like *maritime* sounding like *marine time*, or *wanton* reminding you of the school bully Anton—use your association. Learning is all about expanding your network of associations. Trust us, our mnemonics pale in comparison to yours, because yours are *yours*.

It's usually easier to remember a couple things at a time, so grab a small stack of your notecards and keep them with you at all times. When you have a few minutes, whether it's while you're waiting for the bus or while you're sitting at the DMV for a *ridiculously long time* (seriously, what are they doing between customers?), whip out your notecards and study a few. Once you feel a little more comfortable, throw them on the bottom of the deck and start with another sliver. Once you've gone through them entirely, shuffle them up and start over. It's a lot easier and way more efficient than sleeping on a pile of notecards at 2AM!

NOTES:

Math Highlights

▶ Know that your time will be split between 44 multiple choice questions and 10 "grid-ins." This means that you absolutely *cannot* allow yourself to become absorbed in any one question. Remember: they're all worth the same number of points!

▶ Know what functions you'll need to use on your calculator and *know how to use them*. It is also helpful for many students to bring a simple 4-function calculator for basic arithmetic. More importantly, it's key to remember how to do simple math in your head: button pushing is absurdly time-consuming when your skull contains the fastest, most complex computer this world has ever known. Oh, and make sure that fancy computer of a brain knows how to change the batteries on your calculator.

▶ Do not make math problems more complicated than intended. This is particularly true for factoring and expansions: take a quick glance at the answer list and see what your goal *looks* like.

▶ You will be given some formulas on the SAT, but by no means will they explain *how* to use them. Take some time to practice applying the formulas so you really know what those variables mean.

Writing Highlights

 Your essay will be worth about 30% of your total Writing Section score, so don't even *think* about "winging it." This is your chance to get some seriously easy points. Remember how we recommend that you practice writing essays and even produce a few sample essays? Do it and have your favorite writing instructor go over them with you.

 When dealing with usage questions, remember that *only underlined portions may be changed*. Do not, even for a split second, consider how you would rearrange the sentence. Rather, focus on amending the underlined bits.

 When it comes to sentence correction questions, do not read option (A). Option A is *always* the same thing as is represented in the original sentence; i.e., it is the equivalent of "no change."

 Short and sweet is always better than long-winded ramblings. This goes for your essay *and* for improving paragraphs: the best writing is that which fully conveys an idea in the fewest words.

 When it's time to write your essay, do not forget to BOW. Even if one of your sample essays is so perfect, it's not going to be exactly what you need to write. Take the time to **b**rainstorm how you're going to relate your essay to the question and **o**rganize your flow of thoughts before you **w**rite.

Do you remember a lot of those tips? Fabulous! That means you've done a great job retaining information. We just have a couple more checklists for you before we let you go:

Prior to the Test

 Be sure to read this *entire* book (if you're here without having read the rest of it, shame on you).

 Know the directions. All of them.

 Have your SAT-Conquering Kit prepared *days* before the exam in case you realize the day before the test that you forgot your admission ticket. Include your photo ID (see page 42), your admission ticket, several #2 pencils with soft rubber erasers (most sharp, a couple dull), a couple bar erasers, a pencil sharpener *just in case*, a calculator and replacement batteries (or calculators if you want that handy 4-function buddy), a silent watch, a snack for break time, and a bottle of water.

 Be able to navigate to the testing center and to your testing room with your eyes closed and know exactly how long the journey will take. (We know it's going to be a dramatic drive, so call it your journey—oh, and don't keep your eyes closed if you're driving … please ….) And then leave earlier than you could possibly need, because who knows if a train will appear between you and the testing center, or if a bakery gives away free donuts and causes a traffic jam, or maybe you need to stop at that bakery because those donuts are, after all, free!

 Don't cram the night before the exam; rather, *sleep*. A fresh brain is infinitely better than one beaten into SAT-flavored jelly.

✔ So ... we hope you noticed ... we didn't include the directions for the SAT. But we did it for a reason! (And we seriously hope you caught that since we kept telling you to memorize them without ever actually giving you anything....) We didn't want to pay for publishing rights and then pass on the charge to you. Plus, we want to force you to pick up an official SAT practice test. The directions will be there.

✔ In addition to the official SAT practice test, we have a book chock full of SAT practice drills—26 of them, to be exact. Have you begun looking at these practice exams? Do you plan on using all of them? (Answer yes to both and act accordingly.) Oh, and be sure to score your practice tests so you can actually learn something from them!

While You Conquer

💡 Recall that questions are presented in ascending order of difficulty.

💡 Answer all of the easy questions before you tackle any hard ones. The easiest question has the *same* exact point value as the hardest question. Thus, you should never put too much time and effort into a difficult question when you could be grabbing easy points elsewhere. In a nutshell, *keep moving.*

💡 Eliminate bad answers to increase your chances of correctly answering *or luckily guessing* the answer.

💡 You cannot use scrap paper, but your booklet is fair game: mark it up as much as you need. Put an X where you skip questions and a ? where you made a guess that you're not quite positive about.

NOTES:

 Fill in your bubble sheet *one page of questions at a time*. Going back and forth between the test booklet and answer sheet is A) a waste of time, B) a little confusing, and C) more likely to cause you to … *dun dun dunnnn* … fill in your answer sheet incorrectly.

 Stay positive! Being negative about this whole experience isn't going to help you! Remember, *you're* actually studying: you now know more about the SAT than many of your peers and *you* will have an easier time navigating, understanding, and beating the test. Major advantage? Check!

After You Have Won the Battle of Wits

Go celebrate! Even though you don't know your score yet, you put in one heck of an effort, and that means you deserve some fun.

And now that we've given you all the resources you could possibly ask for, we're going to bow out and let you take the reins. May your journey be smooth and your destination be a giant, gloat-worthy score.